NETHER WORLD

NETHER WORLD

CRIME AND THE POLICE COURTS IN VICTORIAN LONDON

DREW D. GRAY

REAKTION BOOKS

Published by
REAKTION BOOKS LTD
Unit 32, Waterside
44–48 Wharf Road
London N1 7UX, UK
www.reaktionbooks.co.uk

First published 2024
Copyright © Drew D. Gray 2024

Printed and bound in Great Britain by TJ Books Ltd, Padstow, Cornwall

A catalogue record for this book is available from the British Library

ISBN 978 1 78914 854 1

CONTENTS

INTRODUCTION AND THEMES

It is hard to avoid superlatives when writing about nineteenth-century London. London was much bigger and more populous than anywhere else in Britain. Its population hit 1 million as the new century began, rising to 1.6 million by 1831 and more than 2.3 million by mid-century. By the end of Victoria's reign the capital's population had swelled to a staggering 6.5 million souls, only about 3 million short of its current population. In one hundred years the number of people in London had risen by 5.5 million, or 550 per cent. In the previous century it had merely doubled, so change was dramatic, and this was echoed in its geographic footprint. Eighteenth-century London occupied an area that was not much greater than the space now associated with central London and the City. In terms of built-up space London stretched from Soho in the west to Stepney in the east. By the end of the 1700s it had expanded west to St Marylebone, north to Hoxton, and in the south (which was limited to Southwark in the late 1600s) to Kennington and Walworth.[1] John Rocque's 1746 map covered an area of 4,050 hectares (10,000 ac) from Marylebone to Bow, Vauxhall to Hyde Park.[2] When George Bacon published his *Ordnance Atlas of London and Suburbs* in 1888 he included an expansion as far north as Crouch End, south to Brixton and Wandsworth, west as far as Shepherd's Bush and Willesden, and east to Blackwall and the Isle of Dogs.[3] While the London of 1800 may have appeared small and unfamiliar to the modern eye, that of 1888 might seem much less so. London was the largest city in Europe in 1800, twice the size of its closest rival Paris. In 1850 London was the largest city in the world, and five times the size of Manchester or Liverpool, the next most populous urban environments in England. Around a tenth of Britain's population lived in London, so it is unsurprising that the poet William Blake described the capital as 'A Human Awful Wonder of God'.

London was a magnet for people. Migrants travelled to live and work in the capital from all over the British Isles and beyond. There were small enclaves of French, Germans and Italians, all bringing aspects of their culture with them. At the docks there were sailors from across the globe: Portuguese, Greeks, Malays and Lascars from the Indian subcontinent and Africa. Other Africans, slaves and former slaves, mingled with Irish and Scots, and small numbers of Chinese settled in Limehouse in the east. Also in the east, and increasingly from the 1870s, were Ashkenazi Jews from the Russian Pale of Settlement (modern-day Belarus, Moldova, Latvia, Lithuania, Poland, western Russia and Ukraine).

Ludgate Circus and St Paul's Cathedral, c. 1880–1910, photograph.

These last arrivals came to escape persecution, as French Huguenots had done in the sixteenth century. Others came as a consequence of Empire, for work or opportunity, or because they had simply arrived 'pressed' onto an English ship.

And while London was not an industrial city in the way that Birmingham or Manchester were, it was certainly industrious. All manner of trade took place from high-level retailers in the West End to leather, shoe and clothes manufacturers in the East End. Workshops crowded close to the Thames, and canals ferried goods in and out of London and up to Birmingham and the north. The London Docks were the busiest in Europe and the capital profited from the dominance of the British Empire and its command of the oceans. The wealth was reflected in the architecture, especially in the City (the centre of banking then as now) and in the developing western sprawl from Bloomsbury to Marylebone and in the suburbs where Londoners sought to escape the noxious air of an increasingly overcrowded city. Alongside affluent wealth, desperate poverty and overcrowded slums brought issues of sanitation and urban improvement to the fore in the 1800s. London suffered several waves of cholera before action was taken to rebuild the sewers and tackle the problem of a clean water supply.

An industrious and increasingly 'modern' city required a public transport system that catered for all tastes and pockets. Nineteenth-century London did not disappoint here either; alongside the carriages and traps of the rich were hansom cabs for those that could afford them, and trams and omnibuses for those on tighter budgets. From the 1840s trains served London and its locales and after 1863 Londoners could travel across the city on the world's first subterranean railway, from Paddington to Farringdon initially, and ever expanding thereafter. More people, more shops, more businesses, more banks, more transport, more horses, and a more diverse and younger population than anywhere else made London unique. There was nowhere like it. And on top of this London was

King's Cross Underground station, 1868, illustration from Walter Thornbury,
Old and New London (1873–8).

the seat of government, the main residence of the monarch, and
the capital not only of Great Britain and Ireland but also of the
British Empire.

Along with this came social problems associated with urban
areas in the long nineteenth century. Poverty was rife and was even
shown to be worse in the late 1880s than revolutionary socialists
had claimed it to be. Crime was a serious issue and London had
experimented with 'professional' policing sooner than almost anywhere in Britain (Glasgow had the first police force, pre-dating
the Metropolitan force by nearly thirty years). London's legal
system was more extensive than anywhere in England and Wales,
and London judges were sent far and wide to deliver justice to the
counties. The focus of this book is the lower tier of the capital's
justice system, the Metropolitan Police courts, but in order to
understand their function we need to understand how the whole
system operated.

The criminal court system

Nineteenth-century England was served by a three-tiered court system. At the top, dealing with the most heinous offences such as murder, violent robbery and the most serious property crimes, were the assizes. The assizes were organized around the country with judges travelling from London's high courts to 'deliver' all those held in the county gaols on their circuit. Assizes were held twice a year in most English and Welsh counties, with four of the more sparsely populated northern counties only hosting a single assize court annually.[4] Below the assizes were the quarter sessions (or sessions of the peace), which, as their name suggests, convened at four points in the year: Epiphany, Lent/Easter, Summer and Michaelmas. The sessions were presided over by local judges, drawn from the county list of Justices of the Peace, and the business of the court was much broader than that of the assizes. Alongside hearing cases for lesser criminal offences (less serious

Holborn Viaduct, *c.* 1860–80, photograph.

theft, non-fatal violence, frauds), quarter sessions also acted as an administrative body. The fundamental difference between assizes and quarter sessions, the power to hand down a sentence of death, was less distinctive by Victoria's reign as hanging had largely been removed from the suite of punishments available to judges. Both were jury courts where a jury of twelve men (women would not be allowed to serve on juries until 1919) determined guilt or innocence based on the arguments presented by legal counsel for both sides.

The situation in London was different to the rest of the country. As the most populous urban area, the seat of government, centre of commerce, a principal port for import and export, and a magnet for internal and external migration, London presented challenges for law and order well beyond those experienced outside its administrative boundaries. Consequently, London's court system effectively functioned continuously throughout the calendar year, holding its assizes almost concurrently. From 1669 the Old Bailey sessions sat eight times a year and ran at the same time as the sessions of the peace of the City and Middlesex. In the period 1800 to 1830 sessions were held from January to December with the only gaps being March and August, where there were no sessions. From the 1830s there are recorded sessions in all twelve months of the year. Until 1834 the City of London administered the Old Bailey court (as it was situated within the City boundaries) but the court heard cases from both jurisdictions, Middlesex and the City. From 1834 almost all serious property offences went through the Central Criminal Court (as it was called from then on) while less serious crimes were dealt by the sessions at Middlesex and Westminster.[5] In reality, most business was dealt with by magistrates sitting in police courts, where no jury was required. This practice was consolidated in law and extended in the 1840s and '50s.

The Metropolitan Police courts

The Metropolitan Police courts were first established in the late eighteenth century following the passing of the Middlesex Justices Act of 1792.[6] The act's intention was to create a number of police 'offices' on the model pioneered by the Fielding brothers – the famous novelist Henry and his younger brother Sir John – at Bow Street with a 'bench' of stipendiary magistrates supported by a small cohort of paid officers (akin to Bow Street's 'Runners').[7] The City of London had its own courts – at Guildhall and Mansion House – which were excluded from the plan, a shrewd political move to ensure the 1792 legislation was not blocked by vested interest. The City remained staunchly independent in policing, retaining its own police courts and (post 1829) police force. Regardless, the reality was that from 1792 London was served by a connected system of police magistrate courts that was, after 1829, supported by an increasingly professional and organized police force. By 1850 there were 11 police courts and 23 police court magistrates.[8] These courts were the starting point for almost all criminal prosecutions in the capital, as every 'criminal charge, almost without exception, that was brought in London was heard first before a stipendiary magistrate'.[9] In 1879 the courts and their locations were as follows:

Bow Street, at Covent garden; Clerkenwell, on King's Cross Road; Greenwich, near the station; Hammersmith, on Vernon Street; Lambeth, Renfrew Road; Marlborough Street, on Great Marlborough Street; Marylebone in Seymour Place; Southwark on Blackman Street in the Borough; Thames in East Arbour Street; Wandsworth on Love Lane; Westminster in Vincent Square; Woolwich; Worship Street close by Finsbury Square, plus the City courts at Guildhall and Mansion House (plus the City and

Metropolitan Police offices at Old Jewry and Whitehall place respectively).[10]

By the end of the century the police court network had expanded to include the courts that served the growing capital. By 1913 the list included the above plus North London, Old Street, Tower, West London, South Western and West Ham.[11] Bow Street ('tucked away, just like the Opera House, just behind Covent Garden market') was accepted as the capital's superior court, its magistrate the chief among peers.[12] Thames Police court and Worship Street covered the notoriously rough and criminal East End, while Woolwich and Lambeth dealt with the southern half of the city. Thames and Worship Street employed a translator, a Yiddish speaker, by the last decades of the century, in order to function amid such a large immigrant community of Eastern and

Prisoner's entrance, from 'Sketches at the London Police-Courts', *The Graphic*, 16 July 1887.

Central European Jews.[13] In the centre, Marylebone, Westminster and Clerkenwell supported Bow Street. Marlborough Street was synonymous with prostitution and with the high numbers of immigrants (or 'foreigners of shady reputation', as one contemporary described them) who attended the court.[14]

These courts operated six days a week, and the daily, evening and weekend newspapers sent reporters to capture the 'police intelligence' (as they captioned it) for their readers. Throughout the nineteenth century the London, national and regional press gave considerable space to tales from the capital's police courts. This was fuelled by an expansion in newspaper readership, born from improvements in technology (both in terms of production and distribution) and an increasingly literate populace. Moreover, politicians no longer viewed newspaper readership among the lower orders as a threat but as an opportunity, especially following the extension of voting rights under the Second Reform Act in 1867. There was also an increased interest in the lives of the poor and this is reflected in the close, if selective, attention paid to the business of these courts.[15]

This book relies heavily on newspaper reports and so it is necessary to consider for a moment the extent to which they provide an accurate picture of how these courts functioned and the nature of the business that came before them. Throughout this work the newspaper reports will be used to give examples of cases that came before the various magistrates in police courts across the capital in a period between the creation of the Metropolitan Police in 1829 and the turn of the twentieth century. The reality is that newspapers were highly selective in the cases they published. There was a clear focus on certain themes and on cases that would work well as 'human interest' stories or those that were entertaining. The Sunday papers such as *Reynolds's* or *Lloyd's* in particular benefited from the popularity of police court reports that were 'cheap, [and] simple to organize'.[16] There is an evident use of characterization in the articles, often deployed to ridicule well-established targets of public opprobrium, such as petty officials, drunkards and immigrants. The voice of the magistrate is often given the greatest authority while those of defendants and some witnesses are downplayed, or even absent. In this respect the reports echo the published accounts of trials at the Central Criminal Court (the 'Proceedings of the Old Bailey'), where the voice of the defendant was rarely heard and the printed material largely served to cement the authority of decisions made in court (rather than reflecting the arguments made about guilt or innocence).[17]

Crucially the press reports could not possibly reflect the volume of caseloads the London courts dealt with. Hundreds of hearings took place daily, thousands weekly, while the daily coverage in most papers was of between a half dozen and a dozen examples in total. In 1828, by way of example, there were 44,439 hearings involving 48,742 individuals across the metropolis's police courts, excluding the City.[18] The average per court was just under 5,000 and we might reasonably expect this number to rise from mid-century when legislation increased the official remit of magistrates to adjudicate summarily. There will be an attempt to contextualize the limits of this reportage by, where possible, offering statistics that better reflect the prosecution of certain offences and other uses of the courts by the public, police and local government officials. One very clear example is the relative absence of drunk and disorderly cases from the pages of the newspapers, when this was one of the most regular prosecutions in police courts. Cases of attempted suicide are by contrast covered in many examples despite being much less frequent occurrences than other, less well-documented hearings.

Nevertheless, this reportage remains valuable because it occasionally allows us to hear the voices of London's marginalized populace, traces of whom are rarely left in the historical record. The reports also offer a window into the operations of the courts and tell us about societal values, albeit expressed via the printed pages of contemporary newspapers. Editors were sensitive to the opinions and values of their readership and so it is possible to discern differences, however subtle, between papers aimed at an elite, middle-class audience and more 'popular' papers designed for working-class readers. We should also recognize that newspaper readership included more than simply those who were able to read; newspapers and their content were shared orally in public houses, clubs and homes. The city's public – mostly working-class Londoners – regularly filled the public galleries of the Metropolitan Police courts. It is reasonable to think then that the reports of these courts would have had to, at the very least, represent a picture that was recognizable to Londoners. So, here I agree with recent work on the representation of police court coverage, which argues that the newspaper coverage – while 'highly skewed' – remains 'very useful' in many ways.[19]

The police court magistracy

What of the men who dispensed justice in these courts? Who were they and what can we know about them? From 1839 all those serving as magistrates had to be barristers-at-law and could sit in judgment on most cases on their own, without the need to convene a 'bench' as was the case outside of the capital.[20] This formally placed considerable discretionary power in the hands of a small group of individuals but did not represent a change in magistrates' practice. Throughout the eighteenth century and indeed earlier London justices had overseen criminal and civil business without the need to justify their decision-making to fellow justices or a higher authority. The 1839 legislation enshrined practice in law and widened the justices' powers to grant summonses to complainants. It also awarded magistrates an annual salary of £1,200 (approximately £100,000 at present-day values) and arguably helped create a class of men 'of high professional standing who would enjoy a significant voice in the legal and political affairs of the metropolis'.[21]

A handful of magistrates wrote up their memoirs, as justification, self-promotion or an exercise in reflection. Several feature in this book and each needs to be treated carefully. Useful as they are as a record of how police courts operated, they are, like newspaper reports, only a partial and particular view of this level of the justice system and the people that it impacted. Like many autobiographical accounts they present a narrow viewpoint on the past and, given the nature of these particular works (the reminiscences and justifications of male magistrates drawn from a select professional background) they must also be seen as contributors to the construction of a prevailing attitude or narrative of crime, poverty and, more broadly, the working classes in Victorian Britain. This is because, as Jennifer Davis has argued, 'side by side with the new police, stipendiary magistrates were the primary instruments of public order in Victorian London.'[22]

Magistrates were not alone in court; their clerks ably assisted them. The other key individuals in these spaces were gaolers and police.[23] There will be a full discussion of the role and development of Victorian policing later, but it is necessary to give a brief description of the role of clerks. Each court had a chief clerk, a junior (secondary) and 'one or two' others.[24] Chief clerks were paid £500 and their juniors £300 (about £43,000 and £26,000 respectively at today's values), a remuneration established by the 1839 legislation. The position of the clerk seems to have developed in the course of the later 1800s from the largely administrative role they fulfilled in the eighteenth century into a more active one. Clerks at the Guildhall and Mansion House justice rooms in the 1700s merely recorded the substance and outcomes of hearings in minute books that were then signed by the sitting justice.[25] By the late 1800s clerks were more involved, advising magistrates on law and procedure, and punishments, even if the magistrate was 'supreme'.[26]

Their main function was to keep minutes of hearings, write out warrants, summonses and any other paperwork associated with the courts, all of which required 'great accuracy'.[27]

The other character who began to make an appearance in police courts from the 1870s was the police court missionary (PCM). The Church of England Temperance Society, founded in 1862, had begun sending missionaries to police courts from 1876 to encourage defendants accused of drunkenness (or offences where drunkenness was a factor) to sign a pledge of abstinence. As Chapter One will discuss, the impact of alcohol on the lives of the poor was considered one of the most pressing social problems of the age. By the mid-1880s there were eight PCMs serving the police courts and, as their presence began to become accepted and normalized, the magistracy turned to them to play a supporting advisory role in identifying defendants that were deserving of release on their own recognizance, rather than being fined and or imprisoned. They collated pre-trial information about the accused and their circumstances, followed this up on release, and in some circumstances helped them with funds, advice and seeking employment. In doing so they became 'an indispensable counterpoint to the work of the magistrate'.[28]

This role was indirectly established by legislation in 1879 (the Summary Jurisdiction Act) that gave magistrates the formal power to release prisoners on recognizance if their offence was minor. While the legislation allowed for discharge, courts were not resourced sufficiently to monitor this, which is where the PCMs were able to step in. With a further statute in 1887 (the Probation of First Offenders Act), which allowed courts to bind over first offenders for a wider range of offences, the importance of PCMs grew again, since no provision was made for supervising those released.[29] Missionaries like Thomas Holmes are another useful source of information about the nature of the courts and the people that came before them.[30] Again, they were not neutral observers: Holmes (who wrote up his memoirs and a number of works on crime and punishment, and went on to be secretary of the Howard Association (now the Howard League), which advocated penal reform) reflected widely held attitudes towards morality (especially women's sexual morality) and alcoholism, and was an advocate of state intervention into the lives of the poor.[31] He is an example of the intermeshing of charitable endeavours with social reform that characterizes other prominent individuals in this period, including Beatrice and Sidney Webb, Helen Bosanquet, Octavia Hill and the Rev. Samuel Barnett.

Until 1829 London's magistrates had effectively controlled the policing of the capital. In the aftermath of Robert Peel's creation of the Metropolitan Police this control passed to Sir Charles Rowan and Richard Mayne, the first pair of Metropolitan Police commissioners, and to Peel, at the time the Home Secretary.[32] However, this did not shift the balance of power in the police courts to the new uniformed officers of the Metropolitan force. The authority of the magistracy grew in the second half of the century, with the consolidation of practice in legislation allowing these courts to deal with the vast majority of minor crime in London. Magistrates retained their power to determine outcomes for defendants and complainants without the need to refer their decisions and did not automatically find in favour of policemen. That said, the courts and the police were closely linked and increasingly it was the police that instigated proceedings that were heard at court. This was reinforced in the newspaper reports of court hearings, which consistently featured the names or numbers, or both, of London policemen and often recorded their testimony. In the public representation the police and the police courts were synonymous.

A brief history of the Metropolitan Police

The establishment of a professional police force in 1829 was far from inevitable. Arguments for and against a wholesale reform of policing in London had raged across the eighteenth century, driven by concerns about crime and public order as well as those concerning liberty and English identities. Policing was generally organized at parish level and local interest resisted (and indeed continued to resist well into the 1830s and '40s) attempts to remove their oversight and direction of policing of communities. In London the most organized system of policing before 1829 was at Bow Street, where the so-called 'Runners' operated as quasi-professional 'thief-takers' targeting crime and criminals, allowing them to profit from the rewards available for prosecuting felons instigated under Queen Anne.[33] Sir John Fielding (magistrate at Bow Street) and his half-brother, the novelist Henry Fielding, had championed the merits of paid police as a necessity to combat perceptions of rising crime from the mid-1750s. Henry Fielding and the Thames magistrate Patrick Colquhoun both set out their visions for police reform that were based around the developing magistrate courts in the late 1700s.[34] Arguments for police reform were renewed in the aftermath of the Gordon Riots of 1780 and in 1785 a bill was presented to parliament to create nine police divisions in the capital, overseen by the Home Office. The bill was lost because the City of London refused to give up its power to direct policing within its boundaries. In 1792 a reworked bill succeeded as the Middlesex Justices Act. In 1798 Colquhoun established the Thames River Police (so called from 1800) as London's first professional police force.[35]

For the most part, however, London relied on the system of police that had served it throughout the 1700s: a parish watch that patrolled at night, and a relatively small number of parish constables that could be augmented by special constables, sworn in for public events (like public executions, riots and demonstrations).

Suggestions that England might follow the example of other European states like France in creating a professional police force were regularly dismissed, even in debates in the 1820s. Nevertheless, it is clear that from the end of the Napoleonic Wars and in a climate of concern about law and order, opposition to police reform was falling away. Into this debate stepped Robert Peel, who was appointed Home Secretary in 1822. As Chief Secretary for Ireland from 1812 to 1818 Peel had inherited the Irish County Police (established in 1786) and he developed their role with the Peace Preservation Police (from 1814), in effect trialling the notion of professional policing across the Irish Sea.[36] Peel set about an overhaul of the criminal justice system, which eventually included a proposal to establish a professional police force in London. He was able to persuade parliament to pass his bill, in part because of his oratory, and because the House of Commons was fatigued by long debates about Catholic emancipation, but also because the climate was right and he had the support of his prime minister, the Duke of Wellington. Peel's bill excluded the City (removing opposition from vested interests there) and was general enough to avoid too much scrutiny.[37] He also used crime statistics (a relatively new innovation) to demonstrate that certain parts of the capital were experiencing dangerous levels of crime and had become more vulnerable due to a relative lack of policing.[38] The bill passed into law and in September 1829 the first Metropolitan Police officers began perambulating their beats dressed in their swallow-tailed blue coats and tall hats.

The New Police were tasked from the start with the dual role of ensuring the 'security of the person and property' as well as the 'preservation of the public tranquillity'.[39] While few members of the public might have objected to the first duty, there was to be considerable opposition to the way they interpreted the second, especially when communities in the north of London objected strongly to the imposition of the 1834 Poor Law Amendment Act.[40]

In an effort to assuage fears that the Home Office was aping foreign governments by instigating a system of 'domiciliary visit, spies, and all the rest of Fouche's contrivances', as famously expressed by one commentator in 1811, Peel made sure the police looked as much like ordinary citizens as possible.[41] They wore blue tail-coats with minimal ornamentation; their hats were not unlike those worn by men generally – until 1864, that is, when the more familiar helmet was adopted – although they were reinforced in the crown. Most importantly perhaps, they were only lightly armed, with wooden truncheons and not pistols or cutlasses (as the Bow Street Runners were equipped). They largely took over the role played by the night watch

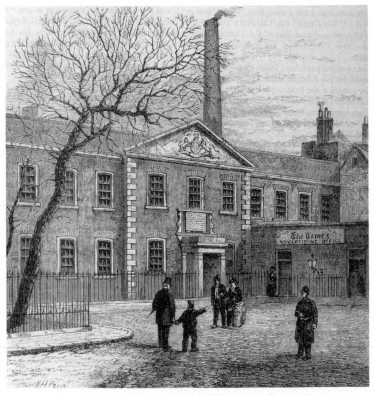

Printing house square and *The Times* office, 1870, illustration from Walter Thornbury, *Old and New London* (1873–8).

and Bow Street patrols of walking a set beat at set times. What distinguished them most was that patrolling now routinely took place night and day, and sergeants made sure police were where they were supposed be, not asleep in their stands, drinking with locals in a public house, or cavorting with prostitutes. This is not to say that these things did not happen. They did, and in the first few years of the force there was considerable churn as the commissioners imposed discipline and weeded out the malefactors.

This force was properly salaried and recruited from a similar demographic to the armed forces. The commissioners (one with a military past, Rowan; the other, Mayne, from a legal background) wanted men who would follow orders, be fit and strong, and independent enough to cope with the demands of street policing. Beyond these attributes, 'no special skill was demanded'.[42] The force of 895 constables, with 8 superintendents, 20 inspectors and 88 sergeants, was smaller than the combined total of parish constables, specials and watchmen that it replaced but it was more clearly organized, with a hierarchical structure, discipline and accountability. The force was also (eventually) trained and so, despite considerable opposition from various sections of society, it had established itself as a permanent fixture on London's streets by the 1850s.

Given that the New Police were mostly focused on preventing crime (a Detective Division was not created until 1842) most of their remit was centred on the control of the streets. In this they were part of a wider mechanism or drive to impose order on Victorian society. In addition, the police were, as David Churchill has so elegantly put it, 'supposed to serve as cautionary signal bearers for the criminal justice system, impressing upon the people the ubiquity of a systematic, mechanical surveillance, and thus the certainty that law breakers would be caught'. The police, Churchill argues, not only attempted to impose this on working-class society by force; by practising this as a body of men they also sought to transform working-class constables into 'a characterful, forward-looking, consequentialist body' who would in turn play their part in improving the morals and behaviours of the communities they policed.[43] Stephen Inwood has seriously questioned the extent to which, at least in the formative decades of the Met's existence, they were successful in inculcating middle-class values on working-class communities.[44] One clear way to investigate this is to look at the ways in which the New Police dealt with those members of the public who transgressed contemporary norms of 'good' behaviour. We can look closely at this in the chapter that follows, by examining the prosecutions brought by police to the summary courts of those accused of some violation of the laws concerning drunk and disorderly behaviour. Before that let us return to the police courts themselves.

A typical day in a police court

In the 1880s most of the police courts were open for hearings from ten o'clock in the morning until five o'clock in the afternoon. The courts at Greenwich, Hammersmith, Wandsworth and Woolwich only operated half a day and shared magistrates. Two sat in rotation at each of the others, covering several days in a row before handing over to their colleagues. The exception was Bow Street, which had three magistrates, the most senior assuming the position of Chief Magistrate for London.[45] With the exception of Sundays, Good Friday and Christmas Day the police courts opened daily.[46] The first to arrive were those seeking summonses. A summons cost 2 shillings and while this was a hefty amount for the poorest to part with, it did not put off working-class Londoners who felt they had legitimate claims to make.[47] Magistrates made themselves available prior to the formal opening of the court to listen to applicants and issue summonses and warrants. Having been successfully obtained these were delivered to the named recipient by police officers attached to the court.[48] Once applicants had been dealt with the business turned to the prisoners held in the cells, brought in by police from the stations or street, or to those making appearances to press charges, seek advice, or answer summonses issued against them.

The procedure was straightforward: the gaoler brought prisoners to the dock, read the name and number from the charge sheet and the case opened. Each defendant had their charge read out and, from the 1840s onwards, was asked if they wished their case to be dealt with by the magistrate or to be heard by a jury. For most the former option was the best one; while they surrendered their right to be judged by a jury of their peers, which in most cases were anything but, they avoided the more serious penalties that a jury court could hand down. For those punished by a magistrate the worst they might expect was a relatively short period of imprisonment or a large fine.

Drunks were dealt with first or, if still inebriated, were sent back to the cells to sober up.[49] For more complex cases solicitors were in attendance and it was usual for magistrates to delay judgment,

Women's entrance, Great Marlborough Street, from 'Sketches at the London Police-Courts', *The Graphic*, 27 August 1887.

request more information and suspend cases while information was sought. In common with the way justices operated in the 1700s, Victorian magistrates were quite willing to lock up those they suspected of criminal activity for a few days even if, when no concrete evidence was forthcoming, they were eventually released without further penalty.[50] Witnesses were sworn in before giving their testimony and could be cross-examined by the accused or their counsel and the magistrate. It is important to remember that these courts were open to the public and while some of those in attendance were there to support loved ones, friends and colleagues, others simply went along for entertainment. On many occasions the newspaper reports record the laughter and occasional applause that emanated from the public gallery. Here indeed were all sorts and conditions of men (and women), and to read the reports of these courts is to open a window into nineteenth-century society and its actors. This was a nether world, experienced directly by many Londoners, but viewed by even more through the pages of daily and weekly newspapers.

Themes and structure

This book focuses on cases brought before the magistrates and while it is interested in the structure of the courts, the magistracy themselves and the way in which cases were reported, it is most concerned to understand how the courts operated as arenas of negotiation for the working classes and as instruments for disciplining them. Self-evidently this presents us with a conundrum: to what extent were police courts effective in either controlling the poor or allowing them a space to voice and ameliorate their disadvantages? Could they possibly do both? Work on the summary courts of eighteenth-century Essex has recognized the ability of the labouring poor to 'triangulate', that is, to choose which magistrates to bring their disputes to (for example with a master, parish official or neighbour) in the hopes of gaining a preferred outcome.[51] As Peter King concludes, the role of the Hanoverian summary courts 'was highly paradoxical': 'On the one hand they were a vital force for the propertied. They resolved inter-parish disputes. They protected property. They provided a means of disciplining troublesome members of the labouring poor. On the other hand, the summary courts could be described as "people's courts".'[52]

In rural Essex in the 1700s, and other largely non-urban districts of England, the poor were not always subject to rigid discipline in the way often characterized by histories of the jury courts of assize and quarter sessions (or indeed in often inaccurate representations of the magistracy in contemporary and modern popular culture).[53] However, the extent to which the limited freedom enjoyed by the poorer classes in rural England was replicated in the summary courts of the capital in the same period is much less clear. In the late seventeenth and early eighteenth century poorer London communities (notably those in the East End, which were to become regular users of police courts) were much more reluctant to go to law.[54] The City of London's summary courts were busy places but the fixed nature of them meant the option to triangulate and play one superior off against another was more limited. The City elite that sat in judgement there consisted of the same City merchants that largely controlled trade and industry and who formed the structure of urban government. That said, the poor still used these courts to settle disputes and the outcomes they achieved, while certainly limited, reminds us that agency existed beyond the drawing rooms and coffee-houses of the middling sorts and elite. These 'people's courts' may 'have been more useful to the propertied but we cannot dismiss them simply as a disciplinary tool of the ruling elite'.[55]

Nevertheless, London's magistracy was a professional elite. As trained barristers with many years' experience, it is likely that they were affected to some degree by groupthink. They were drawn from the same social class, shared a very similar training experience, would almost certainly have encountered each other in chambers, court or a social milieu, and while some level of individual peculiarity, specialism or characteristic is to be expected, a general move towards a consensus position on most matters is likely. Most of the memoirs project an image of considerate but firm justices, determined to uphold the law while standing up for the poor where (crucially) that support was deserved. In this they probably reflected the views of many professional middle-class men in the second half of the nineteenth century.

Most of the work on the summary process has concentrated its attention on the eighteenth century so it is harder to judge the extent to which the patterns of the 1700s were repeated in the 1800s. The development of public offices that gradually evolved into police courts by the early years of Victoria's reign saw use of the summary process by poorer Londoners continue and indeed increase. Jennifer Davis, one of the very few historians to focus attention on the nineteenth century, has argued that 'the purpose of the police courts was not merely to suppress law breaking but to seek to win lower class acceptance of the law and implicitly of the social order'.[56] Magistrates like Louis Charles Tennyson D'Eyncourt recognized that their role was in part to serve a wider constituency than the class from which they came. In 1880 D'Eyncourt (who certainly came from a much higher social class than those he sat in judgment on), writing to Sir William Harcourt, Home Secretary under William Gladstone from 1880 to 1885, stated:

It is very desirable to have a police court within easy reach of a populous and active district for the interests of all classes – but especially for the benefit of the poor – the magistrate advises them – settles their differences – dispenses charity – and the Westminster Court is a kind of institution, nearly a century old, and the poor resort to it for advice in their troubles.[57]

Davis contends that the role of the courts as a working-class resource went into decline from the end of the 1860s, but recent work challenges this, arguing that this decline in fact post-dates the First World War.[58] This book broadly supports this revised understanding of the Metropolitan Police courts. Measuring effectiveness is notoriously difficult at a distance, especially the content of courts for which written records are partial at best. Yet the continued use of police courts throughout the Victorian period by members of marginalized communities (the poor, women, immigrants and so on) suggests strongly that they believed these were arenas that offered them a resource not easily affordable elsewhere. Of course, the dichotomy noted earlier for summary courts in the 1700s is apparent for the Victorian period, as Davis recognizes. The police courts 'clearly functioned as the right hand of the police and of the propertied classes', while at the same time 'attracting a numerous and diverse working-class clientele'.[59] In other words, the poorer classes of the capital were present in huge numbers at the police courts, as defendants certainly, as witnesses often, but also, crucially, as complainants and supplicants. What this means for our understanding of the Victorian criminal justice system and the contextual social relations of London in the 1880s is something this book is intent on exploring.

The following two chapters consider the role that police officers played in maintaining public order in the disputed environment of the street. We focus on the category of offending that, while it received relatively little coverage in the press reports of police court business, was by far the biggest in terms of numbers of those brought before magistrates: drunk and disorderly behaviour, or one of several variants of it. Within this section we will meet two women who gained considerable notoriety during the last decades

of the 1800s, held up as they were as examples both of the debili-
tating effect of drink and the futility of the police courts as institutions that might reform behaviour. The police were at the front
line of prosecutions involving drunkenness simply because most of
those that appeared had invariably been arrested on the street, by
patrolling police officers. The contest for control of the capital's
thoroughfares and pavements is a recurrent theme in this book
and naturally, given their deployment, the Metropolitan Police
were everywhere involved, so Chapter Two looks at the way that
the police (and others) brought prosecutions for obstructing the
free flow of traffic, pedestrians and commerce in the Victorian city.
One definable group that found themselves in conflict with the
New Police was London's itinerant street traders, known as costermongers. The desire for order and the demands of bricks and mortar
retailers were in conflict with costers' ancient and deeply held
beliefs in their rights to set up stall wherever they wished and wherever they were required to serve the needs of poorer Londoners.
This was a battle that they would ultimately lose, but not without a
fight that was often physical, and which placed them and the police
at odds. As previous work on the New Police has shown, the attempt
to control the streets was part of a wider assault on the popular
culture of the working class, even if historians disagree as to the
effect, scope and indeed the intention of this.[60] Chapter Two also
considers the ways in which the police courts mediated disputes
around trade and the use of the streets.

Chapter Three begins an analysis of the nature of crime in
London, beginning with property crime. This starts with the most
serious forms of offending – robbery, housebreaking and burglary,
and forgery and coining. All these offences would have earned a
capital sentence in the early decades of the nineteenth century, each
having this harshest of penalties removed (and largely replaced by
transportation or imprisonment from the late 1820s) as part of
Robert Peel's reform of the criminal justice system. While these

cases often began in the police courts they mostly ended at the Central Criminal Court. It is often possible to trace offenders through the papers and court and punishment records using electronic online resources.[61] Having considered more serious offending, Chapter Three focuses on the sort of crime that, while sometimes prosecuted at the Bailey or the Middlesex Sessions, was more routinely dealt with by police court magistrates. These were the pickpockets and shoplifters who profited from London's pre-eminence as the retail centre of Britain. Others exploited the Docks or places of work, many were opportunistic and sometimes motivated by low pay or a sense of entitlement. London's place as a centre for the import and export of goods also means that the courts were required to deal with smugglers intent on evading the excise. Finally, this chapter will look at those that practised fraud, organized (such as the 'long firm' scam) or otherwise, to con Londoners out of their hard-earned wages and savings.

Having considered property crime, the book next turns its attention to violence, looking at assaults on the police, on wives and partners, and on children – in addition, it explores notions of male violence, including the so-called 'fair fight'. As well as non-lethal violence Chapter Four addresses homicide, murder being one of the subjects that consistently filled the pages of the Victorian newspapers and other forms of sensational print culture.[62] In Chapter Five it is young offenders that are the focus of study; it was in the early decades of the nineteenth century that the notion of the juvenile delinquent was established, and from then on youth offending has dominated debates around criminal justice and penal policy.[63] Youth offending overlaps with discussions of street activities, like gambling, pocket-picking and shoplifting, but the attitudes of magistrates here and developments in punishment warrant the topic receiving a chapter of its own. Here we also discuss the police courts' role in enforcing Victorian education acts and in intervening in families that might, in modern parlance, be deemed dysfunctional. From juveniles in Chapter Five we move to women in Chapter Six. More specifically this chapter looks in detail at another problem that was given prominent focus in newspaper columns and the jottings of social reformers and commentators: prostitution. The chapter examines the law and prostitution and the efforts of reformers to regulate or limit the sex trade. The Victorian state imposed a brutal forcible examination process on street women (the Contagious Diseases Acts, passed between 1864 and 1869) in a largely futile attempt to protect armed forces personnel from being taken out of service by sexually transmitted diseases. This provoked a fervent campaign of opposition by women, which arguably sowed the seeds for the tactical fight for emancipation in the Edwardian period. Trying to track sex workers through the courts is problematic, not least because the act of prostitution was not illegal in the 1800s and the term was rarely used. Nevertheless, it is possible to explore prostitution and the trafficking of women for sexual exploitation in a period in which one of the most high-profile sensation stories of all time was published.[64]

Many of those who engaged in sex work at the time, including several of the women who would fall victim to a savage serial killer in 1888, were part of the poorest section of society, those whom some commentators began to describe as the 'residuum' in the last decades of the century. In Chapter Seven the life of London's poor is explicitly examined, although of course they feature throughout this book. Here we meet those prosecuted by the Mendicity Society's officers for begging on the streets or arrested for knocking doors to ask for alms. Here too are those that came to the police courts for help and advice, sometimes because the parish Poor Law officials had failed to support them. This is a good place to see how effective the courts were in offering support to the poor and again we can discern prevailing Victorian attitudes that differentiated between the 'deserving' and 'undeserving'. Poverty, alcohol and depression, caused by all manner of challenges and hardship, drove some to desperation and to attempt to end their own lives. Here too we encounter some of the arguably lucky ones, those that failed in their attempts to drown in the Thames or London's canals, or who were rescued from attempts at self-strangulation and other means of self-destruction. The courts were expected to uphold the law (attempted suicide was a crime in the 1800s) but also to consider the context and look at ways to help these individuals. As with alcoholism there were limits to what the state could or would do to help, and the outcome for many of those whose attempt to end their life was perhaps worse, given the state of mental health care in Victorian England.

Chapter Eight studies the role the police courts played in reacting to a rising tide of political tension from the 1870s onwards. Britain had enjoyed relative stability from the 1850s once Chartism had been defeated and the memories of the post-Napoleonic War tensions had all but faded. Having avoided much of the revolutionary fervour that swept continental Europe in the 1840s, Britain's complacency was sorely tested by uprisings overseas (notably in India in 1857), by Irish Republicanism from the 1860s, and by continuous imperial conflicts (culminating in the South African War of 1899–1902). And in the 1880s a series of riots and strikes and the emergence of new radical political movements, which corresponded with an economic downturn after decades of prosperity, brought the police and courts into direct confrontation with another sort of offender, those motivated by politics and by a desire to change the status quo for the benefit of the working classes. Some of these people were recent arrivals in the capital or were influenced by imported ideas of socialism or anarchism, brought in by immigrants fleeing persecution overseas. Here again we are able to explore the idea that the police courts were 'people's courts' or arenas in which the poor could obtain help and justice so long as they remembered their place and acquiesced to the prevailing wishes of their social betters.

1

THE POLICE, DRINK AND THE WORKING CLASSES

Although the 'police intelligence' columns of the newspapers offered their readership a varied and often sensationalized selection of cases from the police courts, the reality was often much more mundane. As the records of the Thames Police court from 1881 show, offences involving overindulgence in alcohol resulted in the single largest proportion of prosecutions before the magistrates. There are very few qualitative records of police court hearings and even simple registers of cases have not survived in anything like the numbers that would make a more comprehensive study possible, but the Thames court registers for the 1880s do allow us to place the prosecution of alcohol-related offences in some sort of context.

Between March and November 1881 the register of the court of summary jurisdiction at Thames listed some 3,075 entries for all manner of offences, mostly brought by police officers from H or K division (the police divisions that covered the East End of London). Of these, 1,295 (42 per cent) related in some way to drunkenness.

Most charges for drunk and disorderly (or one of its variants) were heard by the magistrates on Monday mornings, meaning those arrested on Saturday night would spend an extra night in a police cell unless the desk sergeant chose to discharge them on their own recognizance, or because they had sobered up and were no longer considered a danger to themselves or others. For the drunkards who made it before a justice, a dressing down was the minimum they could expect. Many would take an admonishment from the bench and be released with a warning not to appear before the court again. For others a fine would be levied, with the alternative of a few days in prison if they could not find the money.

Magistrates had been officially empowered to deal with all such offenders summarily by the terms of two pieces of legislation passed in August 1839.[1] Under the terms of the Metropolitan Police Act (1839) police could arrest anyone they found on the streets who they thought were either guilty of an offence or they 'had good reason to suspect' of committing one. As a result policemen brought in huge numbers of 'loose, idle, and disorderly' persons of both sexes, many for being drunk. By way of an example, on Monday, 21 March 1881, Justice Saunders was presented with 22 alcohol-related cases at Thames in a row. Of the thirteen women, he discharged three, fined five of them 2s 6d and two others 5s, and sent Margaret Caldon, Margaret Hegethsly and Mary Ann Sullivan to prison for seven days with hard labour.[2] The last two women had been brought in for fighting each other and Caldon had given the policeman that tried to move her on a mouthful of abuse, which compounded her offence.

Policemen were advised, if not always required, to take individuals into custody for their own safety. Police officers had to make a judgment as to whether the person was insensible (not through drink) or just plain drunk. Neither was technically an offence, but the Police Code book offered slightly different forms of procedure depending on what the situation was. Drunken persons were to be left alone unless they were acting in a disorderly manner or were 'so incapable as to be likely to sustain injury'. For those found insensible (who might of course have been rendered so by drink) officers were instructed to consider the position, to look for any signs of the cause of insensibility, and then to carefully place the person in the recovery position (on their back, 'head inclined to one side, the arms by the sides' and the legs extended).[3]

The law that covered public drunkenness by 1881 was the 1872 Licensing Act, section 12 of which stated that: 'Every person found drunk in any highway or other public place, whether a building or not, or on any licensed premises, shall be liable to a penalty,' with additional penalties on a sliding scale for any subsequent conviction.[4] By default anyone unable (or unwilling) to pay the fine would face imprisonment for up to two weeks, although magistrates increasingly seem to have agreed that it did little good.

Prosecutions for offences relating to drunkenness at the Thames Police court, 15 March 1881 to 8 November 1881

CHARGE	MALE	FEMALE	TOTAL
Drunk and Disorderly (D&D)	220 (55.7%)	175 (44.3%)	395
D&D and using obscene language	154 (43.1%)	203 (56.9%)	357
Drunk and incapable	95 (50.3%)	94 (49.7%)	189
D&D and assault	115 (72.3%)	44 (27.7%)	159
D&D and fighting	27 (40.3%)	40 (59.7%)	67
D&D and wilful damage to property	19 (52.8%)	17 (47.2%)	36
Drunk in charge of vehicle/horse	31 (96.9%)	1 (3.1%)	32
Drunk with assault	27 (93.1%)	2 (6.9%)	29
Drunk and refusing to quit licensed premises	12 (75%)	4 (25%)	16
Drunk	6 (50%)	6 (50%)	12
D&D and causing a crowd	2 (66.7%)	1 (33.3%)	3
TOTAL	708 (54.7%)	587 (45.3%)	1,295

Registers only record alternate months, so this represents just sixteen weeks of business

While the sparse records of the Thames court provide little if any detail that explains the context for cases of drunkenness that brought persons before the magistracy, the records of the contemporary London press are more enlightening. Drunks fell into several categories. There were loud and 'disorderly' or 'riotous' drunks, most often found in and around the capital's many pubs and clubs. There were those found lying in the gutter or in shop doorways who were quite literally incapable of making their way home. There were belligerent drunks, and passive ones; drunks who beat their wives (or husbands) and drunks that railed at cab drivers, or at police trying to usher them home. Policemen were advised not to interfere with drunks unless they were a risk to themselves or presented a risk or disturbance to others. Someone walking home quietly from the pub would be unlikely to attract police attention, while another singing or shouting at the top of his voice might. Even then the direction given to the police was to use gentle persuasion to get the person to either go home or accompany the officer to the station. On no account were policemen to leave their beat to take a drunk home or anywhere other than the station, so it is quite likely that police officers applied discretion when dealing with drunks. The number of drunks appearing in court probably represents the tip of a large iceberg. While the registers at Thames indicate that perhaps as many as eighty to one hundred people each week were being prosecuted for drink-related misdemeanours, we can reasonably assume that very many more drunks were left unmolested by police.

Since almost no one was immune from the effects of an excess of alcohol, this was an offence that could bring persons of any social class before the magistracy. In early 1850 a 'town traveller' named Shannon (most likely a travelling salesman, and therefore a member of the lower middle class) found himself hauled before Mr Ingham at Thames charged with being drunk and disorderly and assaulting a policeman. Shannon was arguing with a cab driver and disputing the fare when PC Charles McCarten intervened. According to the officer, a 'mob of night crawlers, prostitutes, and other disorderly characters' had been drawn to the altercation and so the policeman politely suggested that Shannon paid and went home to bed. This drew a stream of abuse from the salesman, who called McCarten 'a _____ Irish vagabond' and put up his fists. Ignoring a second warning Shannon continued his abuse and was arrested. He was fined 40s, which he paid on the spot, indicating that he was sufficiently wealthy.[5] There was a class aspect in the punishment of offenders for being drunk: those with means to pay fines could avoid gaol, while most of the poor could not. By 1880 the law surrounding summary prosecutions and the imposition of fines had been changed by the Summary Jurisdictions Act of the previous year. This meant that even so-called respectable persons could be asked to demonstrate they had the required funds to pay a fine imposed by the court.

Given the proliferation of drunk and disorderly charges, we would not expect reporters to bother submitting copy to editors unless they felt there was either a public interest story or it was in another way newsworthy, since drunkenness was commonplace. Occasionally the circumstances of drunkenness were notable, as in a case from May 1880. Mr Flowers heard the case of Mary Ann Fitzpatrick, an eighteen-year-old charged with being drunk and disorderly in St Giles. PC Butler testified that he had been called to a disturbance at a house in Betterton Street that was almost entirely occupied by young women and girls. Every night large numbers of girls aged fourteen to eighteen congregated in the streets, 'behaving in a most disorderly manner'. They lived in one property, which was home to 'upwards of 70 people'. Mr Flowers thought the problem lay with the landlord for allowing his or her house to be so disorderly, but as Mary Ann had previous convictions for drunkenness her punishment was a fine of 20s or fourteen days in prison.[6] Between 1886 and 1903 Charles Booth, a wealthy businessman and

social reformer, conducted a survey of 'life and labour' in London
with the assistance of School Board visitors and local police.
Betterton Street in the late 1880s, as revealed by Charles Booth's
survey, was very poor (being coloured dark blue denoting 'Very
poor, chronic want'). Around the corner was the St Giles and St
George workhouse in Bloomsbury and so it was at the heart of
the roughest part of the parish of St Giles. Also nearby was the
St Giles mission for fallen women and cloth workers, suggestive
of the attempts of local charity to 'improve' the district as well as
being testimony (with the workhouse) to the deep-seated poverty
to be found there.[7]

Drunkenness was endemic in the capital's slums. As researchers have identified, domestic violence was closely identified with
and a crime primarily ascribed to poor working-class males, but
we should not be blind to the fact that middle-class and elite wives
and daughters suffered at the hands of male abusers.[8] It was simply
easier to hide in wealthier households. Alcoholism and its effects
were possibly just as much of a problem in the homes of the rich
as they were in those of the poor, but their doors were invariably
closed to the prying eyes of the press, who preferred to highlight
the problem of intemperance among the working classes. Sometimes the detrimental effects of alcohol are self-evident in the
reports. When a tradesman named Clarke took his Irish lodgers
to court in September 1850 for neglecting their children, it
revealed a family in the most desperate poverty. The Stewarts lived
in one room in Clarke's house in Hopkins Street, Soho. A parish
officer testified that the space they occupied was 'filthy and destitute' with 'no furniture, and nothing but a bundle of rags on a
truckle bed for all the family to sleep on'. Justice Hardwick was
told that the infant children were 'locked-up all day long in the
room without food' while their parents went out drinking. Mrs
Stewart denied neglect and, less plausibly, denied her drinking.
Her husband said the couple both had to work to make ends meet

but, at present, they had no work and so no money. The landlord and several neighbours gave evidence that when the couple did have money they invariably spent it on drink rather than on food for the children. Mr Hardwick decided the parish needed to intervene. He instructed the relieving officer to 'do something for the children'. He did not fine or imprison the Stewarts, but it is likely that their children would have been removed. To the readers of the *Morning Chronicle* this may have served to confirm their worst prejudices concerning the poor, especially London's large impoverished Irish community. Justice Hardwick showed leniency by not fining the Stewarts and acted to 'save' the children by having them taken into the care of the parish beadle and workhouse.[9]

The effects of endemic poverty are clear in many other reports of drunkenness and its prosecution in the police courts. The records also highlight examples of poor mental health. In January 1861 Ann Field was locked up for being 'drunk and creating a disturbance' in the street. It was not the first time that Field had been in trouble with the law: she was a 'well-known prostitute' who had appeared at Clerkenwell Police court on more than fifty occasions. On this occasion, just ten minutes after being locked in a police cell she tried to take her own life. Inspector Mulvenny found her half-dead, her face turning black as she slowly strangled herself with a scarf. Mulvenny wrestled the scarf free, saving her life but earning no thanks. Within moments of being rescued Field was tearing at her clothes trying to fashion another piece of cord to hang herself from. It must have been evident to anyone present at Clerkenwell that she needed help but, despite her promise not to make an attempt on her own life again, the magistrate sent her to the house of correction for a month of hard labour.[10] Women like Ann Field, with long histories of offending related to alcoholism, were all too regular occupants of police court docks. As the century drew towards its close more voices joined those that called for legislation to help prevent women ending up like Ann. Until the last quarter of the century, however, the police and the summary process continued to treat public drunkenness as a social problem that should be dealt with as a personal failing in the individual concerned, not something best understood by environmental factors or as an example of poor mental health.

The 1800s saw the growth of the Temperance movement, a campaign aimed at reducing the problems of alcohol abuse. Its adherents adopted two approaches: either to encourage and promote individual abstinence and/or to campaign for legislation to restrict the availability of alcohol (prohibition). Teetotalism was equated with self-control and 'respectability'; its opposite was highlighted as a path to immorality, poverty and self-destruction. Historians have identified the Temperance movement as an example of 'moral regulation' in the second half of the nineteenth century representative of large-scale efforts to 'compel people to behave differently'.[11] British Temperance had its origins in resistance to the passing of the Beer (or Beerhouse) Act of 1830, which liberalized the brewing and sale of beer by opening up the industry, reducing process and allowing more beer to be made and consumed.[12] The act was designed to encourage beer drinking and discourage the consumption of gin, which was deemed a worse social evil. This echoed attempts in the previous century to restrict the sale of Dutch gin, *genever*, and establish beer as Britain's national drink. Negative attitudes towards drink and drinking had existed previously, but in the words of one recent historical study, following the Beer Act 'alcohol as a substance was problematized.'[13] An individual's commitment to Temperance began with 'the pledge', a signed public statement promising to abstain from alcohol. The 1830s and '40s saw a growth in teetotalism that stressed the benefits of drinking tea or coffee instead of alcohol and embraced members from across the social divide. Temperance influenced debates about morality, work and education, and adherents held 'tea parties', public talks and set up their own coffee-houses.[14] Throughout the

George Cruikshank, *The Bottle*, 1847, engraving: 'Unable to obtain
employment, they are driven by poverty into the street to beg,
and by this means they still supply the bottle.'

1800s a series of licensing acts attempted to control or regulate
alcohol consumption, with limited effect. The most significant of
these was the act of 1872, which made it an offence to be drunk in
a public place or while in charge of a horse-drawn vehicle.[15] The
penalty was a fine, the amount of which would rise on each subsequent conviction within a twelve-month period. Serial drunks
could therefore find themselves up before a magistrate with alarming regularity and, given that many did not have the money to pay
a fine, having spent it all on drink, as a result became extremely
familiar with imprisonment.

In the 1870s a long campaign led by two prominent doctors
prompted parliament to pass legislation aimed at treating those
suffering from the 'affliction' of drunkenness. Donald Dalrymple,
a Liberal MP, with the support of the British Medical Association
(BMA) introduced a bill to deal with the problem of alcoholism in
1870. The BMA played a leading role in arguing that drunkenness
was not simply a moral failing, as it was generally seen in the

1800s, but was in fact a condition that could be treated by medicine. Dalrymple's co-campaigner, Dr Norman Kerr, insisted that 'if medical treatment were allowed to replace imprisonment it offered a real possibility of cure.'[16] This represented a radical shift in the approach to working-class drunks who were generally dismissed as undeserving of sympathy or care. Opinions varied, and some magistrates were open to alternative ways of dealing with habitual drunks but, for the most part, the law frustrated them. They had little option but to fine or imprison the accused and so, since most alcoholics were unable to sustain the employment that would enable them to fork out for financial penalties, the revolving door of the prison beckoned.

Dalrymple ran Heigham Hall Lunatic Asylum in Norwich and had first-hand experience of working with mental illness. He recognized that the system failed those suffering from alcoholism. Anyone deemed insane by reason of drink could be committed to an asylum but only for a short period while they dried out. Thereafter they had to be allowed to leave or the asylum could face charges of false imprisonment. This hamstrung the efforts of magistrates in police courts to deal with the problem of habitual drunkards because, as one historian has put it, without alternative sanctions all the officials did was 'impose sureties and enforce repeated and futile short periods of imprisonment'.[17] Dalrymple faced opposition when he introduced his bill to parliament. It drew fire from those who continued to see drunkenness among the working classes as something best punished by imprisonment and not by care in a more comfortable reformatory. The latter, it was said, was more suited to more genteel drunks, the unfortunate sons or wives of the middle class and elite, who fell into alcoholism as a result of mental weakness or peer pressure. As a result Dalrymple's bill was amended to exclude those 'charged with criminal offenses'. The 1879 Habitual Drunkards Act, like so much of the beer served up in London's alehouses, was watered down as it passed through parliament.[18] While it ended up as an entirely voluntary and largely ineffectual tool to deal with a widespread social problem, it was a step in the right direction. The act allowed individuals to be admitted to an inebriate reformatory (rather than a lunatic asylum) so long as they consented both to surrender their liberty on arrival and pay for their keep and treatment. This meant that if a person agreed to enter a reformatory he could not leave until he reached the end of his period of care; if he absconded, staff could forcibly bring him back.

Critics complained that the legislation only helped those wealthy and 'reasonable enough to agree to be committed' to an asylum, not ordinary working-class drunks.[19] This can be seen in a case that came before the Thames court in 1880. A 'gentlemanly-looking man' (whose name was not published in the press) appeared to make a 'statutory declaration' that he wanted to enter an inebriate asylum. The magistrate, Mr Lushington, asked him a series of questions to ascertain that this was indeed what he wanted to do.

> The applicant said he was quite aware that he should have to stop in the retreat when once he got there for the time agreed upon, whether he liked it or not. He was also aware that if he escaped from the retreat he would be liable to be sought after, apprehended, and taken back there on a warrant; and he was perfectly cognizant of the fact that he was liable to certain penalties if he misbehaved himself whilst an inmate of the home.

Having established all of this, Lushington authorized the man's declaration.[20]

The act was ineffectual but did succeed in defining what a 'habitual drunkard' was: 'a person who by means of habitual intemperate drinking of intoxicating liquor is dangerous to himself, or herself, or to others, or incapable of managing himself or herself, and his or her affairs'.[21] Dalrymple died in 1873 without seeing his legislation passed, but the medical profession was now set on a course of gaining state recognition (and thereafter state action) for the need to treat alcoholism as a mental health and social issue and not merely a criminal one. This was influenced by Dr Kerr's own definition of inebriety as a mental disorder 'characterized by an irresistible impulse to indulge in intoxicating liquors or other narcotics, for the relief which these afford, at a peril'.[22]

While the 1879 act was of limited practical use, it did provide a foundation for campaigners to build upon. In the years following its implementation campaigners continued to press for further legislation to deal with the problem of alcoholism. The press (consciously or not) helped keep the debate in the public eye by carrying regular reports of notorious offenders appearing before magistrates who could do nothing but imprison them with little hope or expectation of reform. The modern concept of the revolving door of recidivism is applicable to late Victorian criminal drunkenness.

Drunkenness was increasingly associated with degeneracy, and this contributed to concerns about the state of the working class, particularly the existence of an underclass (the so-called 'residuum'). Women represented a special area of concern, it being argued that they could pass the taint on to their children if they drank during pregnancy.[23] Drunkenness in married women was also viewed as a contributory factor in alcoholism among men. This was conflated with concerns about women 'invading' the 'public male social sphere' by drinking in pubs.[24] Drink was clearly a gendered social issue, made more obvious by the focus of press attention on notorious examples of drunken womanhood.

Following a government enquiry, the Departmental Committee on the Treatment of Inebriates (1893–4) concluded that the only way forward was the compulsory long-term confinement of persistent offenders in reformatories.[25] The resulting bill was again diluted in the Lords but became statute in August 1898 as the Inebriates Act. This amended the 1879 legislation and extended its reach to include those deemed to be criminal habitual drunkards.[26] Perhaps most significantly it adopted the term 'inebriates' rather than 'drunkards', reflecting the medical profession's approach and, in particular, that of the Society for the Study and Cure of Inebriety. The act allowed magistrates to send guilty persons to a reformatory for up to three years if the individuals had been convicted four times already for an offence relating to drunkenness. This was in addition to any other penalties (such as fines). But this extra sanction was dependent upon the court being convinced that any indictable offence the accused was charged with 'was committed under the influence of drink or that drunkenness was a contributing cause of the offence'.[27] The accused also had to admit to being a 'habitual drunkard' and the court had to have been informed of this before the case was heard. Both those who 'committed serious criminal offences whilst drunk' and those habitual drunks who clogged up the police courts 'could be detained for up to three years, in order to keep them away from drink long enough to fortify their will to abstain', as Lucia Zedner noted.[28] The act also prohibited the sale of alcohol to someone who was a registered 'inebriate' (although one wonders how effective that might have been in practice).[29] A London magistrate writing in 1897, a year before the act was passed, had commented: 'How can you cure a drunkard by sending him to a common prison, with hard labor, for a month? The thing is impossible, absurd.'[30] The 1898 act only addressed this failing in part; it did not offer a panacea for alcoholism. Having provided some background context, we can now look at the lives of two of London's most celebrated alcoholics, who occupied the police court report newspaper columns more than any other named individuals in the late 1800s.

Tottie Fay was possibly born Amy Anderson in Seven Dials sometime in the 1850s.[31] Her father was reportedly a costermonger, but we must accept that as with so many working-class lives much of the detail is speculative. Seven Dials was notorious in the 1800s as a place of poverty, immorality and crime. It had areas where the police simply did not go, even if the notorious Church Lane rookery had been demolished to make way for New Oxford Street in the 1840s.[32] Tottie's father, it was alleged, had been a member of a street gang in the Dials, one of many local gangs that pre-dated the 1890s 'hooligan' panic. Not surprisingly then, given the cards dealt to her, Tottie Fay's most pressing concern was to leave her upbringing a long way behind her. Fay attempted to create a new identity for herself, one that took her out of the slums and placed her in 'respectable' society. One of the saddest things about Fay's story is the way in which the papers ridiculed her attempt to rise above her station, to try to be someone she was not. Victorian society did not embrace social mobility; it preferred people (especially women) to know their place.

Between 1879 and 1890 Tottie Fay (using a variety of names) was convicted of various offences at different police courts and the Middlesex Sessions, including theft, illegal pawning and soliciting prostitution.[33] Fay's criminal career probably began around the age of fourteen and by eighteen she was prostituting herself. This should come as no surprise to anyone that has studied the lives of poor women in nineteenth-century London. We have ample evidence to suggest that prostitution was rife in the Victorian capital.[34] Fay's modus operandi in the 1880s was something like this: dressed fashionably, she would accost men as they left clubs or music halls and theatres in the West End and persuade them to buy her a drink. She would then lead them to a nearby hotel where a quick bribe to the porter would secure a room. While this was safe by comparison to walking the streets it still held risks, especially if she asked the wrong man or was observed by a policeman. In Fay's case it seems that the alcohol, taken initially as part of the strategy and partly to numb the experience, began to take over until it became the driver for her actions. Moreover, when she was in liquor she became increasingly rowdy, which attracted crowds and policemen. From the late 1880s Tottie Fay started to become a regular in London's police courts for her drunkenness, where she captured the imagination of the newspapers.

One of the earlier occasions that Fay appears in print was the spring of 1887, when she had already earned a reputation. In its 'occasional notes' section the *Pall Mall Gazette* referred to her as the 'wickedest woman in London'. The report noted she had amassed a variety of pseudonyms that included 'Lilian Rothschild', 'Violet St. John', 'Mabel Gray', 'Maud Legrand' and 'Lily Levant'.[35] The paper thought she was about thirty years of age (although she may have been younger) and dressed well, if slightly eccentrically. On this occasion the magistrate, Mr Mansfield, sent her to prison for a month, as she was unable to pay a fine of 40s. If Mansfield's intention was to teach Fay a lesson, then he was clearly unfamiliar with her history. Offenders like her knew that the best strategy was to not be caught too many times in the same place and thus appear too often before the same magistrate. Being known to the police and the magistracy reduced your chances of avoiding a heavy fine or a prison sentence, or both. This explains her consistent use of false names and a well-rehearsed justification for her appearance in court. For Fay it was pretty much always the case that she had been led to drink by someone else (such as a man) or reduced to it by some cataclysmic event (the death of a close relative or friend). Both her actions in court – lambasting the police as 'mean', overbearing or violent – and her appearance and contrived persona fascinated court reporters. Her frequent visits were reported in great detail with space given to describe her clothes, jewellery, hats and accessories, and in recording her words and demeanour. On 11 April 1888 Fay appeared in a police court after being found drunk and surrounded by a crowd in the early hours of the morning. She claimed she was due at the funeral of her 'poor sister', a declaration met with laughter. 'Last time she said it was her "dear mamma",' interrupted the assistant gaoler, adding that she had only been let out of Millbank Prison the day before. Convicted of being drunk and disorderly, Fay was led away to begin another stretch inside, this time for 21 days.

When she appeared again two months later she almost fooled the bench with her disguise. Calling herself 'Lilly de Grays', it took a gaoler and a court reporter to identify her as a regular at Marlborough Street. The charge was drunk and disorderly but the circumstances were different. This time she had taken lodgings in Langham Street only to cause chaos in a series of examples of drunken bad behaviour that culminated in her being found running 'naked' (which probably meant in her underclothes) throughout the house. Worried for the reputation of her house, the landlady threw her out on the street, where a policeman arrested her. She was sentenced to another month inside. This was the pattern of Fay's offending in the late 1880s, sporadic if frequent arrests for drink and disorderly behaviour, which produced colourful stories to amuse the reading public. At some point, however, the ground began to shift underneath her and Fay's relatively trivial brushes with the law became more serious. But before exploring Fay's continuing decline let us consider another woman who was to impact the debate around inebriety in the late 1800s.

Jane Cakebread was older than Tottie Fay, well into her fifties or sixties by the late 1880s. She had also appeared in front of mag-istrates many more times. She was a habitual drunk but there is no evidence that she was involved in prostitution. Cakebread came from just north of London: Enfield or Hertfordshire. Nearly all her court appearances were at North London Police court and her offences were committed in and around Stoke Newington and Dalston. In late July 1888 Cakebread was charged with being drunk and disor-derly. According to the gaoler, she had been up before the bench there three times since April. She disputed this: 'Only twice,' she insisted. A policeman had arrested her for causing a disturbance at Finsbury Park, drawing a crowd about her as she lay on the ground drunk, swearing loudly at those gawping at her. Cakebread claimed to be 'a lady' and said she had 'a fortune left me'.[36]

Like Fay, Cakebread was often delusional. In July 1888 Cakebread had only recently been released from prison and the sitting magistrate remanded her while enquiries were made into her mental health. A reporter noted that she had built up a staggering 209 appearances for drunkenness at London police courts in her life: 209 became 210 just over a month later when she was picked up in Victoria Park in the East End for being drunk and 'reminding [passers-by] that she was a lady' with property. In court she denied using bad language and claimed to have been singing a hymn. The magistrates who dealt with Cakebread showed more leniency than they did Fay, perhaps on account of her advanced years. In April she reappeared at Dalston (her 219th conviction), where she denied striking a police officer in the chest as he escorted her from a public house in Stoke Newington. When the magistrate enquired as to Cakebread's occupation she claimed she had been 'an upper parlour maid in a gentleman's family' at Stamford Hill. This may have been true; it is possible that Cakebread had been a servant who lost her position and ended up on the streets, with drink her only solace. The magistrate at Dalston sent her to prison for a month with hard labour. 'Thank you, sir, kindly. I hope it will be the last,' said Cakebread as she was led away.[37] It was not; in August, aged 62, she was fined 10s after biting a constable in Green Lanes.

In January 1889 Tottie Fay was back before a magistrate, Mr Hannay, at Marlborough Street. He had not encountered her before, which gave her the opportunity to try and convince him that she was the victim of a malicious prosecution and police brutality and not guilty of being 'drunk and riotous' on New Year's Eve. She had been arrested at Piccadilly's Bath Hotel after the proprietor had thrown her out for disreputable behaviour. He testified that (again)

Fay had been 'running undressed all over the hotel'. When challenged she locked herself in a room and refused to come out. The door was forced; Fay was dragged out and led away by police. She had been using a room there to meet clients. Hannay fined her 40s, which, as she never had any money, meant another month inside.[38] In June 1889 Fay was back in court, calling herself 'Lily de Terry' and giving an address in Grosvenor Square. She was dressed more quietly than usual – either to attract sympathy, or because she was unable to afford anything more glamorous. PC Evans had arrested her after he found her surrounded by a crowd on Porchester Road protesting that someone had stolen her purse. She was 'very drunk' and when questioned she tried to get away, saying 'Oh, I have got it [the purse] now, thank you.' When the officer stopped her she gave him a mouthful of verbal abuse and threw herself to the floor. At first she would not budge and a fellow officer ran to fetch an ambulance.[39] In the end Fay decided that getting up and walking to the station, instead of being dragged there on a cart, better served her self-esteem and public image.

In court she told her well-rehearsed tale of being a lady, pleaded not guilty, apologized and promised not to err in future. The magistrate took pity and gave her a small fine. She thanked him. By now she was so infamous that the *Illustrated Police News* included an artist's impression of her arrest.[40] She was pictured again in August as 'the well-known Tottie Fay' after she appeared in court using the name 'Mabel Granville'. This time drunkenness was compounded with theft and fraud. PC Orchard testified that he had been called to a pastry shop after Fay had refused to pay for 'two pots of tea, four eggs, and a considerable quantity of bread'. She had drunkenly complained that the eggs were undercooked ('they were like water') and a row had broken out.[41] Within a few weeks she was back in court, this time at Bow Street, where a gentleman testified that Fay had tried 'to push into his house' and molested him. This was another tactical ruse on her part. When she had no money to pay for her cab, she would solicit it from a nearby man and, if refused, she would push him and accuse him of assaulting her in the hope that he would 'settle up' to avoid 'further annoyance'. She reportedly conducted her defence in 'her usual simpering semi-hysterical manner'. The gaoler reminded the justice that she was a regular, well known to all the police courts in the capital, and that she had been given opportunities to mend her ways. Apparently a 'Jewish lady from Kensington took a great interest in her and took her to a home. She stayed about a fortnight, and during that time her behaviour was very bad.' Fay was either fraudulently intent on avoiding paying for services (like transport, accommodation and food) or hopeful of making the acquaintance of a man that would pay for them in return for her company or, perhaps, something more intimate; or perhaps she simply had become lost in her own fantasies and, fuelled by drink, could no longer separate truth from fiction. The court ordered her to find two sureties of £20 each for her 'good behaviour for six months', a tall order for Fay.[42]

Fay's 31st court appearance, in April 1890, was dramatic. She arrived wearing a 'light blue silk ball dress' with 'a profusion of lace flounces'. Over this she wore a 'purple brown costume, relieved by a large white silk bow at the back, an enormous dress "improver", and she carried, as she entered the dock, a bright scarlet lace-trimmed opera mantle'. On her head was a 'jaunty little cricket cap', which only partly hid her 'greasy black hair', and on her nose were a pair of opera glasses. She must have been a remarkable sight. Yet for all her gaudy glamour she could not hide her desperate circumstances or her unwashed hair and face. The policeman who arrested her had cleared away a crowd around her once that night, but she had simply caused a disturbance nearby. She claimed to have been robbed, which was probably a distraction to win sympathy (although drunks were often the victims of street robbery). Having listened to Fay's excuses and promises of reform, the magistrate,

Mr Newton, decided to remand her for a week so that enquiries could be made and assigned a plain-clothes officer to her case.[43]

On 17 May she was brought up from the cells to hear what the enquiries had discovered. She cut a sad figure, clutching a bunch of artificial flowers and attempting (and failing) to conceal some bread and cheese. Constable Bush reported that she had been twenty times before the court at Bow Street. Mrs Sullivan, a matron from Millbank, said she had known Tottie since 1879, when, as 'Lilly Cohen', she had been convicted of a felony.[44] She recalled her being imprisoned for six months in 1886 for stealing 'a case of surgical instruments'. Fay spoke in her own defence: 'those "velanies" [felonies] you charge me with were a long time ago, you know.'[45] She then gave her usual excuses, provoking laughter, almost as if she was a music hall performer regaling an audience with a much-loved act. It was clear that her criminal career was catching up with her and Mr Newton was determined that it 'must be stopped'. Despite her pleas that a criminal trial and the long prison sentence that might result would be injurious to her health, he committed her to face a jury. On 27 May 1890 Fay (as 'Dolly le Blanc') was tried at the London County Sessions on a charge of stealing with intent to defraud. She claimed to be an actress at the Alhambra in the West End, but the theatre manager refuted this. She next wove an elaborate story of taking a train from Paris, having breakfast with her daughter and forgetting her luggage at Victoria, before denying both charges (of stealing clothes and food). Despite a 'tearful appeal to the Court' the jury convicted her, and she was sent to prison for six months with hard labour.[46]

In December 1890 Tottie Fay was back, charged at Marlborough Street with being drunk and riotous. PC Carter had found Fay arguing with a cab driver over her fare and complaining that she was 'a respectable young lady' and demanding to be admitted to her 'mamma's' house. She had been trying to ring the bells on several doors and the policeman had roughly pulled her away. Since she could hardly stand, he led her back to the station, where she spent a night in custody. In court Fay said she had been trying to secure work as a maid but was being thwarted by policemen who kept locking her up. Mr Hannay sent her to prison for another month.[47] This took Tottie Fay into the New Year. And, on release in 1891, right on cue, she was back to her old ways. Appearing as 'Violet le Bell', she was charged at Bow Street with disorderly conduct and obscene language. Dressed eccentrically in 'an opera cloak fastened with a spray of imitation diamonds', her hands festooned with brass rings, Fay tried to interrupt the police testimony. She loudly complained about these 'wicked policemen [who] club together to ruin me'. When the gaoler pointed out her extensive record before the courts, she turned on him. 'Oh look at the wicked lies you have told. I'll have you for this.' The magistrate ordered her to find sureties for her good behaviour for three months. 'Oh my God!', she responded, 'three months', before being led back to the cells.

The *Daily News* headed its report of the incident as 'HOPELESS DEPRAVITY', and repeated the court's insistence that 'every effort had been made on her behalf by charitable ladies', all to no avail.[48] What they did not, and could not, understand was that Fay was suffering from a form of mental and physical illness: an addiction to alcohol and a personality disorder that needed treating, not punishing with imprisonment. On 25 April 1891 the *Penny Illustrated Paper* offered a pen portrait of Tottie Fay for its readers. This was almost a full-page 'splash' on one of London's 'many notabilities', as the paper described her.[49] The accompanying sketch was taken as she was being prosecuted for another alleged fraud, this time on Fischer's Hotel in St James's. Fay, as pictured by the paper, was diminutive; just 5 feet tall, and 'squat', dressed, as ever, in a dazzling combination of fake fur, gloves, cheap jewellery and with a pearl coronet on her head. Mr Magnus Heirlei complained that Fay had arrived at his hotel in Clifford Street in the early hours of the

Miss Tottie Fay, portrait from *Penny Illustrated Paper*, 25 April 1891.

morning and claimed that she 'had engaged room No. 5', where her father and mother had stayed the week before. The porter showed her up and in the morning she was served breakfast. At eight o'clock in the evening she was asked to leave and given twenty minutes to pack. When she was still there beyond that Heirlei insisted she leave. She refused and the police were called to take her away. In court Fay tried to deny it all, claiming that the prosecutor had promised not to proceed with the charge and tried to undermine the porter's evidence by intimating that he might have been open to a bribe: 'he must have known that no respectable lady would have been out at that time of night, particularly without an escort,' she argued, not implausibly. The magistrate remanded her for a week so that other staff could be brought to give evidence.[50]

A week later the hearing reconvened and a housemaid explained how she had brought Fay 'a chop, with tea and bread and butter' in the middle of the afternoon, followed by three bottles of ale, which explained her boisterous and belligerent mood. She was committed to the Middlesex Sessions of the Peace. Her trial took place in May 1891 and Fay gave her name as 'Lilly St John' and her age as 42. She offered a plea of 'not guilty, mon cher' and promised to mend her ways. The court found her guilty of obtaining goods by false pretences and sentenced her to twelve months' imprisonment in Wormwood Scrubs, which the papers dubbed her 'temporary retirement'.[51] In September, while the real Tottie Fay languished in prison, a stage comedy focused on a police court included her as a 'notorious' character, 'creating hearty laughter and applause'.[52]

In May 1892 Tottie Fay (aka 'Mabel Carlton') was prosecuted for disorderly behaviour with obscene language. She had only just been released from Wormwood Scrubs prison and had immediately 'commenced plying her occupation'. She had been arrested after being seen with a man in Portland Place. She claimed he had invited her to share a 'glass of champagne' and offered to pay for a cab, both of which she, as a 'modest young lady', had refused. At that moment 'a horrid policeman' had come along and the man had quickly moved on. She had been arrested for using bad language and was probably correct in suggesting that was all the officer could arrest her for. To have evidence of her soliciting he would need the man to testify, which most would have been reluctant to do, or to have overheard their conversation. Fay argued she was the victim of harassment: 'I really cannot walk in the streets now. If I have been in trouble before, am I to be locked up?' Mr Newton warned her not to come before him again and let her go. Fay thanked him and promised to join a Young Women's Christian Society.[53]

The same paper reported that Jane Cakebread had been up before Mr Corser again, only a day after being let out of gaol. She promised to return to her sister in Ware if he let her off again. The magistrate remanded her so enquiries could be made as to whether her sister existed or would take her in.[54] Mr Corser's leniency was not rewarded by any change in behaviour though. On 27 May Cakebread was back at North London for her 246th court case. PC 489J described how he had been called to a disturbance in a pub where she was refused service for being too drunk. He asked her to go home but she 'became very abusive' and she was so incapable he had been obliged to call for an ambulance. Mr Bros sentenced her to a month and as she was being led away she was heard to mutter that 'it might have been a different story if Mr Corser had been here.' Her pleas for lenient treatment clearly worked better on some magistrates than they did on others, a reminder that the exercise of discretion was part and parcel of the police magistrate's role.

When Jane Cakebread next came back before Mr Corser in late July 1892 it was for what the paper recorded as her fiftieth at North London. Jane came in clutching all her worldly belongings in 'her usual bundle' and bowed to 'His Worship'. Having heard a familiar report of her drunkenness, bad language and the necessity to carry her away on a police ambulance, the magistrate told the gaoler to take her back to the cells while he decided what to do with her.[55] Jane Cakebread's story was recounted nationwide. The *Yorkshire Evening Post* reported that one London police court missionary, Robert Smith, had described Cakebread as a 'physical enigma, and morally she has no more backbone than a jellyfish'.[56] This reveals a prevalent contemporary attitude towards women like Cakebread, that they were weak willed and lacked the moral fibre required to resist alcohol. He stopped short of saying publicly that she required medical assistance but implied in his statement that Cakebread's 'power to resist drink is wholly gone'.

In June 1892 Fay was arrested in Oxford Street having been found drunk and dancing in front of two cardboard boxes. She had drawn a crowd, and a policeman asked her to leave but she refused, saying she was waiting for her sister to fetch her in a carriage. Fay claimed that a 'gentleman' had tried to intervene and speak to the inspector at the station house on her behalf. The police confirmed this but added that as soon as the man had been informed of the prisoner's name, he had refused to leave his name. The Good Samaritan presumably thought the police were harassing an innocent, if mentally unstable, woman.[57] After being remanded for a week she was brought up again and had a solicitor appointed to represent her. This was unusual as Fay would have had no funds to instruct one, but Arthur Newton had been paid for by 'a gentleman', possibly the person that had attempted to help when she was arrested. Newton pleaded for leniency. He asked if her week in custody on remand would be sufficient punishment. Mr Hannay recognized it as 'a melancholy case', and as one that made him 'despair': 'if she is sent to prison she is again here almost directly after she is released. Fortunately, in London there are very few of such cases. In mercy to the woman, I must send her to gaol for a month.' Fay did not seem to mind much; it was a roof over her head and some basic food. 'God bless you, sir,' she said as she was taken down.[58]

In August 1892 Fay was charged at Marylebone for another episode of drunk and disorderly behaviour in Great Western Road. Her resort to 'abominable language' earned her a night in the cells.[59] This arrest prompted a change of heart from the writer of an article titled 'Yorkshire Echoes'. He suggested that Fay and Cakebread might be better served by an initiative proposed in

Tottie Fay dances, from *Illustrated Police News*, 11 June 1892.

Germany: 'enforced restraint under proper medical care'. Fay was, like Cakebread, 'past reclamation'. 'She cannot be kept in ordinary refuges,' he stated, 'she is beyond moral restraint, she is a disease.'[60] While hardly sympathetic, it did at least signal that an alternative viewpoint was in circulation. The simple locking up of inebriates in prison increasingly came to be seen as inappropriate. The continued and widespread reportage of these women's desperate lives had crossed a line in 1892. Now they were not merely being seen as objects of ridicule or examples of the moral degradation of their class of womanhood; now they were beginning to emerge as a problem requiring a new solution.

Fay had also reached a critical point in her life. In Sepember 1892 she attempted suicide. She was brought up at Marylebone on Saturday, 17 September, giving her name 'as Lilian Vivian, 37', adding she was 'a governess residing at Kentish Town-road'. While dressed in her own eccentric style she exhibited less bravado. PC Gatrell reported that he had seen her by Gloucester Gate Bridge, Camden Town, at two in the morning, staring into the water. As she threw away her possessions and looked about to leap into the canal the policeman ran and caught hold of her. 'Oh, do let me alone,' she cried, 'I'm in low spirits.' She denied the charge and said she was only stooping to tie her bootlaces. She also denied being drunk. The gaoler confirmed that Fay had only just come out of prison after serving a month and the magistrate discharged her, either because he had some sympathy for her or because there was insufficient evidence to support a charge of attempted suicide.[61] A few days later Fay was up again. Arrested for drunk and disorderly behaviour in Paddington after an argument with a cab driver, she got a warning and three days inside.[62] In October 1892 it was fraud and theft that landed her in gaol. When a commercial traveller named Mr Heatherington answered his door at the Temperance Hotel on Queen's Square he was met by a woman wearing a shawl over her head. 'I beg your pardon,' she said, 'I thought this was the waitress's room.' She complained of being ill and asked him to fetch her some brandy. As he went off to do so she entered his room and stole £3 of his money.[63] She was charged at Clerkenwell Police court where Heatherington explained that Fay had first threatened him with a counter suit if he proceeded with the charge against her and then promised to repay the money if he dropped them. In custody at Hunter Street police station Fay vehemently denied taking the man's money: 'I would not be so mean as to do a thing like that. If I wanted to thieve I should steal diamonds.' The magistrate committed her to face a jury trial. Fay begged not to be incarcerated again, saying 'she would lose her reason if placed in solitude'. Given her recent suicide attempt there is good reason to think that she was genuinely concerned about being sent to prison for a long stretch. Not that this cut much ice with the judge, who sentenced her to three years' penal servitude.[64] In November the press carried reports that a Mr J. C. Phillips of Holloway had written to the Home Secretary 'requesting him to reconsider the sentence of three years' penal servitude passed on Tottie Fay'. The Home Secretary (Herbert Henry Asquith, the Liberal MP and future PM) declined his request.[65] Fay's fears of being driven insane by the confines of prison were realized in December that year. Under the headline 'The Last of "Tottie Fay"', the papers carried variations of the following story:

> The unfortunate woman who is known as 'Tottie Fay' has ...after a careful investigation, been declared a lunatic. This means that she will be removed from the prison at Wormwood Scrubs to a lunatic asylum. It also means that, though she will henceforth be treated with much consideration, she is not likely to make her appearance again in London.[66]

That asylum was Broadmoor, where she was formally admitted on 14 December 1892. When two journalists from *The Sun* newspaper visited Broadmoor in February 1894 ('for the purpose of visiting the criminal lunatic supposed to be "Jack the Ripper"') they reported that Fay was 'stated to be very violent – "maniacal" was the word used in the official document – and had to be removed from her room to a cell where there was no furniture to break nor glass to smash'.[67] Fay stayed in Broadmoor until her release in October 1895.

Throughout her police court career Tottie Fay often declared that she had left luggage at one of London's railway stations. In June 1896 her possessions were said to be at the booking office of the Great Western railway company. *Lloyd's* reported that 'some three years ago' she had deposited a basket of clothes, a 'parcel wrapped in newspaper, and six pots of flowers'. She left instructions for the flowers to be watered and promised to return in a few days. On that occasion she left the station under arrest having caused a scene and the report noted that no application had been made by the St Giles' Board of Guardians (of the Poor) to collect them.[68] And this, it would seem, is the last time Fay troubled the newspapers in person. Her name was used either in connection with debates on habitual drunkenness or when some occupant of a police court dock resembled her or her transgressions in some way. So, for example, in January 1893 'Mary Buyers, a woman who is known to the police as "Poll", was charged with being drunk and disorderly in Coleshill Street' in Birmingham. 'On Wednesday night she was locked up by a constable for being drunk', the report in the *Daily Post* continued, 'when she said she was "Tottie Fay".' The woman was fined, and the paper noted that it was 'the second time within two days a woman has professed to rejoice in the name of "Tottie Fay".'[69]

It is worth reflecting on what we can sensibly say about Tottie Fay once we remove the hyperbole surrounding her court appearances. Fay grew up in Seven Dials, an area of central London that was notorious for both its poverty and criminality. In creating the character of 'Tottie' and adopting the persona of 'a lady', Fay was distancing herself from her humble origins. Her modus operandi was set quite early on and changed little. She was caught up in a cycle of poverty and prostitution, fraud and theft from at least her mid-teens, possibly being forced into this as many girls and young women were. She dressed flamboyantly, wearing cheap but showy jewellery. She drank, possibly as part of the ritual of attracting men as customers at first, and then as a form of numbing anaesthetic to allow her to cope with the awful set of cards that life had dealt her. Thereafter she became alcohol dependent. This probably undermined her ability to command a better sort of client. She would visit hotels to find clients, or picked them up in the West End's many theatres and drinking venues and took them to hotels, so she would probably be well known to the porters, possibly having to tip them from time to time. Her comment that the porter at Fischer's would have known the sort of woman she was when he let her in is suggestive of a practice that, while nominally illegal, was prevalent and hard to police. By the 1890s she was reduced to alcoholism and in a cycle of imprisonment that she seemed unable to break, so would often be homeless with very little means of support. With no money for food or lodging, or for drink, once out of prison she headed back to her old haunts and attempted to bluff her way in and live 'for free'. In some cases she may have been successful, on the simple basis that those she encountered were either fooled by her or did not want the attention of a court hearing. Increasingly this became difficult and with a string of convictions behind her she inevitably started to collect more prolonged terms of imprisonment. Given the nature of the Victorian prison system, which did its utmost to break the spirit of its 'victims', this cycle of incarceration would have had a severely detrimental effect on Fay's health, physically and mentally.[70]

For Jane Cakebread the pattern of recidivism was similar but less destructive, because she served shorter sentences as a result of not compounding her alcoholism with serious crime. It was still a desperate existence and is a reminder that the lives of working-class women were extremely hard. Choices were limited; opportunities to fall foul of the law were ever present, and the chances of getting back on the 'straight and narrow' were severely hampered by police surveillance. The Inebriates Act was not much better than the legislation it replaced, but it was an important recognition of alcoholism as a mental illness and not simply a sign of character weakness. The point is made by Roy McLeod:

> Not until the last half of the 19th century did the scientific appreciation of alcoholism become general. Only then, under the guidance of a few doctors and reformers, was the image of the drunkard as a disorderly, ill-disposed social unit gradually transformed into one of a neglected patient suffering from a mental disease with well-marked clinical features.[71]

Cakebread, like Fay, eventually ended up in an asylum – Claybury in Middlesex, which opened in 1893. She was sent there in February 1896 and so was one of its earliest residents. The police court missionary Thomas Holmes visited her in 1896 and described her as suffering from 'delusions'. Lady Somerset, who founded a 'farm colony' in Surrey and helped 'rescue' women like Jane from alcoholism, was adamant Cakebread was severely ill and belonged where she was. In her opinion Jane was 'unquestionably insane, and the smallest amount of liquor will so affect her as to render her a most dangerous lunatic'.[72] Cakebread saw herself differently: 'Mad am I?' Jane is reported as saying, 'I wish everybody had the sense, memory, ability, and education that I have.'[73]

Fay died in Horton Asylum on 1 February 1908 having spent the previous seven months there. Years of alcohol abuse and almost constant periods of incarceration would have taken a severe toll on her health. We can view Tottie Fay as a victim of a society that cared little, or as a self-destructive individual who was quick to blame her misfortune on others. Both of those sentiments would have had currency in the 1890s. Perhaps we might rescue Fay from the 'enormous condescension of posterity' by placing her extraordinary 'ordinary' life at the centre of debates to change the way habitual inebriates were viewed and dealt with by the justice system.[74] In some small way Tottie Fay, and those whose similar experiences touched the lives of newspaper readers through the reports of the police courts, changed the world.

FAY AND CAKEBREAD are unusual in having their encounters with the police courts recorded in such detail. Most of those brought before the magistrates charged as drunk and disorderly, or some variant thereof, did not make the newspapers. As one informed observer noted, while there were huge numbers of persons being charged 'a large proportion make but a single appearance', never to trouble the courts again. Very few, he added, were 'habitual drunkards'. That said, he and many others recognized the 'vast amount of misery' caused by drunkenness and alcohol dependency among the working-class population of London.[75] Organizations like the Salvation Army were in part founded to intervene to help those who succumbed to the 'demon drink'. The Army rescued an 83-year-old woman from Leeds who had been brought up on charges of drunkenness on at least 240 occasions, rivalling even Jane Cakebread for notoriety.[76] Alcoholism and poverty were intertwined and there seems to have been very little concern with the consumption of alcohol by middle- or upper-class men, unless, of course, it resulted in an embarrassing hearing in court. When it did their names were generally withheld, unlike those of the working class.

As for legislative attempts to improve the situation, I think it is markedly clear that without a system to support those with alcohol problems properly, so that they could overcome their addiction, then little progress could be made. For much of the century drunks were treated as societal problems to be fined, locked up and chastised. James Greenwood may have reported that the police court magistrates he spoke to viewed the 1898 Inebriates Act as 'a boon and a blessing', because they had so many drunks to process on a Monday morning, but the reality was that there were insufficient resources to support intervention.[77] Drunkenness was a core problem for the New Police because drinking was an important part of working-class culture in London.[78] Pubs were centres of community life, and drink lubricated occasions for celebration and sorrow in equal measure. While Londoners were not drunkards, their drinking brought them onto the streets, where they were, after 1829, engaged in a struggle for the control of space with Peel's 'bobbies'. That contest manifested itself in all manner of disputes, many of which led to police court hearings. This is the subject of the next chapter.

2

REGULATING THE CAPITAL'S STREETS AND BUSINESSES

Every one commits a common nuisance who obstructs any
highway by any permanent work or erection thereon, or injury
thereto, which renders the highway less commodious to the
public than it would otherwise be.[1]

As this quote from the 1889 Police Code book notes, anyone
causing an obstruction was liable to prosecution before a
police court magistrate. This regulation was, however, open to interpretation. In many, if not most cases, offenders were simply asked
to 'move along' and only resistance or confrontation provoked
arrest. For some infringements a summons would follow, bringing a prosecution days or weeks later. The usual penalty for these
'nuisances' was a fine, although inability to pay could result in im-
risonment by default. Given the wide range of activities that might
earn someone a court appearance, the prosecution of obstruction
offers an opportunity to explore the streets of Victorian London
through a particularly nuanced lens.

In this chapter we will meet the itinerant market traders of their
day, London's costermongers, whose daily brushes with 'Peelers'
were described by Henry Mayhew, journalist and author of *London
Labour and the London Poor*.[2] However, costers were not the only
ones to fall foul of the police. Men and boys gambling in the streets
and alleyways, preachers and Salvation Army marching bands: all
contributed to the fines collected at police courts. All these

individuals and social groups were victims of a move towards a more tightly regulated society in the Victorian period. The New Police enforced this change by their physical presence on the street, and by their conscious intention to control it. As David Churchill puts it: 'Better than "moral reform" or "civilization", "nuisance" captures the spirit of urban ordering under the police.'[3] Gradually those experiencing this new form of urban discipline adapted to it and, albeit grudgingly, accepted its reality.[4] Change did not happen overnight, spaces continued to be contested, and the 'rights' of persons to use them as they had previously done brought many into the police courts.

Before 1829 London's streets were not patrolled during daylight hours; only after sunset did the night watch leave the watch-houses to perambulate between their boxes. Poorly equipped and paid, watchmen had acquired an unfairly negative reputation by the late 1700s and this is cited as a causal factor in their replacement by full-time professionals in 1829.[5] Once Robert Peel's officers began their daytime beats it was inevitable that they would come into regular conflict with those that used the city streets as their workplace and playground.[6] However, the policing of 'nuisances' was not an innovation born of professional policing in the 1830s, it had much deeper roots. The police were enforcing a new discipline and continuing a tradition of local self-regulation.[7] Increasingly arguments for improvement drove agendas to clean up areas of the capital and rid the streets of nuisances. This was manifest in the removal of the cattle market at Smithfield in 1852, and in the shifting of most 'dirty trades' to east London, north and south of the river. Here police took on a role that had been performed by non-policing agents previously. While the prevention of crime by the patrolling of streets was a continuation of the work of the watch, the intervention of the police to deal with obstructions (and a variety of other infringements) represented a takeover of the work of urban scavengers. So as well as fighting crime the Victorian policeman was 'the obedient servant of the local propertied community, and its representatives in local government'.[8] This role brought them into direct conflict with those who believed that they had a right to use the streets and who rejected attempts to prevent them earning a living, as well as those who simply resented being told what to do by policemen.

The costermonger: London's market traders

Costermongers were independent traders, generally selling fruit and vegetables from barrows on the street. Overwhelmingly costermongers were London born, even if they had immigrant ancestors. No doubt this has helped cement the image of the costermonger as the archetypal cockney, supposedly embodying 'the virtues of good-naturedness, determination, and individualism'.[9] It is fair to say that contemporary views of costermongers were mixed. The *Sunday at Home* was critical: 'The costermonger is seldom at home. He rises early, works till dark, and gambles, drinks, or occupies a seat in the gallery of his favourite local theatre in the evening. His home is therefore neglected.'

Costers tended, the article suggested, to shun religious services and many followed the 'wrong' faith – Catholicism.[10] Costermongers were a close-knit group; many handed down their business to their sons, while a significant number of the poorer traders were 'driven' to the streets by economic hardship.[11] Costermongers were obliged to live close to the source of their produce: the capital's wholesale markets.[12] As a result of this, and the casual and poorly remunerated nature of their work (they typically earned less than 10*s* a week), costers were found in London's poorer districts.[13] They lived in cheap and insanitary housing and when the Artisans' Dwelling Act (1875) ushered in a decade of slum clearance, they were disproportionately affected.[14] Huge numbers of costermongers were forced out of accommodation in Whitechapel,

Limehouse, St George-in-the-East, St Giles and Southwark. As Gareth Stedman Jones noted, this 'disastrous' piece of legislation contributed considerably to 'the crisis of overcrowding' that so blighted London in the 1880s.[15] This was a second purge of the area; between 1842 and 1847 the Church Lane rookery was demolished in order to build New Oxford Street. In the process more than 5,000 of the capital's poorest were displaced. Residents did not disperse across the capital, as designers had intended, but decamped locally to streets around Seven Dials. As a result, while the average number of persons per house in London was around 7.8, in St Giles it was double that by 1871.[16]

Alongside the image of the coster as a 'cheerful cockney' is that of a casual worker with no liking for imposed law and order. Costers may have been culturally conservative, but they had little respect for police authority. This was linked to a general disdain for wealth and privilege.[17] As a body the costermongers represented an urban workforce that valorized independence and opposed regulation. This meant that a running battle with the forces of law and order – the Metropolitan Police – was inevitable.

Much of the contemporary material we have describing the people of the capital in the 1800s was written by, and for, a middle-class audience. As a result, historians have been reticent to take such sources at face value, preferring instead to read them as a 'discourse of alterity' created by a dominant class intent on imposing its own values on society.[18] In the writings of Mayhew we might just be able to see what Ole Münch described as an 'intercultural exchange between a middle-class journalist and his poor informants'. This is because not only did Mayhew often represent the costermongers sympathetically, but costers 'actually read what Mayhew wrote about them'.[19] Mayhew described the costers as independent and dismissive of shared societal values and practices.[20] Having made efforts to present himself as a friend of the casual street trader, Mayhew managed to alienate them with some

Bleeding Heart Yard with costermongers, illustration from
Walter Thornbury, *Old and New London* (1873–8).

of his observations and allegations of their reticence to marry and
comparisons of them to 'nomadic races'.[21] Most costers saw themselves as respectable tradesmen, rejecting Mayhew's slights on their
character and culture. These sleights were common currency in the
1800s and reflected what were probably widespread views among
middle-class Londoners that costers were loud and vulgar, and
were falling behind in the race for respectability by comparison to
fixed shopkeepers. A cartoon in *Punch* from November 1863 con-
trasted the 'Costermonger as he is' (standing in front of his barrow,
a string of onions in one hand, the other cupped to yell 'Ya? Ho! –
cauliflowers – Ho!') with 'as he might be' (smartly attired in top hat
and tails, asking his lady customer, 'Yes, Ma'am! Is there any other
article?', as she selects her purchases). The cartoon makes it plain
which version of the street trader the periodical would like to
see.[22]

The most obvious way costermongers represented a problem in the eyes of the police was by blocking the free flow of traffic and pedestrians.[23] Traders would place their carts where they might expect to find customers, whether they were selling pots and pans, seasonal fruit and vegetables, or street food. Drawing a crowd was integral to the way in which these street sellers traded. They 'cried' their wares, shouting to attract customers to the goods they had for sale and the price they were asking. A stationary cart attracting a small crowd could occupy a section of the highway, making it harder for other vehicles to pass safely, or spill onto the passageway forcing pedestrians into the road. Additionally, the presence of casual street traders represented an economic threat to London's fixed traders, its shopkeepers. Costers would often position their carts outside a row of shops, hoping to benefit from the foot flow of customers. In some cases this was a symbiotic relationship: a coster's goods bringing in custom to shops, or vice versa. But other times they represented unwelcome cheaper competition. Costers themselves were always at pains to highlight that they represented a mobile, cheaper alternative to the fixed high street grocer. They sold affordable fresh produce and brought it into poorer communities where money and time were at a premium.

Press reports give a clear indication of the sorts of problems associated with costers. In 1870 William Hiscocks, a City constable, was busy removing barrows causing an obstruction on Lower Thames Street, opposite Billingsgate Market, when Edward Kelly waded in. Kelly was a 'tall, powerful-looking man' who had earned a reputation as an unsavoury character. The policeman insisted the traders remove their barrows, but they refused. Kelly urged his fellow traders to continue to resist this infringement of their 'customary rights' and, when the others folded and complied with PC Hiscocks's request, he remained and began to restore the baskets to the pavement. When asked to stop he gave the officer a mouthful of abuse and was arrested. At Mansion House Kelly denied doing anything wrong but previous appearances counted against him. The Lord Mayor sided with the policeman, telling him that he was 'a very bad character': 'If you would only live quietly without annoying other people, there would be no difficulty, but you are always using abusive language, causing obstructions, and "finding"... property that does not belong to you.' He sent him to prison for fourteen days with hard labour.

Charles Lee, 23, was brought up before the same magistrate, also charged with obstruction in Lombard Street, the heart of the capital's banking community. Lee had been selling shirt studs and other goods on the pavement. In mitigation Lee said he 'always kept on the move, and never remained in the City after four o'clock'. He had been fined 2s the last time he had been in court and added that 'paying fines was not very pleasant.' 'I don't impose them because they are pleasant,' the Lord Mayor snapped. He accepted that the life of a street trader was hard but that did not excuse him

Petticoat Lane with Jewish traders, illustration from
Walter Thornbury, *Old and New London* (1873–8).

causing obstructions. He fined him 4*s* or seven days in gaol.[24] Both examples show the constant battle between the authorities (the police and magistracy, and the vestry as the representatives of the ratepayers) and those who relied upon the streets for making a living.

When several itinerant traders gathered, an obstruction was almost inevitable. This sometimes infringed existing by-laws and necessarily involved the police. Yet it is also a clear example of the changing nature of the capital and the pressures on space caused by a rising population. Earlier in the century, and before the passing of an important defining piece of legislation in 1867, the battle for use of the streets regularly brought police and costers into conflict with each other. The following case is an example of how coster-mongers could be doubly penalized by the application of the law by unsympathetic policemen. In October 1858 James Murray was charged at Guildhall with obstructing Beech Street in the Barbican. Murray had been arrested and his barrow confiscated and taken off to the City's Green Yard in Whitecross Street. This was a long-established pound where stray animals and abandoned carts and other vehicles could be taken. In order to retrieve it Murray had to pay 2*s* 6*d* in fines. Alderman Finnis was content the law had been correctly applied, as Murray had refused to move, but unhappy that the barrow was impounded. This had not only rendered the man liable to a fine, but undoubtedly caused his stock of fruit to spoil. The policeman had acted as judge, jury and executioner and that role belonged to the magistrate alone. The policeman justified him-self: 'The obstruction caused by these men with their barrows and fruit is a very great nuisance, and . . . I am bound to bring them before you.' The alderman reprimanded Murray, warned him not to offend in the future, and let him go without further sanction.[25]

In September 1860 Sir Robert Carden fined several coster-mongers in the City half a crown each and threatened them with prison if they continued to block the junction of King William

Street and Cannon Street. Local shopkeepers had complained repeatedly about the nuisance caused by barrows and, while it may have been the competition they really objected to, the magistrate was informed that the 'spot [where they pitched] is very steep and slippery, and the effect of the barrows being there is not only to cause great obstruction to the carriage trade, but also to the tradespeople of the neighborhood'.[26] The shopkeepers had a valid point but were pressing it because it suited their common interest in denying competition for their trade. The police were still targeting costermongers in Hammersmith in late February 1874. They brought summonses against several costermongers for 'standing their barrows [in King Street] longer than was necessary for loading or unloading goods'. One coster said he had only stopped to serve a customer, but the police argued that this had taken twelve minutes, which was too long. The magistrate at Hammersmith Police court said twelve minutes was reasonable and thought it understandable that people went to buy from barrows. The police stated that a market had been built at Hammersmith but the costermongers 'would not use it'. King Street had shops on either side and the presence of so many barrows meant the street was congested. One of the defendants complained that plenty of the shopkeepers displayed goods for sale on the pavements in front of their shops but the police did nothing about them. In the end the magistrate compromised, levying minimum fines.[27]

As Inwood argued, in the first decades of their existence the New Police applied the laws available to them with considerable discretion.[28] What constituted reasonable was clearly open to interpretation and police officers were susceptible to all sorts of pressures (from superiors, local businesses, vestrymen and the general public). It would be remarkable if they applied the law completely without 'fear or favour' in such difficult circumstances. When William Mayhead was brought before the Westminster Police court for obstructing the footway in Grosvenor Row, Chelsea, he stoutly defended himself. While he was selling fish from a cart placed outside a butcher's shop, the butcher himself was offering meat at cut price, causing a crowd to gather. As Mayhead was serving a customer a policeman intervened and arrested him, not bothering to discover what the actual cause of the congestion was. The customer was in court to support the costermonger and the magistrate, Mr Arnold, dismissed the charges. The magistrate criticized the police for allowing some traders to operate but not others, when it was 'not part of their duty to make such distinctions'. Mayhead grumbled that when he sold fish from a basket the 'police followed him about and trod upon his heels'. That was harassment and the inspector present told him he should report any officer doing that at the nearest station house.[29]

It is evident that a war of sorts was underway for the control of the streets and highways. The police were the de facto face of authority on the capital's thoroughfares but there they encountered classes of men and women who had claimed the streets as their workplace or entertainment venue for decades, if not centuries. In the 1850s this was still hotly contested, and the police could not be sure that the magistracy would always find in their favour. As the century unfolded, however, the interests of fixed trade (shopkeepers) and the local authorities (the parish and later the London County Council from 1889) won out and across London itinerant traders like William Mayhead were increasingly restricted to fixed markets where they could be better regulated and where they would not obstruct pavements.

One of the frustrations voiced by shopkeepers was that they were held to different and higher levels of account than their itinerant competitors. The difference between a fixed trader and a costermonger became the key distinction in a case heard before Mr Woolrych at Westminster Police court in December 1870. William Haynes, a fruiterer and potato dealer with premises in Pimlico, was summoned to explain why he had obstructed the carriageway. He was prosecuted under the 'new Street Act' for 'allowing two barrows

Cock Lane with costermonger, illustration from
Walter Thornbury, *Old and New London* (1873–8).

to rest longer than necessary for loading or unloading'.[30] The court
heard he had left them there for five hours. His defence lawyer
accepted the facts of the case but tried to argue that since his client
sold apples from these barrows he might be classed as a costermonger, and therefore be allowed to do so. Woolrych admired the

creativity of the defence but rejected it. The word 'costermonger' might have derived from 'costard', a large apple, as the lawyer suggested, but 'that term had become obsolete', the magistrate explained, as 'the present acceptation of the word costermonger was an itinerant trader [who] went from place to place.' Haynes owned two shops and did not move them around. Woolrych let the fruiterer off the fine but insisted he pay the costs of the summons. The lawyer said he would take the question of 'whether a tradesman cannot be a costermonger if he please' to the Court of Queen's Bench for a higher authority to determine. Two weeks later Haynes was back in court and the charge was the same, as was the defence. This time he was fined.[31]

The Metropolitan Streets Act (1867) had several regulations aimed at ensuring the streets were kept as free moving as possible. No one was to leave goods on the street, or 'be otherwise allowed to cause obstruction or inconvenience to the passage of the public', for any amount of time 'longer than necessary'. Contravening the act carried a penalty of up to 40 shillings.[32] However, complaints from costers and other itinerant tradesmen caused a small amendment to be made to the act allowing them to be exempted from it. It was recognized that an inability to stop and sell their goods would effectively undermine their businesses. Inevitably this was going to cause some resentment among shopkeepers. In April 1872, two years after his previous court appearance, William Haynes was back, this time as one of three Pimlico greengrocers brought before the Westminster magistrate for obstructing the pavements. The court heard that the trio occupied premises 'where costermongers are allowed to assemble in accordance with the provisions of the Metropolitan Street Act' and that the area was a 'a regular market on a Saturday night'. Once again the defence lawyer presented the argument that his clients had as much right to trade from stalls outside their shops as costermongers did to sell from barrows, so long as they 'did not infringe the police regulations'. But it seems they did infringe those regulations. Inspector Turpin said that Haynes's stall was fully 50 feet (15 m) long while Joseph Haynes (his son or brother) had one that was 35 feet (11 m) (a coster's barrow would typically be 5–8 feet (1.5–2.5 m) long). Both stalls forced pedestrians to walk out into the road to get past. The defendants pleaded guilty, promised to 'make better arrangements' in the future, and were fined between 10s and 40s each, plus costs. They paid up but with some protest.[33] This was not something that was going to go away. The greengrocers could afford to keep paying fines and may well have thought it a necessary expense to be able to compete for trade with the costermongers. In the United Kingdom today high streets have very few independent grocers and greengrocers as the supermarkets have captured most of that business. In the 1800s, then, we can see the future unfolding as Londoners competed for space and the right to use it as they saw fit.

Obstructions came in many forms. Under the headline 'LIVING PLACARDS' the *Morning Post* reported the case of Thomas Ellis, who was brought before Mr D'Eyncourt at Worship Street in December 1853 charged with obstructing the highway. Ellis was an elderly man who won the sympathy of both reporter and magistrate. A policeman testified to seeing Ellis on the City Road carrying two advertising boards: 'one in front and the other behind', the classic 'sandwich-man'. His boards advertised 'lectures' at Crosby Hall, which, before it closed in 1868 to become a restaurant, was the home of a literary and scientific institution in Danvers Street.[34] Ellis was clearly something of a novelty, so presumably sandwich-boards and their wearers were not common. D'Eyncourt expressed surprise that the policeman had thought Ellis was doing anything wrong since the boards were no wider than he was. He was told that the constable was enforcing a new order issued to prevent all such 'exhibitions upon the footpaths', so perhaps the police commissioners were responding to an innovation in advertising that they feared might create a new problem. Ellis was apologetic and stated

Birch's Shop, Cornhill, with a sandwich-man, illustration
from Walter Thornbury, *Old and New London* (1873–8).

that he had not known that he was infringing any laws. He had
taken the work as it was not too 'laborious' for someone of his age,
however he promised to forego the sixpence a day he was paid and
return the boards to his employer and was discharged.[35]

The problem of street gambling

The 1867 legislation could also be applied to those whose intentions
were arguably less honest than the purveyors of fruit and vegetables,
household goods or sandwich-men: for example, gamblers (usually
using coins or dice). Gambling had been represented as a threat to
public morality for centuries. In August 1870 a detective approached
a small crowd that surrounded three individuals taking bets on
horse racing and arrested the trio, who, it turned out, had no betting

licences and so were fined £5, the maximum for persons causing an obstruction. Since betting was such a lucrative business, they were able to avoid prison by paying it.[36] The Metropolitan Streets Act was not the only weapon in the police armoury; in 1873 an amendment to the Vagrancy Act enabled police to bring prosecutions against those engaged in gambling in the streets.[37] Two young men were prosecuted for obstruction while running some sort of betting scam on Tottenham Court Road. A plain-clothed officer picked them up after he was able to get close enough to see what they were up to. Regular uniformed officers would have little chance of catching organized gangs in the act because small boys were routinely posted as lookouts and could spot uniformed police coming some way off. When the officer made the arrest he discovered that one of them – William Tripp – had a pocketbook that contained an annotated list of 'all the racing events of the season'. It was the nuisance they had caused that brought complaints about them, but it was illegal betting that Mr Vaughan decided to punish at Bow Street. Tripp was fined £5 (or one month in prison) as he was seen to be the ringleader (or 'duper'), while his second – Robert Leader – was given a fine of £1 (or ten days). They paid the fines and were discharged, again demonstrating the money to be made from street gambling.[38]

Given humanity's long and deeply divisive relationship with games of chance the problem of street gambling often resurfaced. To get some indication of the nature of the games of chance Londoners could risk their hard-earned wages on, consider the case of William Davis, brought before a magistrate in the City in April 1880. Davis had set himself up in a street near Petticoat Lane (or Middlesex Street as it was renamed in the 1830s) with a wheel-of-fortune board. A large crowd of people gathered round as gamblers placed their bets on various 'lottery' numbers. The board supposedly randomly selected a winner. However, Davis had rigged the board so that 'he could make the indicator stop in his own favor', thereby ensuring the house invariably won. The police had tried to eradicate such sharp practice, but lottery men like Davis placed lookouts at several vantage points to signal whenever an officer appeared. This time the police got lucky and shut down the game, confiscating the board. Davis denied owning the gaming board but was fined 5s.[39] A very similar scam had been temporarily shut down in Bethnal Green seven years earlier. John Hambledon's table (dubbed a 'spinning jenny') was numbered and players placed bets on where the spinning dial landed, rather like a modern roulette wheel. Since this game was taking place on a late December evening the board was illuminated by candles placed on the ground around it, lighting up the faces of the eager gamblers. This probably helped the police catch them unawares. Most ran away, but Hambledon was arrested and dragged back to a police station. The Worship Street Police court magistrate sent him to prison for six months with hard labour.[40]

Street musicians and other entertainers

London was already a multicultural urban centre in the mid-1800s, even if numbers of immigrants were relatively small, around 13,000. By the end of the century around 3 per cent of Londoners were foreign born, and in the 1890s the capital could 'justly claim to be the most cosmopolitan city in Europe'.[41] Among those arriving were two Frenchmen, De Love Chamary and Agas Jean. The duo escaped penalty when they appeared before Mr Corser at Dalston in 1890. More than two hundred people had gathered in Homerton to see the 'picturesquely-dressed' men force a muzzled bear to dance. This entirely blocked the street and a policeman asked them to move along. They only went a few yards before restarting the entertainment. A gentleman complained that, along with the obstruction, the bear represented a threat to the public, having seen the beast 'make for a servant girl twice'. The magistrate, assured by the defendants that the bear was harmless, said there was little he could do beyond making them aware that they were to obey police instructions in future, and he let them go.[42]

The press reported several instances of performing bears in the capital. Messieurs Coll and Delanne were charged at Lambeth with obstructing the streets. On this occasion three hundred or so people had stopped to watch a bear holding a staff do a series of 'peculiar dances mingled with growls'. A policeman told the men to move along, which they did, but not very far, so he arrested them. At Carter Street Police station the bear was tied to a post, where, without its owners, it grew restless, began growling aggressively, and almost managed to escape. The magistrate fined the men 20s each or fourteen days in gaol for causing a nuisance. Since they did not have the funds to pay, prison looked likely, but what would be the fate of the bear? The justice first suggested the Green Yard (where missing cattle were sent) but this was probably a joke. He was advised that in previous instances bears had been sent to the zoo in Regent's Park, so that was what he ordered. The men were advised to pay the fine and return to France, which is what eventually happened, the bear being reunited with them.[43]

In 1889 a gentleman complained at Westminster Police court that a 'band of Salvationists' (meaning the Salvation Army) were continuously causing nuisance outside his property. He told Mr Sheil that there were 'at least 20 persons singing to a tambourine accompaniment' and he had called the police after they refused to stop. A policeman intervened and 'begged the people to go further off', but they refused. Instead they continued, making an even more 'hideous' noise than before. The man described how he had told the group's leader that his wife was 'lying dangerously ill' having had complications in her pregnancy. He just wanted her to be able to rest but the officer in charge of the Army band refused to believe him. He had come to Westminster to seek a summons to bring the Army to court. Sheil was sympathetic but not very helpful. Could the police have done more, he asked? 'They have no power,' the complainant told him, or at least 'they don't like to interfere.' Had an itinerant organ grinder stood opposite his house the police would have happily taken them away, but not, it seems, the men and women of the Salvation Army, however disruptive they were. The magistrate refused a summons, instead suggesting the applicant visit the 'headquarters of this so-called Salvation Army, and see why, in the name of religion, they continue to disturb a person who is ill'. In other words, challenge their Christian principles and beliefs rather than apply the same rules to them as would have been applied to itinerant street musicians.[44]

This echoes a similar case concerning the nuisance caused by the Salvation Army in its early years. One Sunday morning in late April 1896 a Mr Eamonson had settled down to write in his study when his peace was broken by the sound of music playing in the street outside. He set aside his work and went outside to remonstrate with those responsible, as he had apparently done more than once before. Disturbances like this were a perennial problem and we might imagine Eamonson's rising anger as he strode across the road from his home on Burdett Road to confront the band members assembled there. A small crowd had gathered around them and Eamonson pushed his way through towards a man who was banging a large drum. He asked them 'to stop, or go away', but the bandsmen took no notice and played on. Eamonson tried again, cupping his hands and shouting for them to stop or play somewhere else. Ignored three times he set off in search of a policeman. Eventually he found one who accompanied him back to Burdett Road to ask the band to desist. The officer tried to take their names and addresses on the grounds that they were causing a nuisance and obstructing the pavement, but it was difficult given the 'infernal din' they were making. As a consequence of their refusal to disperse, two members of the band (John Murfitt, the drummer who would not stop, and Charles White) were summoned before Mr Mead at

Thames Police court on the dual accusations of refusing to stop making a disturbance after having been requested to, and of obstruction of the thoroughfare. They denied both charges. In essence the men tried to argue that they could not hear what was being said to them, so were not aware that Eamonson had requested them to stop. Their solicitor (Mr Frost) told the court that the Army 'always cheerfully acquiesced in any suggestion' that they should refrain from disturbing the peace, but hinted that on this occasion his clients were the victims of an 'organized attack'.

Perhaps Eamonson was a serial complainer and simply did not like the Salvation Army. He would not have been alone; in its early years Salvationists like Murfitt and White suffered abuse from all classes in society. They were ridiculed, chased down the street and prosecuted as a nuisance. Mead was a stickler for the law and trod a careful path around this pair of summonses. He agreed that the playing of music was not illegal and that any obstruction was minor, and not worthy of a summons. However, he was also clear that Eamonson had been disturbed by a band playing loudly outside his home on a Sunday morning. He told Frost that if his clients gave an undertaking not to play there in the future he would dismiss the summons. The lawyer waivered, not wanting to commit the Army to signing up to self-enforced restrictions, but Mead pressed him. Further prosecutions could follow if others objected to the Army setting up a band outside their homes but hopefully if they took sensible cognizance of this action they could continue their form of recruitment without the need to defend themselves in court. It was an invitation to common sense: leave Eamonson and others like him alone, and the Salvation Army band could continue to play.[45]

William Booth had founded the East London Christian mission in 1865 and adopted the name 'The Salvation Army' in 1878. Booth and his wife Catherine were Methodists, and their intention was to bring religion and abstinence from alcohol to the poor of the East End. They did this by public meetings and marches, accompanied by brass bands made up of members, a military system of organization (with 'General' Booth at the head), and by selling their weekly paper, *The War Cry*. This they sold on the streets and in public houses and, as this case from 1882 shows, could sometimes bring them into dispute with the local constabulary. Thomas Dawson was an unlikely looking occupant of the dock at the City Police court. He was described as thirty years of age, 'delicate looking' and wearing the uniform of the Salvation Army. He had been summoned for 'obstructing the footway in Liverpool Street' while attempting to hawk copies of the Army's publication. Appearing for the City of London police, Chief Inspector Tillcock said that there had been a growing problem with Army men and women standing on the streets and drawing crowds. It was 'a great nuisance' he stated, because of the 'peculiar actions and dress' of those involved. In these early years it is likely that many members of the public were simply curious and stopped to hear what the soldiers of Booth's 'Army' had to say; others probably stopped to harangue them as misguided or laugh at their costumes. The City officer tried to move Dawson on several times but each time the man had simply returned to the same position and carried on his business. When challenged in court Dawson declared that he had just as much right to sell the paper as anyone else and was causing no more obstruction than a Punch and Judy show and the Salvation Army was 'something they wanted everyone to know about'. Sir Robert Carden found for the police and begged to differ regarding the merits of an organization that took a doctrinal position that differed from the established Anglican Church. A fine of 2s 6d plus costs was imposed with a warning that this would double for future breaches of the law.[46]

Carden's prejudices were clear and were shared by others in the Army's formative years. As a deeply religious Protestant sect it attracted criticism from middle-of-the-road members of the established Church of England. Such sneering criticism from above was matched by ridicule and antagonism from below, as some members of the working class resented the temperance message the Army preached. Many others simply disliked the awful row they made when they marched through London playing brass instruments badly and singing off key. On some occasions the actions of the Army provoked violent reactions, especially when they chose to march through areas where the prevailing beliefs were at odds with the message they preached. John Sullivan was a labourer living in Lisson Grove, an area with a large Irish community. One Sunday in 1880 an Army parade of up to sixty members was marching down Paul Street and a crowd of hundreds had turned out to watch them. A sizeable number resented the presence of the Army and the numerous missions that had been set up locally. Missions were Protestant, most London Irish were Catholic and so we might imagine the conflict that this engendered. Sullivan was convicted of assaulting a 63-year-old Salvationist and fined 1s. This was a token gesture by the magistrate at Marylebone, Mr Clarke, who advised the Army to desist from marching through these small streets as 'they were sure to lead to disturbances.'[47]

The Metropolitan Streets Act (1867) along with other pieces of legislation provided the police with a wide array of powers to move on, arrest or summons street users. Once a person came before a magistrate accused of an offence under one of these laws there was relatively little room left to the magistrate to apply common sense. Obstruction and nuisance could include anything from costers wishing to continue to trade as they had done for generations, or anyone leaving goods in the street that caused 'inconvenience to the passage of the public', to games of pitch and toss or dice, foreign street musicians or Salvation Army bandsmen and women.[48] As they had with the capital's drunks it was the police officers who found their authority challenged when they attempted to apply the law, as their superiors understood it. As a result, the police courts bore witness to dozens of prosecutions daily for obstruction. Very little of this would we consider to be 'crime', which reminds us that the police courts played an integral role in regulating everyday life in Victorian London.

Magistrates, regulation and the 'improvement' of London in the 1800s

As it had been for their Georgian predecessors, a role fundamental to magistrates in the 1800s was the regulation of the capital's trade and industry. As London grew, so too did the opportunities for commerce, the pressure on space and the possibilities of conflict arising from competition. Throughout the Victorian period there was a burgeoning awareness of the harm that industrialization and urbanization – the twin components of economic growth in the 1800s – brought. Victorians were increasingly able to organize resistance to unsavoury practices (such as the adulteration of food-stuffs or release of pollutants in residential areas), and this built upon a more general pursuit of urban improvement begun in the previous century. While actions were brought against unscrupulous traders and polluting manufacturers by agents of local government, the laws were mostly enforced by the magistracy and reported in the newspapers alongside tales of drunks, thieves and abusive husbands. By studying these reports, we can build a picture of the Victorian capital and the people that lived and worked there, trading, going about their business, competing and complaining as their lives were impacted in the seemingly never-ending pursuit of profit. It reveals the dynamic nature of London in the nineteenth century but also the roots of many of the problems we live with in the twenty-first century.

Regulating the food industry

The City of London authorities actively policed the sale of meat at London's markets to protect the citizens of the capital from the

Old Smithfield Market, 1837, illustration from
Walter Thornbury, *Old and New London* (1873–8).

ill effects of diseased produce. Prosecutions were brought to the
Guildhall by the Commissioners of Sewers' inspectors, backed by
doctors from the Medical Board of Health. Those caught selling
meat deemed unfit for human consumption could expect hefty
fines. In the earlier part of the century farmers brought their cattle
into London to be sold at Smithfield and then slaughtered, but
drovers were increasingly being prevented from driving cattle and
sheep though crowded city streets dominated by pedestrians, omnibuses and cabs. Smithfield's livestock market was eventually shut
down in 1855 following a series of investigations, and its business
moved to Islington.[49] Before 1855 Smithfield was not a 'dead' meat
market; meat was sold primarily at Newgate, but also at Leadenhall
and at Farringdon (on the west side of Farringdon Street near New
Bridge Street, Blackfriars).[50] The new Central Meat Market on the
old Smithfield site opened in 1868.[51] This move, taking the ancient

function of the market and replacing it with something more fitting for a modern commercial city, was part of a process of urban improvement in the long nineteenth century that aimed to clean up Britain's towns and cities.

To give an example of prosecutions at Smithfield here is a case from June 1889 brought to the Guildhall. John Stafford, a Leicester butcher, had sent four pieces of beef to the market in May that year. These had been inspected and found to be unfit. Stafford pleaded innocence, declaring the meat was fine when he had dispatched it. Dr Sedgewick of the Board of Health disagreed. He testified that he had seen the meat himself, and it was 'wet and emaciated . . . very dark, and had a very offensive odour.' He added, 'It had the appearance of coming from an animal that had been ill for some time.' The court heard from an officer from Leicestershire constabulary, Detective Sergeant George Crisp, who had been asked by the

Metropolitan Meat Market, illustration from
Walter Thornbury, *Old and New London* (1873–8).

commissioners in London to make inquiries. Stafford claimed that he had purchased the animal at a local fair and had killed and butchered it himself. The evidence convinced the magistrate that the butcher had known the meat was bad before he brought it south, and so fined him a huge sum, £60 (£15 for each piece), with an additional 3 guineas to cover the commissioners' costs. The next defendant was also from the East Midlands. Francis Height was a butcher who gave an address in Northamptonshire, and a police inspector from that constabulary accompanied him. Height had sent a sheep to the market for sale that had been seized by one of the market inspectors. Dr Saunders, for the Board, said the animal suffered from a lung disease and the meat was not fit to be eaten. The Northamptonshire man admitted sending the sheep but like the previous defendant assured the court that he thought the meat was fine when he let it go. This was deemed no defence and he was fined £20 plus costs. So on that day alone the Commissioners of Sewers and the Guildhall court were awarded £80 in fines, plus significant costs.[52]

Alongside the scrutiny of meat and poultry the police courts were involved in the regulation of the trade in other consumables. Restrictions on what went into food and drink, along with attempts to police illegal practices, are synonymous with the growth of the Victorian state. From the early years of Queen Victoria's reign her governments oversaw a tremendous increase in bureaucratic systems aimed at monitoring and controlling all aspects of daily life. While a focus on health and safety may often be presented as a modern, post-war phenomenon, closely associated with bureaucrats in the European Union, the process of closer regulation began in the 1800s. It was manifested in the Factory Acts (to regulate the number of hours children could work), in legislation to determine the width of streets, house building, and the amount of adulteration allowed in the production of foodstuffs.[53] So whether it was chalk in bread (to make it whiter), water in milk (to thin it and make it go further) or the sale of meat that was off, the Victorians led where we have followed in trying to protect the consumer from physical harm and being ripped off. Throughout the 1800s food was adulterated and beer was watered down. These actions were done to improve margins and increase profits, but by the last quarter of the century they had been made illegal and offenders could be prosecuted after legislation finally brought meaningful change.[54]

Joseph King fell foul of the law in late July 1881. On Friday, 29 July, King was up before Mr Marsham at Greenwich Police court to answer a summons brought by Joseph Edwards, a local sanitary inspector. Edwards had approached King as he made his rounds and asked for some milk. Suspicious, King refused the request. Revealing himself as an inspector Edwards opened one of the cans on the cart. King now admitted selling milk mixed with water, at 4d a pint. He said that his customers were aware of this, and so there was no deception. If they wanted pure milk they could have it, at 5d a pint. Edwards then walked across to where he had seen the milkman last make a sale and asked his customer what she believed she had bought. She vehemently denied being aware that she was buying milk mixed with water. Edwards's sharp practice was exposed and Marsham fined him 20s plus 2s costs for trying to deceive his customers and drive up his margins.[55]

In April 1894 Frederick Lock and Edgar Simmonds were summoned to appear before the magistrate at Worship Street Police court. The summons was issued on behalf of the Bow Sanitary Authority and their officer was in court to press charges against the two men who kept shops in the district. The sanitary officer had visited each man's premises and reported that both were selling butter from large tubs kept behind their counters. In the late nineteenth century butter was sold loose and by weight, so customers bought exactly what they needed. When the officer entered Lock's and then Simmonds's shops he asked for a 'half-pound of that', pointing at the butter in the tubs. There were no labels on the wooden tubs, but he insisted it was widely understood they contained butter. However, when the butter was analysed it was shown to be adulterated. Lock's butter only contained 40 per cent pure butter, while Simmonds's was a little better at 53 per cent. Both men had allegedly contravened the law. Instead of butter they were selling margarine, a cheaper, less pure substance. Neither man denied selling margarine, and said that they had never labelled the tubs as butter anyway. They argued that there had been no deception involved, and Mr Bushby (the magistrate) agreed. This seemed like an overeager sanitary officer who had not appreciated how small shopkeepers like this operated. Nevertheless, there was a breach of the law even if there was insufficient evidence of any intention to defraud or deceive. Mr Bushby fined each of them 10s and awarded costs of 12s 6d to the sanitary officer. Both tradesmen would have to ensure that in future their labelling was clear to avoid unwanted attention from the inspectors.[56]

When two sausage makers appeared at Worship Street in early 1869 the case was much more serious. George Simmonds and his brother Charles, both based in Bethnal Green, were charged with making sausages from meat that posed a very real threat to human health. George Simmonds entered his shop as two of his men were discovered cutting up meat that was clearly 'bad'. The defendant said his employees had been given it by mistake and since he was able to show that he had not seen the meat before the inspector seized it, he was let off with a hefty fine and costs. In total it cost him £23 16s, which he paid on the spot. His brother was not so fortunate. He was found preparing a side of beef to make into sausages, and when the inspector pointed out that the meat was diseased he said he had not noticed. The inspector confiscated the meat and brought it to court to show the magistrate. The Hackney medical officer of health, Dr Sarvis, declared that its consumption 'would be attended with the most injurious consequences'. There was no mitigation for Charles Simmonds and the magistrate told him he was going to send him to prison for three months, with no option to pay a fine.[57]

The regulation of public nuisances

In February 1862 a 'respectably attired man' presented himself at Clerkenwell Police court and asked the magistrate to help him. He wanted to raise awareness of an issue that he said affected everyone in London, but the children of the poor in particular. The man stated that 'should any person wonder why the mortality amongst children runs so high at the present time, they have only to take a walk to the church of St Peter, Great Saffron Hill'. If they carried on towards the rear of St Peter's, 'across the ruins to the arches of Victoria Street', they would find '[a]n issue of sewerage of the most abominable description, [which had created] a pool of large dimensions, into which has been thrown dead dogs, cats, fish, etc, till no words can convey an idea of the abomination that exists.' This was next to a school where more than one hundred children breathed in the 'fever-engendering miasma' daily. The anonymous complainant said the pool had existed for more than a month and nothing was being done about it, which was a disgrace. The magistrate told him to take up his complaint with the parish.[58] Compare that example with one from 1875. Maria Dunning was a dealer in hogwash, better known as pigswill. Dunning collected kitchen waste, which she sold to those rearing pigs in the capital. Unfortunately for the residents of Princes Gardens, Kensington, where she lived, the kitchen waste she collected had an unpleasant pungent smell. Since she had taken to temporarily storing it on the street, locals complained to the Westminster board of works. It was not the first time that Dunning had been prosecuted for infringing by-laws and it ended up with her being summoned before a magistrate. The sanitary inspector explained the defendant had been cautioned more than once, but on the day in question allowed more than two quarts of offensive liquid to run into the road. It was sour and smelt 'very bad'. The magistrate fined her 10*s* plus costs and warned her not to repeat the offence if she wanted to avoid a much stiffer penalty in the future.[59]

So what do these two examples tell us about the role of the magistracy in regulating everyday life and, more broadly, how might they help us understand the challenges facing the growing capital in the second half of the nineteenth century? As London grew so did the competition for space. With a huge urban population that needed to be fed but also required work, housing, heat and water, the authorities (at parish and, later, London County Council level) had to balance the needs of industry and work with those of health and domestic living. The case of Maria Dunning reveals an increasingly 'modern' city that was still relying in part on customs and ways of working that were medieval in origin. The earlier case is informative because it is from the period after the so-called Great Stink of 1858 when raw sewage had turned the Thames into a major public health hazard. In the aftermath parliament legislated for the building of a network of underground sewers designed by the engineer Sir Joseph Bazalgette. It was also just over a decade after the last major cholera outbreak in London killed over 10,000 people and the outbreak in Broad Street, Soho, in 1854.

At the time that the anonymous complainant appeared at Clerkenwell work on Bazalgette's new London sewers was well under way, and in the public consciousness. Sewers existed prior to the 1860s and were overseen by sewer commissioners, unpaid holders of ancient titles originally established by Henry VIII.[60] The system, however, relied on householders paying their sewer rates, which they were notoriously reluctant to do. Wealthier residences were not always connected to the public drains and their householders often argued that they were therefore exempt from the charge. Poorer residents saw the sewer rates as a low priority and 'burdensome' charge on their already limited resources. Sewer commissioners frequently had to resort to the law, issuing summons to force payments. A parliamentary committee investigated the problem in 1834 (following an outbreak of cholera in 1832) but failed to do much, if anything, to improve matters. It was the political rise of Edwin Chadwick in the 1830s and '40s that focused public attention on change. Chadwick was convinced that public health was impacted by clean water and clean air and while his ideas were not original (others had proposed changes before he did), his 1842 report was influential.[61] His report led to a parliamentary commission that in turn published two reports (in 1844 and 1845).[62] The recommendations were watered down as parliament debated the legislation required to make them into law, but eventually emerged in 1848 as the Public Health Act, which established a Central Board of Health.[63] In 1848 and 1849 parliament passed the Nuisances Removal Acts, which, once extended in 1855, made it 'easier to prosecute owners of foul dwellings' and 'enforce local improvements in drainage', as Jackson has argued.[64] The Metropolis Management Act (1855) created the Metropolitan Board of Works as a central body concerned with the capital's sanitation.

It is possible to see the impact of the work that Chadwick and others undertook to raise awareness of sanitation and public health in the 1840s and '50s. In late September 1854 the police court at Southwark was packed as the Bermondsey Improvement Commissioners brought a series of actions against local businesses. The complaints, presented by Mr Ballantine of Messrs Drew and Gray, solicitors, lasted several hours and focused on activities being carried out underneath the railway arches of the South Eastern Railway Company, near Russell Street. This area of south London was associated with the leather trade and there were numerous tanneries and curriers operating from under the arches of the railway. This presented exactly the sort of problem for locals identified above where industrial and domestic usage came into conflict. The fumes produced by the various trades housed in the arches were, according to the commissioners, causing illness, injury and death.

Moreover, this was not confined simply to the locals (invariably poorer Londoners) but extended to anyone travelling on the railways above, and especially those coming into London from the countryside. Thus it was affecting the lives of wealthier middle-class commuters and visitors. James Oates operated a bone boiling works under the arches and this was particularly unpleasant to travellers. It was, the prosecution alleged, 'dangerous in the extreme ... and parties coming in from the pure air in the country ... were sickened by the noisome effluvia emitted from the defendant's premises'.[65]

Jane Prior's work involved melting used cooking fat and the smell was obnoxious. The commissioners condemned her trade as 'filthy in the extreme, and dangerous to the health of the locality'. Ralf Sockhart had a similar business. His involved boiling offal to make pet food and was equally disgusting and offensive to locals. The magistrate listened carefully as a string of cases were brought against the occupants of the arches, many of whom must have been practising their trades for several years. These actions against the 'dirty trades' of Bermondsey can be seen in the context of 'improvement'. In all the cases the magistrate sided with the commissioners even if he sympathized with the business owners, none of whom were rich. All were given a month to find new premises, hopefully far away from the homes of residents. Mr Ballantine hoped that press coverage of the proceedings would also warn the railway companies that they were expected to take more responsibility in letting out the arches they owned.[66] When chemicals and gases were being used in enclosed premises there was a risk of disease, fire and explosion, and the Victorians recognized that some trades had to be separated out and placed a long way from peoples' homes. The people concerned were, more often than not, those that could not afford to bring private prosecutions against large companies and rich businessmen.

Enforcing the Factory Acts

London was too far from the source of energy, coal, that powered industry in the second half of the nineteenth century to compete with the Midlands and Lancashire as an industrial centre. Nor did London have the space for the building of large factories of the type most often associated with industrialization. Nevertheless, the capital was a major port, 'by far the largest single consumer market in England', and through its pre-eminence as the seat of governance it had a long-established luxuries market.[67] While it may not be accurate to describe London as an industrial city, industry was everywhere in the Victorian capital. Small manufacturers were rife, with areas closely associated with the making of particular goods (such as clothing and footwear). This brought the capital under the scrutiny of the inspectors appointed to enforce the Factory Acts.

A series of acts were passed from the early 1800s onwards, notably from the mid-century, to regulate workplaces, especially larger factories, and the conditions of employment within them. A maximum sixty-hour working week was established by the 1850 and 1853 acts, and the 1867 act restricted the employment of children, although in both areas the focus was on larger workplaces and considerable abuses and exploitation were allowed to continue.[68] The 1844 Factory Act had limited the working day to twelve hours for women (and children aged thirteen to eighteen). This was reduced to ten hours in 1847.[69] This legislation was extended to include all workshops employing more than fifty persons in 1867.[70] As with complaints brought against traders who polluted their environment, prosecutions under the Factory Acts were occasionally brought before the capital's magistracy.

An example is the prosecution of a theatrical costumier in 1869 for working his staff over hours. Samuel May was well known for supplying the theatrical trade, and Christmas and the New Year were particularly busy periods for business. Inspectors had called at his premises in Bow Street (directly opposite the police court) and warned him that he was infringing the regulations. May countered that in order to fulfil his obligations to customers he had no choice but to ask his workforce to work late into the evening and at weekends. This led to a summons and a court appearance. A medical officer testified that May's workshop was overcrowded, with some of his 'sewing rooms' having twice as many (eighteen) working within them as the law permitted. The costumier pleaded for allowances to be made given the 'exceptional' circumstances his 'extensive orders' required. He had to make costumes for 'Gnome Kings down to the humblest member of the ballet, and all requiring to be completed by a certain time'. Mr Vaughan was unsympathetic; there would be no exception in his court. May was fined £1 and told to improve the working conditions for his staff or risk further sanction.[71]

Later that month several traders in tobacco and cigars were crowded into the dock at Thames so that they could be made aware of the regulations as stipulated by the recently passed 1867 Factories (extension) Act. All the defendants were Jewish and they were brought in because Mr Oram, sub-inspector of factories, had discovered that they were requiring their staff to work on Sundays. Most of those employed were young people, men and women, under eighteen. This was a technical infringement of the act, but the traders were at pains to point out that this was peculiar to their religion. They employed fellow Jews and asked them to work Sundays because they could not operate on Saturdays, which was their Sabbath. This is an example of how laws passed to protect workers (and restrict Sunday trading) did not take into account the culture and practices of a significant minority in late nineteenth-century London. In the end the magistrate took a pragmatic view, charging the manufacturers a small amount in costs but issuing no fines on this occasion.[72] It is evident that while they might not always have been selected as newsworthy stories by the press, the courts played a key role in regulating work in the capital and not least in protecting employees from unscrupulous masters. Indeed employers were under the spotlight as never before in the second half of the nineteenth century as the drive for improvement and public health gained significant momentum. The police court was central and widely used by public servants who found the summons a cheap and effective tool to enforce the law and demonstrate their authority.[73]

Transport and animals

As an industrious city London's population required an organized and extensive public and private transport system for people and goods, a system that grew and developed across the century. At the heart of this was the horse. Horses were ubiquitous in the nineteenth-century capital: they pulled hansom cabs, omnibuses, trams, and carriages for the wealthy or carts for tradesmen. Individuals rode horses and so horses were everywhere. When horses grew old or sick, they were slaughtered and invariably their carcasses were processed and reused as meat or glue or some other by-product. Legislation in 1849 and 1850 allowed prosecutions of those that wilfully mistreated horses (and other animals) and many were brought by, or with the support of, what was to become the Royal Society for the Prevention of Cruelty to Animals (RSPCA), which had been founded as early as 1824. There are many accusations of cruelty revealed by reports in the papers; some were linked to issues prior to the acts in 1849 and 1850 that the Society had campaigned to establish.

It may be that the long-running campaign of the organization empowered or persuaded policemen like PC Carlyon to act. In September 1870 he was on duty in Charlotte Street when he noticed that a cab driver's horse was injured. Impounding the horse and cab, he asked an officer of the RSPCA to examine the animal. Mr Young (for the charity) testified that the horse had a

4-inch wound on its back and was unfit to work. Mr Tyrwhitt handed down a 10*s* fine with a warning not to repeat the offence in future.[74] That same year several cases of cruelty to horses were reported in the press, suggesting perhaps that the Society was successfully managing to highlight the issue. The reporting of cases was vital given that coverage of the courts, while daily, was highly selective.[75] Repeated instances of certain types of prosecution are common in the nineteenth-century press, if only appearing in short bursts before giving way to the next newsworthy topic. Tyrwhitt was again presiding when Richard Bartlett was prosecuted for cruelty to his horse. William Peet from the RSPCA testified that he had seen Bartlett driving on Jermyn Street and 'on examining the horse, found it quite unfit for work'. It was, he explained, 'old, lame, . . . and bore the marks of flogging'. Bartlett's employer tried to mount a defence by bringing in his own vet but that backfired as the man simply concurred with the view of the RSPCA's officer. Once again a fine was issued.[76]

Prosecutions brought against or by cab drivers and coachmen were more commonly for reasons unrelated to animal cruelty. In early March 1890 Nathan, 1st Baron de Rothschild, was being driven in a brougham coach along Queen Victoria Street in the City. A policeman was holding up the traffic and had his arm extended up, palm out, to signal this. Lord Rothschild's driver eased his horses to a halt to wait for the officer's signal to continue. Suddenly, the coach was hit from behind by a hansom cab. One of the shafts of the cab broke through the brougham, narrowly missing its occupants. Rothschild was shaken but unhurt. The baron stepped down from the damaged coach and approached the policeman. He handed him his card and said, angrily: 'These cabmen always drive furiously. Take my card and give it to the Inspector.' The incident ended up with the cab driver, James Povey, being summoned before the alderman magistrate at the Guildhall court and charged with 'driving a hansom cab wantonly'. Povey pleaded 'not guilty' and one of his passengers that day was in court to give evidence to support him. He testified that the baron and his driver could not possibly have seen what happened as they were facing the opposite direction, adding that Povey had attempted to stop. The collision was an accident, and not 'wanton' or dangerous. The alderman agreed and dismissed the summons, adding that a claim for the damage to the brougham could be made in the civil courts.[77]

Traffic accidents were fairly common, as were prosecutions for dangerous driving. The most usual outcome was a fine, and occasionally a short spell in prison if the cabbie was unable to pay the fine. The Metropolitan Police courts were arenas where all levels of Victorian society might coalesce, as cases could be brought by a wide cross-section of society. The drivers of hansom cabs were as likely to appear as complainants as they were to occupy the dock. For the most part drivers complained about their passengers, or about other road users and pedestrians, or about under- or late payment, and being made to wait for an unnecessarily long period. It was a part of the role of the magistrate to resolve disputes if possible and so avoid costly and lengthy actions in the civil courts. These sorts of cases were made that much more difficult because they were rarely conducted between social equals, occupants of cabs being from a very different social class to the drivers.

Complaints about fare dodging were more common on the omnibuses and this was an offence that might bring 'respectable' defendants to a police court dock.[78] A case heard at Thames Police court of Alfred Pearl, who was charged with dodging his fare to Dalson Junction, reveals the system that one tram company deployed to ensure passengers paid. It reveals also that the North London Tramways Company was concerned about the honesty of its employees. It had adopted a system whereby none of its conductors could collect fares from those boarding their trams. Instead, a collector would board the car, take the fare and issue a ticket, which the passenger surrendered when alighting. Pearl had boarded a tram somewhere before Kingsland Road on a Saturday afternoon in August 1873. At Kingsland Road Philip Egerton, one of the company's collectors, 'demanded his fare in the ordinary way' but Pearl refused. He said he would not pay his fare in advance, only once he had reached his destination, which was the Junction. Once the tram arrived, Pearl insisted he wanted to continue further, and remained adamant that he would only pay on arrival. The collector asked him for his name and address, and when Pearl refused Egerton called over a policeman. The policeman was not inclined to waste his time, but Pearl decided he was going to make a point, so he took himself to the nearest police station where he again refused to pay or give his name. The desk sergeant had him locked up and brought before a magistrate in the morning. In front of Mr Bushby at Thames, Pearl insisted he had done nothing wrong. He 'denied the right of the [tram] company to demand or receive his fare before he had completed his journey'. In response the company's solicitor cited the firm's rules and regulations, which clearly demonstrated that they were perfectly entitled to do just that. Bushby was unsure how to proceed. He adjourned the case and released the prisoner, who went off complaining loudly about being detained.

The case came back to court in October 1873 where both parties were represented by barristers. Astonishingly, here it was revealed that Pearl offered the policeman 10*s* to arrest him, and the collector Egerton a whole sovereign if he would prosecute. This was a case of principle to Mr Pearl. Pearl's defence was that when he had been asked to pay he had explained that he had refused because 'his mother had on the previous day lost the ticket given on payment being made and had been compelled to pay again'. He had told the collector in August that his own ticket had 'blown away in a gust of wind'. Evidently Pearl was not the usual fare dodger and Bushby had no desire to punish him as such. He (the magistrate) also felt the circumstances of the arrest and imprisonment had been unjustified and so agreed Mr Pearl had been treated poorly. The by-law, however, was 'a very excellent regulation' but 'it was informal, and consequently not to be enforced'. The whole matter was, he was told, to go before the Queen's Bench court for consideration, so there was little for him to do but discharge Mr Pearl without a stain on his character.[79]

There were cases of road users being embroiled in hearings before magistrates, but these troubled the police intelligence columns less frequently. Trains, trams and omnibuses in London were all venues for crime and anti-social behaviour. Trams and railways were the preferred option for the working classes, as horse-drawn omnibuses commenced running a little later and were a bit more expensive. Most working men had to be at their place of employment very early in the day, so they either needed to live close by or required reliable public transport to get them there. Given that wages were low, transport had to be cheap, which is why men like Alfred Shepperson took the train. Thousands used the workmen's trains from the beginning of the 1860s. These usually ran early and charged just twopence return (instead of the flat rate of a penny per mile that was the cost of third-class travel on the railways). It was an imperfect system, some train services ran too late, others too early, and casual workers were particularly badly affected by this. On 27 July 1867 Alfred Shepperson arrived at Walworth Road station at 7 a.m. as usual, ready to start work nearby as a sawyer. He presented his ticket to Henry Ricketts at the gate, but the Chatham & Dover Railway employee refused it. It had expired on Saturday, Shepperson was told, and he would need to pay 4*d* for his travel. Shepperson bridled and an altercation seemed inevitable. But then a smartly dressed man stepped forward and paid the sawyer's fare. Shepperson was in no mood to be reasonable, however, and he continued to protest until he was asked to leave the station. Angry and perhaps a little embarrassed, he refused, shouted abuse at Ricketts and threatened him. The ticket inspector was called and when he tried to steer Shepperson out of the station the sawyer's rage intensified and he became 'extremely violent', assaulting both men and ripping the inspector's coat in the process. Eventually he was subdued and hauled off to a police station. On the following morning he was up before Mr Selfe at Lambeth Police court where Shepperson claimed he did not know the ticket was out of date. 'Can you read?' the magistrate asked him. 'Yes, sir.' 'Then you must have seen the ticket was not available, for it is plainly printed on it.' Despite his show of contrition, he was fined 20*s*, a sum he did not have. He was led away to the cells to start a fourteen-day prison sentence that might well have cost him his job. Men like Pearl could risk a court appearance for a point of principle, men like Shepperson could not.[80]

When drivers risked the lives of other road users by driving too fast ('furiously') they would also find themselves in court. The offence of 'furious driving' was included as one of many clauses of the 1861 Offences Against the Person Act, which attempted to refine and consolidate the laws relating to violence in England and Wales.[81] The act stated that:

> Every person who rides or drives furiously, so as to endanger the life or limb of any person, or to the common danger of the passengers in any thoroughfare, may be summoned, or, if absolutely necessary, apprehended, and is then liable to a penalty, or in default to imprisonments.[82]

Those found to have caused injury as a result were deemed guilty of a misdemeanour and were liable to imprisonment.[83] Such cases were usually brought before police court magistrates, as happened 32 times in the five months of Thames court records surveyed for this study.[84] Anyone driving a vehicle could be charged with furious driving, but hackney coachmen more often than not occupied the dock.

In 1870 John Wheeler was prosecuted at Clerkenwell for causing damage and endangering the public, by 'furiously driving a
horse and cab' while drunk. A policeman watched Wheeler's cab
career down Caledonian Road and turn into Pentonville Road
without slowing. He was going so fast that Wheeler was unable to
pull up and avoid crashing into a larger cab coming down the hill
towards him. The horse pulling that cart was sent flying over on its
back, its harness broken by the collision. The cab was damaged and
the horse so badly hurt that it was off the road for several days.
The magistrate fined Wheeler 20s plus 30s costs, with a month's
imprisonment if he could not pay. Wheeler did not have that sort
of money, so was led away to the cells.[85] Earlier the same year a
young man named George Hudd was charged with being drunk
and driving furiously. He was described as a 'horsekeeper', but
frequently drove his father's cab. On this occasion, having had one
drink too many, he had been driving a young woman when he lost
control of the vehicle on Harley Street. A policeman watched as the
cab crashed against a lamp post, extinguishing the light, before
mounting the pavement and up on to the steps of one of the houses,
breaking five of the iron railings. All the time Hudd was thrashing
his horse 'most unmercifully'. Thankfully his passenger was un-
harmed but the expensive fan she was holding was smashed to pieces.
The young woman had attended at the police station to sign the
charge sheet but was not in court. This gave Hudd the opportunity
to blame her for the accident, claiming she had been 'hissing' at the
horse and urging him to drive faster. Given the evidence that he had
been drinking, the magistrate fined Hudd 40s with the alternative
penalty of a month in gaol at hard labour.[86] Unsurprisingly the
press commonly reported the behaviour of cab drivers, their middle-
class audience probably delighting in seeing one of the objects of
their irritation exposed in print, confirming their prejudices.

3

THIEVES AND SWINDLERS

The police courts were full of thieves. From the 1850s there was an increase in prosecutions as a series of acts allowed minor, young and first-time property offenders to be punished by a magistrate without the need for a lengthy jury trial.[1] This shift meant that by the end of the 1850s three-quarters of larceny cases were being dealt with at this level, without a jury.[2] This had some advantages for offenders; by accepting a short sharp prison term handed done by a magistrate they could avoid the very real risk of being sent down for several years in a national penitentiary.

In the records of the Thames Police court from March to November 1881, 30 per cent of the entries in the main court register list complaints associated with some sort of property crime. These vary considerably, as we might expect, since property offending covered a wide range of activity in the 1880s. In many instances the cryptic nature of the sources reveals only that a 'felony' was alleged to have been committed, with little more that would allow the reader to identify these with any confidence as 'theft'. However, many of the cases that reached the jury courts in the 1800s started life in magistrate hearings as felonies, so it is reasonable to include them here. At the bottom end of the scale were cases where the act of taking or stealing was unclear, but the individual concerned was found to be in possession of someone else's property. In others the theft was obvious, and sometimes violent. Not surprisingly magistrates dealt with these variants differently.

The perpetrators of theft were a mixed crowd and yet while this group included children I exclude them here, choosing instead to deal with them separately in Chapter Six. Historians of crime have agreed that gender was an important factor in the nature of theft, with male or female offenders tending to steal property most clearly associated with their spheres of influence or place in society.[3] Women were more likely to steal food, household goods, linen and clothing; men more often took tools, goods associated with manufacturing, metals such as lead or imported products unloaded at the London Docks. Both sexes stole money, and 'dippers' of both genders pinched whatever was easy to find in the pockets of those careless enough to brush against them. We have also established that men and women committed different sorts of property crime. Female offending was invariably less direct and open, and therefore much less likely to involve confrontation or violence. There were exceptions but most robbers were men. Women were also disproportionately accused of shoplifting, and London, as the Victorian capital of retail trade, offered almost unlimited opportunities for stealing from shops.[4] The London Docks had been a focus for pilferage for over two hundred years by the end of the 1800s and historians have identified the shift from a grudging acceptance of pilfering – seen as an unofficial benefit of the job – to its criminalization in the 1700s.[5] One of the property crimes that occasionally saw offenders brought before the police courts was smuggling, another activity that might be considered, along with pilfering from work, as a 'social crime' as identified by historians.[6]

Identifying social criminality, actions that neither the perpetrators nor their communities saw as 'criminal', also helps with understanding why crimes were committed. In so many of the records of property offending ascribing motive is almost impossible. A defendant was hardly likely to explain why they stole something if the central plank of their defence was that they did not steal it. It might be assumed that discovering motive became easier in the later 1800s as the penalty of death, applied in a blanket form for almost all property crimes in the eighteenth century, was systematically removed by Robert Peel in the 1820s. But that would be to ignore first the horrors of transportation to Australia and then penal servitude with hard labour. In most cases we are left to infer why people stole and, given the very real experience of poverty in nineteenth-century London, are bound to consider the reality that many of those charged with theft did so out of need not greed, especially at times of high unemployment, low wages or other periods of economic stress.

Not everyone could claim such a justification for offending. This chapter will also look at the individual or collective attempts to separate the vulnerable from their money. Some of this was cunning, well organized and indicative of 'professional' crime, however we might wish to define that. Other actions were spontaneous or opportunistic. Both had the capacity to ruin lives. Much of the history of crime that focuses on property offending has sought to demonstrate that it is here that we see the power of the state, its rulers and beneficiaries, handing down harsh penalties to protect privilege and wealth. While there is considerable merit in an argument that sees the power of the wealthy expressed in laws that protect and uphold an inherently unfair economic system (capitalism), there have been too few words written on the victims of property crime, many of whom were not rich or privileged at all.

Serious property crime

The overwhelming majority of prosecutions of non-violent property crime that reached the Central Criminal Court at the Old Bailey, the main focus of historical research on crime in the capital, were for 'simple larceny'. Prior to 1827 larceny (theft) had been differentiated into 'petty' and 'grand'; the distinction being that petty larceny was the theft of goods valued at under one shilling. In reality magistrates in summary hearings prosecuted nearly all petty larcenies, and in the nineteenth century the powers of justices to sit in judgment on petty thieves was extended and confirmed in legislation, removing many cases from jury trial.[7] This move was not new in the 1850s. Throughout the long eighteenth century justices had the power to determine guilt in specific property crimes, such as the theft of metals.[8] Simple larceny accounted for 36 per cent of trials for non-violent property crimes at the Old Bailey during Victoria's reign but this figure was significantly higher in the first two decades, indicating a tendency for less serious offending to be filtered by the summary process (continuing a trend that had started in the previous century).[9]

The next highest category was 'stealing from master', although this also declined, both as a proportion of property crime and the number of cases brought before an Old Bailey jury, falling from more than 4,000 in the 1840s to just over 200 in the 1890s.[10] Burglary and housebreaking represented 12.6 per cent of cases, with theft from a specified place adding another 8 per cent. In the eighteenth century the archetypal criminal was the highwayman, or highway robber, but by the 1820s highway robbery was in steep decline, gradually being replaced in the public consciousness by burglary. Nevertheless, there were still significant numbers of prosecutions for robbery in the nineteenth century (more than 3,000 between January 1837 and the end of 1899).

Robbery, albeit in decline in its classic form, remained a problem for the unwary pedestrian in 1880s London. John Roots had come to London to get treatment at Guy's Hospital. The elderly labourer caught a stage to London, arriving at London Bridge with 29*s* to his name. After dining at a pub, he set off in search of lodgings. As he rested on a bench near the gates of the Mint three men approached him. 'What are you doing here? Let us see what you have got about you,' one of them asked. Roots told them to go away. He was seized and punched hard in the face before having his pockets rifled. This was highway robbery and was carried out by a notorious gang of known criminals. The labourer's cries alerted police and Sergeant Menhinick quickly set off in pursuit of the gang. He caught one of the assailants, who gave his name as Edward Sweeny. Appearing in court at Southwark a week later (Roots had been too sick from his injury and general ill health to attend earlier than then) Sweeny pleaded his innocence, claiming he had seen Roots lying on the pavement and had tried to help. When the policeman came up, he ran away fearing he would be blamed. This was undoubtedly a lie, but nothing had been found on Sweeny that linked him to the crime.

It was not an easy case to prove; nevertheless, given its serious-ness, the magistrate committed Sweeny for trial. The case was heard at the Old Bailey where Sweeny (aka Shanox) was acquitted for lack of evidence. Roots was left temporarily penniless by the robbery and his ability to pay his hospital fees must have been in doubt.[11] He is an example of how the history of property crime, most often considered from the perspective of the harsh penalties imposed, has tended to neglect the victims.

In another example, robbers attacked John Palmer, a casual labourer, as he made his way home from work. Palmer may have enjoyed a few pints after work, which would have made him more vulnerable to being attacked, as drunks were easy prey. James Tyson and John Sadler jumped him, knocked him to the ground and stole 7s. Palmer reported the incident, a search began and the culprits were caught a few hours later. When Sadler was frisked he was discovered to have several pawn tickets for 'valuable gold and silver watches', some 'Albert' chains and broken watch-bows. Items such as these, commonly engraved, were identifiable. The most significant find was a gold locket and a Freemason's gold medal. At Marlborough Street police reported that Tyson and Sadler were well known 'magsmen', a contemporary slang term for members of the so-called criminal class and which probably covered a range of offending.[12] Mr Mansfield was confident that the men were suitable objects for further enquiries to be made and so he acquiesced to the police request to remand them in custody. However, there is no record of either man in the higher courts in the immediate aftermath, which suggests the evidence was thin or the pair were able to buy off Palmer as a potential witness against them.[13]

In August 1880 Clarence Lewis was working at the Aldgate shop of his master Mr Barham, a grocer who also operated premises in Kensington. Barham instructed his eighteen-year-old apprentice to travel to Kensington to pick up the day's takings. Lewis collected a bag containing nearly £100 in cash, a considerable sum of money, indicating the trust placed in him. Concealing the package in his pocket, Lewis headed for High Street Kensington station to catch the train back to the City. As he passed the ticket office someone called his name. 'Don't you know me?' the stranger asked him, adding, 'I am Perry, of Aldgate; I thought you were too proud to speak to me.' Lewis recognized the young man as Henry Perry, who once worked at Barham's shop. Perry insisted Clarence join him in a first-class carriage and waived aside the younger man's protest that he did not have the fare: 'Never mind,' he said, 'I will pay.' The train rattled through a couple of stations before Perry produced a small phial of liquid that he said was Zoedone. Described as 'the king of non-alcoholic beverages' in its marketing material, Zoedone was a tonic drink available throughout the late 1800s. Perry offered it to Lewis, who swallowed a mouthful that tasted awful and fizzed in his nose. Lewis immediately felt sleepy and was unable to resist when Perry poured some onto his handkerchief and suggested he sniff it. They continued their journey for a few stops, then, just before they reached Farringdon, Perry pounced, hitting Lewis with a stick and knocking him to the floor. It was a savage attack: Perry hit him about the head and back, knelt on his chest and put his hand over his mouth, demanding the money Lewis was carrying.

Drugged, beaten and robbed, Lewis crawled under the seat to hide, only emerging when the train pulled into Aldersgate Street station (now Barbican). Perry was nowhere to be seen. John Bell and his brother Thomas saw Lewis staggering out of the compartment covered in blood and moved to help. Pointing to the disappearing figure of Perry, Lewis shouted: 'Stop that man, he has stolen my money.' The brothers overtook Perry and handed him to the authorities. It took weeks for Lewis to recover sufficiently to be able to attend court. Perry was accused of drugging him with laudanum and chloroform and then assaulting and robbing him, charges he denied. 'We are friends,' Perry reminded the apprentice; 'I have not robbed you; that is my own money.' The alderman at Guildhall committed Perry for trial.[14] At the Old Bailey the jury heard evidence from several witnesses as well as testimonials to Perry's general good character. This was not enough save him. Perry was found guilty of violent robbery and was fortunate to avoid a charge of attempted murder. The judge sentenced him to thirty lashes and twenty years of penal servitude.[15]

While these cases are newsworthy (offering a cautionary tale or highlighting contemporary concerns) they are not unusual. Lewis's experience of being robbed on the railway echoes many other incidents reported by the press and, while Perry's actions were particularly unpleasant, many other rail travellers were robbed. While Perry targeted his victim, John Roots and John Palmer fell victim to opportunistic thieves who preyed on their vulnerability. Professional policing and expanding urban spaces contributed to the waning of the age of the highwayman. The villainous Bill Sikes from Dickens's *Oliver Twist* epitomized his replacement, the burglar. The newspapers were quick to focus on burglary as a crime that presented a similar level of threat to robbery, albeit with a different context. Burglars invaded the home and so brought the public sphere into the domestic.[16] From the middle of the century the press carried adverts for anti-burglary and anti-theft devices,

and home insurance against burglary 'soon became a common transaction' after it was first introduced in 1899.[17]

In 1881 John Reynolds, a potman at the White Horse tavern on the Haymarket, locked up the premises before going upstairs. Reynolds noticed his employer's bedroom door was open. This surprised him because his master (a Mr Austin) was out of town. When he entered the room, he found it 'in a state of confusion' with drawers 'broken open'. Reynolds rushed downstairs to fetch a fellow servant. The pair found a loaded revolver and cutthroat razor on the bed and realized several things were missing, including

Francis Holl, *The Railway Station*, 1866, engraving after
a painting by William Powell Frith, 1862.

silverware, some clocks and an umbrella. The police were called,
and an inspector found an earring near the skylight and a large
amount of clothing in an unoccupied house next door, possibly
dropped as the intruder escaped. There was no sign of the culprit,
who might have got away with theft had it not been for a sharp-
eyed landlord at a rival establishment, Charles Cooper at the Dog
and Duck in Frith Street, Soho. A day after the break-in three men
tried to sell him two clocks. Cooper recognized the timepieces as

belonging to his fellow publican so, telling the men he was interested, informed the police. When the trio returned the police were waiting. The magistrate at Marlborough Street listened to the witness and the police, who produced the umbrella. This had borne Austin's monogram but the letters had almost been obliterated as the thieves tried to disguise its ownership. The justice remanded Charles Edmunds and Henry Watkins in custody.[18] They faced trial at the Central Criminal Court on 12 December but were acquitted.[19] The pair were tried for two other burglaries in December 1881. The first was for burgling the house of William Evans in St John's Wood, which was let to an Ann Turner. Despite some evidence that the pair had pawned stolen items, a jury once again acquitted them.[20] Their luck held for a third time when they were accused of burgling a counting house. This time the prosecution offered no evidence against them, and they walked free from court.[21] Perhaps they were innocent victims of mistaken identity; more likely a lack of forensic knowledge at the time made their crimes hard to prove.

In February 1861 a spate of burglaries in Clerkenwell placed police on heightened alert. Sergeant Robinson and Constable Blissett adopted plain clothes to keep watch for any unusual activity near Mecklenburgh Square, where several incidents had been reported. At eight o'clock in the evening they saw three men 'loitering about in a very suspicious manner'. As they watched, one man started trying doors on the street to see if any would open. The others were 'piping' (slang for keeping watch), and when they saw the policemen they ran away. The officers quickly overtook them and attempted an arrest. Instead of accepting their fate the trio attacked the policemen. One broke away and threw something into the gutter, while another tried to discard a set of skeleton keys, which the sergeant recovered. Eventually, once they were safely locked up, Robinson returned to the scene and recovered a chisel that one of the gang had jettisoned and which matched marks made on nearby doors.

Before Mr D'Eyncourt at Clerkenwell the three gave their names as William Green, James Higgins and William Smith. They were all well known to police who suspected them of being responsible for the minor crime wave in the district, but on this occasion they had not actually broken into anywhere. There was some strong circumstantial evidence however. A local man, named Abrahams, explained that his property had been burgled and the culprits had gained entry using a set of skeleton keys. Abrahams said thieves had broken into his house on Bedford Row and had stolen property valued at £50. 'What made the matter worse', he continued, was that 'his servant's savings, amounting to over £11, besides some of her clothing, were stolen'. This was not simply a case of stealing from someone that might afford it; it was the plunder of the life savings of some poor domestic. The men denied doing anything wrong. They admitted picking up the keys – innocently, without intent to use them – and as for the chisel 'they knew nothing of it.' D'Eyncourt told them that had they managed to break into a house that evening he would have had no hesitation in committing them for trial where, if convicted, they might have faced several years' imprisonment. As it was, they were lucky that he could only punish them for the attempt and the assault on the policemen who had arrested them. They would all go to gaol for three months with hard labour.[22]

Burglars did not always target domestic environments: commercial properties could often prove more profitable and less risky. In March 1865 John Crane's City warehouse in Birchin Lane was raided. Crane was a gunmaker's agent and the thieves that 'wrenched' the padlock from his door stole several pistols. Three men were arrested while attempting to sell the guns. However, police believed at least one other man was involved. In April 1865 Robert White, who went by the nickname of 'Long Bob', was charged at Mansion House for his involvement in the burglary. White, a 'commercial traveller', had been brought in by City police officers Hancock and Harris after being found trying to sell a pair of revolvers to a pawnbroker in Blackfriars. The pawnbroker's assistant told Alderman Carter that a man fitting White's description, but giving the name 'Martin', pledged two 'six barrelled revolvers'. The man was loaned £2 5s against the weapons. Later that evening White (aka Martin) was back with five more guns. Asked about their provenance, White told him they belonged to a friend who had asked him to sell them. He explained that they were part of a large order for the u.s. Federal Army and were surplus to requirements. (In early April 1865 the American Civil War was almost at an end: General Robert E. Lee surrendered to Union troops in Virginia on 9 April, ending four years of bitter conflict.)

There was some dispute about the facts presented at Mansion House and it cannot have been easy for the alderman to work out who was telling the truth. The magistrate sent Robert White to join the others accused of stealing Crane's pistols.[23] On 10 April John Campbell, James Roberts, Edmund Collins and Robert White appeared at the Old Bailey, charged with stealing fifty revolvers from the warehouse of John Crane. The pawnbroker's assistant Henry Parker explained that, while he had been made aware of the robbery, he had not associated White with the theft because 'Martin' was a regular visitor. This fitted with White's image as a commercial traveller and suggests that he was part of a shady underground in Victorian London where thieves worked together to shift stolen goods through the second-hand market. All four were convicted. Collins received a good character reference and got away with six months' imprisonment. Campbell received ten years' penal servitude and was transported to Australia, while White and Roberts each got seven years.[24]

Burglary and housebreaking involved breaking and entering a premises, the former at night, and the latter generally during daylight hours.[25] It was the invasion of a home after dark that added fear to theft, making burglary a serious crime in the public consciousness. Included in the general category of such crimes was 'theft from a specified place', which might mean domestic lodgings, but included commercial properties such as shops, workshops or warehouses. Despite being seen as a lesser crime, it still carried considerable penalties for those convicted. Sometimes it made sense for the accused to plead guilty to the lesser offence, to ensure a reduced sentence. Equally this might benefit the authorities that were then relieved of the burden of proof required at a jury trial. This was illustrated in a case from 1851.

On 11 August Mr D'Eyncourt was beginning his spell at Worship Street in the East End. He had replaced Mr Arnold, who was off to the calmer atmosphere of Westminster. The men that served as magistrates in the police courts of the capital were not appointed to a single court indefinitely. The policy was to move them around after a period of time so that they had experience of a variety of locations. This would serve several purposes: some courts, notably Bow Street, were more prestigious; others, like Worship Street, were particularly busy with drunks and petty criminals. It also ensured that no single magistrate could establish a fiefdom in any one part of London, and so guarded against corruption. It also served to share the experience of the magistracy around the metropolis and make it that much harder for repeat criminals to avoid recognition, incurring heavier sentences as a result. D'Eyncourt's first task was to determine whether there was sufficient evidence to commit a burglar for jury trial. In the dock stood an 'athletic middle-aged man' who refused to give his name. He was charged with breaking into the house of Miss Jane Harriett Burgess, a 'maiden lady', on the City Road. Miss Burgess had played an active role in the arrest. She had retired to bed at 10 p.m. on the Saturday and as she entered her bedroom, she noticed the window was open and the room had been 'thoroughly ransacked'. Quickly realizing that some of her possessions were missing, including 'a mahogany writing-desk' and a carpet-bag, she rushed to the window and looked out. She saw a man moving carefully along the parapet to the next house along. When he got to the partition wall in between the houses he stopped, being prevented from continuing further. When Miss Burgess demanded to know what he was doing, the man 'coolly replied that a burglary had been affected, and that he had made his way up there to assist in apprehending the thieves'. He then turned around and tried to retrace his steps back past the lady's window as quickly as he could. Miss Burgess grabbed his leg as he passed and clung on tight. She was almost pulled out of her window and over the parapet, letting go just in time. Meanwhile PC Matlock had been summoned by a gentleman in an adjoining house who had seen a man emerge from the window of an unoccupied house next to him. Matlock made his way up to the roofs of the buildings and found Miss Burgess's property, arranged so the thief could retrieve it. Matlock caught the thief and took him into custody. In court the accused refused to identify himself, so D'Eyncourt remanded him in custody to await trial.[26] At trial the man, now revealed as George Andrews, pleaded guilty to the lesser charge of 'theft from a specified place' and was sent to prison for twelve months.[27]

Forgery

In the nineteenth century several activities came under the umbrella term of forgery. Forgery existed on several levels; from serious but simple acts of passing off counterfeit coins as genuine to the creation of forged instruments of monetary exchange (bank notes, coins, share certificates or stamps). At the higher end, forgery was prosecuted before a jury and offenders could expect lengthy prison time; for less serious offending a magistrate might punish the guilty at summary level. Regardless of where these cases ended up, many of them would have begun with a hearing at a police court, where those involved would have been concerned to convince the sitting magistrate of the guilt or innocence of the accused.

Mrs Sarah Cameron ran a tobacconist shop on the Broadway, Westminster. One evening William Meeton approached her counter and asked for a cigar. He handed over half a crown in payment and she gave him the cigar and 'two shillings and four pennyworth of halfpences' as change. A half-crown was worth two shillings and sixpence, so the cigar cost Meeton two pence. However, when Meeton examined his change he rejected a shilling declaring that it was 'bad' (counterfeit). He accused the tobacconist of trying to fob him off with forgeries, but Mrs Cameron was sure the coins she had handed over were fine. Suspecting Meeton of committing a crime she shouted for a policeman, who arrested the young man. Meeton was charged at Queen's Square with uttering, a variant of coining, exchanging counterfeit coin for genuine money, breaking down a higher denomination coin into smaller ones, thereby switching 'bad' money for 'good'. The magistrate demanded to see the coin in question, but this proved impossible as Meeton had swallowed it, along with several other shillings in his possession. It was a common enough ploy to get rid of the evidence.

The chief usher explained that Meeton was 'well known' to the court, which might have counted against him. However, without the proof that the shillings were bad there was little the justice could do. After some conferring Mr Burrell told Meeton that, while today he 'had been too sharp for his prosecutors', his card was marked and warned him about his future conduct. He was discharged but highlighting the case in the newspapers would alert other traders to such sharp practice.[28] A year later another supposed utterer was brought before the police courts. William Collins had entered a butcher's shop in Charles Street and attempted to pay for a 'quarter pound of beef' with a 'bad' fourpenny piece (or groat). The butcher, George Garland, rejected the coin and demanded another. Collins produced a shilling and a sixpence from the same pocket and handed them over. Garland carefully examined each, told him the shilling was 'bad' but accepted the sixpence. Collins left with his supper and 2*d* in change. Next, he went to the Anchor and Crown pub in King Street, Covent Garden, and ordered a pint of beer. When the landlord, Edward Hoey, asked him to pay he tried the shilling that had been refused earlier. Hoey declined it and so Collins tried a halfpenny, which was accepted. He drank his pint and left. Some moments later a police detective approached the bar and spoke to the landlord. He asked if a person fitting Collins's description had been in and revealed that he had been keeping him under surveillance for some time. Collins was arrested and taken to the nearest police station for questioning.

On the following Saturday the butcher and landlord were in court to give evidence against Collins. The young man 'strenuously denied' knowing that the money in his possession was counterfeit and the sitting justice, Mr Jardine, seemed ready to believe him. Jardine asked whether any other 'bad' coins had been found on him. None had but the accused was in possession of a bottle of quicksilver (mercury), which he kept in the same pocket as his money. The mercury would have tarnished the coins. This seems to have confirmed Jardine's belief in Collins's innocence, but at the insistence of the other witnesses and the police he had the coins tested. A jeweller testified that the coins were 'genuine, but discoloured in consequence of being placed with quicksilver'. The magistrate apologized to Collins for having held him in custody while the facts were checked and said he hoped he understood that, while he was now cleared, the 'affair [looked] very suspicious' based on the witnesses produced in court.[29]

While both these examples of uttering were relatively small-scale, the following shows more organized offending. James Brennan, a former detective, had left the force to join a specialist team at the Royal Mint. Their role was to actively pursue prosecutions against those involved in forging and distributing counterfeit currency. In April 1860, acting on information, Brennan and his team visited the Penton Arms beer shop in Islington. He saw his target, Harry Mason, talking with two or three others. Brennan approached him declaring: 'Harry, I am instructed by the Mint authorities to take you into custody. You are suspected of dealing in counterfeit coin.' With that he reached into Mason's pocket and removed a small bag containing '31 florins and 25 shilling pieces, all of them counterfeit'. There was also a tobacco tin that concealed a 'good' florin used to make a mould. Mason was escorted to a waiting cab and ferried to his last known address – 2 Pembroke Street, near Caledonian Road – where one of his known accomplices, Margaret Sawyer, was discovered. A search also revealed a mould in a cupboard, 'two galvanic batteries fully charged, another mould, two or three cylinders, a number of bottles containing acid, and all the necessary implements for making and colouring counterfeit coin'.

Brennan took the case to Clerkenwell, where Mason was well known, having been charged and convicted of felony more than once previously. Mason denied the charges. Margaret also claimed to know nothing about any of it and begged to be discharged.[30] Bail was refused and the pair appeared at the Old Bailey just under a month later. Margaret Sawyer was acquitted but Mason was convicted and sentenced to eight years' penal servitude.[31]

Pickpockets

Finding evidence against counterfeiters was difficult and took time, but catching more opportunistic thieves was just as hard. Catching pickpockets or shoplifters red-handed was most likely to result in convictions. The opportunities to get away unnoticed, to blend into a crowd or simply to ditch stolen items if discovered made a conviction for picking pockets among the hardest to achieve. While an individual policeman in plain clothes might position himself strategically to catch thieves in the act, it was often victims who were best placed to do so. In the summer of 1864 Daniel Vincer was pushing his way up the crowded stairs of the Royal Victoria Theatre when he felt his watch move. Reaching to his fob pocket he discovered it hanging half out and carefully pushed it back in. Seconds later he felt the watch leave his pocket altogether. Turning on his heels he saw it in the hands of a man who was in the process of trying to break it away from its guard. As soon as the thief realized he had been noticed he fled, with Vincer in pursuit. The odds favoured the pickpocket, but Vincer managed to keep him in sight as they moved through the theatregoers and eventually caught him with the help of one of the venue's staff.

The following day Vincer gave his account of the theft to the sitting magistrate at Southwark. The thief, who gave the name Charles Hartley, was an old offender also known as 'Giles'. The magistrate questioned the victim closely: had he seen the man actually take his watch, did he have it in his hands? 'He put his hand along the chain', Vincer explained, 'and [he] saw the prisoner break it off.' Hartley denied everything. As he tried to escape he had thrown the watch away and was prepared to brazen out a story that he was nowhere near the incident. Given the difficulty of securing a conviction without concrete evidence Harley might have got away with it. Unfortunately for him his identification by court officers played against him. A police sergeant told the magistrate that he believed Hartley was a 'returned transport'. In other words, he had previously been sentenced to transportation to Australia and had either escaped or, more likely, had served his time and earned a ticket of leave to return. Hartley denied this: 'I never was in trouble before in my life,' he declared. The gaoler insisted he could prove at least twenty previous convictions against him. The magistrate remanded Hartley in custody so that his identity and previous criminal record could be investigated.

When Hartley came back up on the following Friday PC Harrington told the court that the prisoner had indeed been transported and in prison several times. By the middle years of the nineteenth century the criminal justice system's ability to track a criminal's life history had improved significantly and a retired police sergeant recognized Hartley as a man he had helped put away several years previously. According to him the prisoner had been sentenced to four months' imprisonment in 1851 for a street robbery, before being transported for seven years in July 1853. He had earned his ticket of leave in January 1857, but attempted to steal a watch and got another twelve months instead. He was committed for trial.[32]

Previous convictions (and the ability of the late Victorian justice system to trace them) were one of the most likely ways to convince magistrates to commit defendants for jury trial.[33] In 1883 William Williams and John Nesbett were brought to Westminster accused of picking pockets at an exhibition of global marine life on the Royal Horticultural Society's grounds in South Kensington. The pair were well-established members of London's criminal fraternity, allegedly involved in crime for the entirety of their lives. Now, heading into late middle age, they were still at it. Crowds provided easy pickings for practised thieves. As men and women pressed themselves up close to the glass of the aquariums to gawp at the strange creatures within, Williams and Nesbett took advantage of the cramped conditions to dip pockets and lift purses and jewellery. However, when they attempted to steal an old gentleman's watch and chain they were seen. Realizing this, they tried to escape but the packed halls worked against them and they were captured. The following day they were presented before Mr Sheil at Westminster. The men denied doing anything and nothing was found to incriminate them. A detective gave evidence that they were known offenders and the 'associates of thieves', and that was enough for the magistrate to remand them.[34]

Crowded theatres and exhibitions were an obvious draw for pickpockets, as was public transport, which brought people of all stations of life together in the crowded Victorian metropolis. The London omnibus provided the thieves with opportunities to

Bus, Euston Road, London, *c.* 1857–70, photograph.

prey on the unsuspecting or careless commuter and practised pickpockets could hope to avoid detection most of the time. Just occasionally offenders slipped up or were unlucky. This is what happened to the 'respectably dressed' Jane Clark in 1865. Clark was riding an omnibus in Oxford Street for the express purpose of 'dipping' pockets.[35] Mrs Amy Massy probably did not notice the unremarkable woman sat beside her. As with Daniel Vincer, though, something prompted her to reach into her pocket to 'see if her purse was safe'. To her horror she discovered that the band used to keep it secure had been forced and 'two sovereigns had been taken'. Mrs Massy summoned the conductor and accused Clark of stealing. She claimed she had seen Jane's hand in her pocket, but this is unlikely; Clark was a practised thief, and it is doubtful anyone saw anything untoward. Jane denied the theft and the conductor found no coins on her. Later, however, a young lad found two sovereigns on the floor of the bus and he handed them in when it reached Islington. Police eventually traced the coins back to Mrs Massy.

Clark was detained and presented at Marlborough Street the following day, with a lawyer in tow. Her defence was that Massy must have dropped the coins when she took out her handkerchief to wipe her face. With only circumstantial evidence, Clark should have felt confident of walking away, but Mr Tyrwhitt probably believed that Clark was guilty, even if that was hard to prove. He told her lawyer that he was minded to send the case for a jury to decide. This was a risky outcome for Clark; if she were a known offender this would undoubtedly be exposed. If convicted she faced a lengthy spell of imprisonment, much longer than any sentence the magistrate could impose. As a result, her lawyer pleaded with the justice to deal with the case summarily. Tyrwhitt was reluctant, but when Clark agreed to plead guilty (as was her right after 1855) the magistrate sentenced her to two months in prison with hard labour, not ideal but not penal servitude with all that entailed. Jane

Omnibuses on Poultry, London, *c.* 1890s, photograph.

Clark would be back on the streets by the summer, and able to go back to 'work'.[36]

There were plenty of other women like Clark who preyed upon travellers on the omnibus. Catherine Kelly was a 'dipper' well known to the police. Using the alias 'Margaret' or 'Mary', she had been arrested on many occasions for picking pockets. The omnibus allowed the smartly dressed thief to get close to unsuspecting victims while their dexterity enabled them to lift items of value without being noticed. Kelly often worked with a partner, an effective ploy because she could pass the stolen goods to an accomplice, minimizing the risk of goods being found on her person if searched. In January 1864 Kelly was arrested for picking pockets with Sarah Williams while the pair were out in Regent's Street. Sergeant Charles Cole of C Division had seen them the day before on an omnibus and had positioned himself to watch as they approached passers-by in Argyle Place. Kelly tried to pick the pocket of a lady but vanished into the crowd before the officer could catch her. Soon afterwards he found the pair again, mingling with crowds, and noticed Kelly had her hand close to a woman's side. He moved in and grabbed her before calling for help to arrest Williams. The women knew the sergeant as well. 'For God's sake don't take me Mr Cole,' Kelly pleaded. The plea fell on deaf ears and both women were taken to Marlborough Street where they gave a flat denial of their alleged crimes. Sergeant Cole emphasized that these were known offenders, recognizing this was the most effective path to a conviction or committal. He told the magistrate that her previous companion was currently serving six months in gaol for picking pockets on the buses, adding that Kelly had taunted him saying she 'could earn as much in a minute as he could in a week'. That was probably accurate and helps explain why women like Kelly and Williams chose crime over badly paid manual work like sewing, shop work or domestic service. So long as you accepted that you might spend some time in prison the rewards of crime were considerably higher than the day-to-day drudgery of working-class lives in Victorian England. The magistrate had nothing but circumstantial evidence to go on and without proof that Kelly or Williams had been seen stealing, or a victim appearing to claim it, there was little the magistrate could do except remand them for further enquiries. The remand process was important in bringing new evidence to light, particularly if stolen goods could be identified and witnesses' memories jogged. It is likely that he was keen to find proof of her guilt of some offence, but without a confession of the type Jane Clark made, there was nothing to do but hold her and hope evidence emerged. In that respect the police, courts and defendants were engaged in a game of blink; if Kelly could hold her nerve and calculate that she would not be committed for trial (or that a jury would convict her) then all she would suffer was a few days in police custody before being released.[37]

Shoplifters

Shoplifting ('stealing privately from a shop') was equally hard to prove. It had been made capital in 1699 and remained a hanging offence until 1832, although it was rare by then for offenders to be executed. The severity of the punishment reflected the difficulty of capturing shoplifters and proving guilt. It was relatively easy for thieves to discard stolen property or to simply deny an intention to steal. Many were convicted of simple theft rather than shoplifting, and so the suggested figure of theft from shops in the nineteenth century is probably an underestimate. Looking at the statistics of cases brought before the Central Crown Court at the Old Bailey between January 1820 and December 1910, of 796 offences prosecuted under the category 'shoplifting' fully 88 per cent were brought before 1850, and thereafter just 81 cases reached the Bailey.[38]

In the mid-nineteenth century shopping was a fashionable pastime among ladies of the upper and middle classes and shoplifting was rife. Shopkeepers were well aware that female thieves were known to dress up to resemble wealthier 'respectable' shoppers in order to perpetrate crimes without attracting suspicion. In this context the 'extraordinary conduct' of one City of London shopkeeper in the early 1850s can be much better understood. A 'respectably attired' lady and her sister entered Mr Meeking's shop on Holborn Hill supposedly intending to buy a dress for a forthcoming occasion. The woman (not named in the newspaper report) was obliged to wait for an assistant as two ladies were already being served. One of these placed a £5 note on the counter with a sovereign coin on top, as payment for the items she had selected. The assistant turned over the note and asked her to endorse it, then walked off to the other side of the shop to fetch the cashier. However, by the time the cashier arrived the sovereign was missing. The customer swore she had put it there and the assistant was just as adamant. Suspicion now fell on anyone who was in the general area, including the two sisters waiting to be served. The customer whose sovereign had disappeared now turned to them and asked them not to leave until the matter had been settled.

A policeman was summoned so the women could be searched. However, the 'respectably attired' shopper demanded that a female searcher be brought to the store. She was informed that the police searcher was busy at Smithfield station house and that she would have to be taken there if she wished to be searched by a woman. Since the woman refused to be marched through the streets by a policeman like a common criminal there was nothing to do but wait. They were all forced to remain in the store for three hours before it closed and Mr Meeking returned from business elsewhere. Now the women could be taken into a private room where they were stripped of all their clothes (save 'their shoes and stockings') by one of Meeking's female servants, but nothing was found on any of them.

The unnamed woman was so outraged by this invasion of her privacy and being held against her will that she applied to Sir

Robert Carden at the Guildhall court to complain. She told him she had fainted twice during her ordeal and had been ill ever since. So ill, she said, that it had taken her several weeks to gather the courage and energy to come to court. She was a respectable married woman and the whole episode was a disgrace, which explains why she did not wish her name to appear in the newspapers. Sir Robert was sympathetic but legally impotent. He explained no crime had been committed, but she did have recourse for a civil prosecution for false imprisonment should she wish to pursue it. However, pursuing the case risked the lady's name being dragged through the civil courts and newspapers. The public airing of her experience would also have had an adverse effect on Meeking's business, deterring others from risking a similar one, and this might explain why she chose to complain at the Guildhall.[39] It illustrates how risky accusations of shoplifting could be for a retailer if they were not absolutely certain that a person was guilty. The tactics of the 'professional' shoplifter, which aimed at blending in by appearing to be something they were not, made it particularly hard for shop staff to identify them.

Given that shoplifting was a mundane, everyday crime, when cases did get highlighted in the newspapers it was the unusual or enticing ones that garnered attention. While this limits our ability to use newspaper records statistically, they still serve to present important examples of the nature of shoplifting and those engaged in it. One of the tropes that emerged from the nineteenth century was that of the 'lady shoplifter', the well-heeled offender who had no obvious financial imperative to steal. This phenomenon is much better understood today but in the 1800s the term 'kleptomania' was 'coined to explain a supposed mental weakness in women' who could not help but steal items they could well afford to buy.[40]

One Friday in May 1832 Joanna Garth entered a haberdasher's shop in Percy Street, Marylebone, and bought a piece of lace for 2s 7d. She then asked the assistant if she might have a look at some

Tree at the corner of Wood Street with London shops, 1870,
illustration from Walter Thornbury, *Old and New London* (1873–8).

stockings and other items. Joanna took a seat by the counter as the
man brought the goods out for her to examine but did not buy any
of them. Garth was dressed 'fashionably' and carried a muff. The
assistant watched Garth carefully secrete a pair of the stockings in
the muff and then get up to leave. He challenged her, finding the
stockings in the muff and another pair in her hand. By the chair
where she was sitting he found some discarded lace. The assistant
called a policeman and Garth was taken away. She was charged at
Marylebone with shoplifting. It was a clear case, but the haberdasher
(Harris) was reluctant to prosecute. Garth was unmarried but not,
it seems, a member of the working class. Had she been things might

have been very different. Harris tried quite hard to have the case settled summarily and without penalty, but the magistrate was less keen to let it go. He let her leave his court on the promise she would return when requested but set bail at £200. This in itself speaks to the wealth of the woman. The police were not obliged to press charges and there seemed little to gain by anyone doing so. Joanna Garth was not the sort of offender that society was concerned about or that the Metropolitan Police was created to combat.[41]

By contrast Mary Anne Stanniel more obviously fitted the profile of a working-class female thief. Stanniel was only eighteen when she appeared before Mr D'Eyncourt at Clerkenwell in 1860 but had already established a reputation as a 'well-known shoplifter'. On this occasion she was charged with taking two samples of silk ribbon belonging to John Skinner, a linen draper on Pentonville Road. Stanniel had entered Skinner's shop with a friend and engaged the shopkeeper in conversation, a classic distraction technique. The women asked to see two completely different sorts of product, but Skinner was on his guard. He had been robbed before and was wise to the attempted deception. However, having two customers in his shop, each demanding to see different things at the same time, meant he was hard pushed to keep his eyes on both. He called his wife to help, and she soon noticed that a piece of blue ribbon had gone missing and came round the counter to take hold of Stanniel's hand, turning it over to reveal a roll of ribbon. It was not the missing ribbon, but it was their property, so they called a policeman. Her accomplice fled, but Stanniel was taken to a police station and searched. No ribbon was found on her, so the policeman came back to the shop to check again. After a quick search the ribbon was found on the floor, where the defendant had ditched it. The constable told D'Eyncourt that he had arrested Stanniel before and that she had been up at Westminster Police court on similar charges. Stanniel was able to afford a solicitor who urged the magistrate to deal with the matter summarily. He promised that after she had served whatever time the justice felt was appropriate her father would 'take her home and look after her'. Whether D'Eyncourt believed him or not he did as requested and sent the shoplifter to the house of correction for four months and told her she 'was fortunate' she had not got longer.[42]

Indirect thefts, such as shoplifting or pocket-picking, were much more likely to feature females than the direct and violent or dangerous crimes of robbery or burglary. Thieves mostly took items that fitted within their social sphere. So women took clothes, or linen and lace, lengths of materials and ribbons. Men, by comparison, stole tools, money and precious items such as watches. The explanation is straightforward: women took things they could use or easily get rid of. There was a huge market in second-hand clothes and materials into which thieves could 'invest' their loot. Suspicions might be raised by a woman walking through town with a bag of workmen's tools but not by a basket of ribbons. This sort of theft worked best if the perpetrator was plausible and more so if they could convince the victim that they were genuine. Shoplifting was akin to picking pockets in that a fair degree of skill and dexterity was combined with bravado and no little courage.

Those accused of committing shoplifting in late Victorian London generally fell into one of two categories. There were working-class thieves who exploited the trade in second-hand goods and the widespread pawnshop network, stealing cloth, lace, clothes and other items that were easy to dispose of. In this respect they were similar to many other sorts of thieves who took advantage of the exchange economy of the time. Where they differed perhaps was in their ability to pretend to be someone they were not, to practice deception and to exploit the innate nature of retailing, which is to treat the customer at face value. The other type of shoplifter was notably better off economically. Middle- and upper-class shoplifters arguably had no need to steal the items they were accused of taking, and most likely had plenty of funds with which to pay for them. For them the act of taking represented something different, not a desire to profit from a theft but perhaps to experience a thrill from doing so. Kleptomania is an impulse control disorder, an inability to resist the urge to steal. It can also be associated with other forms of mental illness such as anxiety, obsessive-compulsive behaviour and addiction. Most of the cases we have seen here had female protagonists, and given the nature of goods stolen, such as linen and lace, and the locations of offences (linen drapers, haberdashers) this is understandable. The association of kleptomania with women, however, fits a broader Victorian trope about the weakness (physical and mental) of women. While many shoplifting cases were heard before police courts it was not here that most cases were concluded. Shoplifting was a felony that could attract a long prison sentence and so magistrates seem to have been inclined to send them on to be heard before a jury at the sessions. This was more likely if the perpetrator was working class and if they had a record of previous offences.

Pilfering and smuggling

Another crime closely associated with lower-class offenders was pilfering, something that rarely troubled the jury courts. This was a petty offence with which magistrates like John Arthur Cairns were all too familiar, as this excerpt from his memoirs confirms:

> The ordinary person has no conception of the wealth of the commodities that pours into the Thames day after day – every necessity and every luxury of food, and drink and clothing – grain and sugar, spices and fruit, and nuts, tinned foods of every description, wines, spirits and liqueurs, silks and satins and woollens ... The quantities are so vast that a little taken away can make no difference! Stealing at the Docks has become a disease.[43]

Cairns was writing in the aftermath of the First World War but his reminiscences of his time at Thames Police court are useful in understanding the London Docks throughout the previous century. Cairns regretted having to send dockers to prison for their depredations but claimed it was the only way to stamp out the 'disease'. Thefts were commonplace and considered by many working there no theft at all, but a perk of the job. Dockers worked extremely hard for very low pay, as the Great Dock Strike of 1889 revealed, and a culture of customary rights had persisted despite attempts to eradicate it from the late 1700s.[44] One case from 1870 neatly illustrates the problem.

William Bayley was a 'sober, steady, honest, and industrious workman' in a gang loading a merchant ship, the *Malvina*. Despite this he had been stopped and searched by a dock constable and was struggling to explain why he had a 'bottle of pickles, a pound of dried plums, and two tubes for drinking wine and spirits from casks in the docks' on his person.[45] The Thames magistrate sentenced him to two months' imprisonment, reduced to six weeks on account of his previous good character.[46] William Pitt also felt the full force of the magistrate's frustration that dockers continued to 'plunder their employers'. Pitt had been found with three and half ounces of tea, which he shrugged off as 'sweepings' from the hold of the ship he had been unloading. It was a small amount, but tea was a valuable commodity. Tea was also very much a part of the working-class diet by the 1850s, championed for its health properties.[47] By taking home a few pence-worth Pitt was making the family budget stretch that little bit further ('I have got a wife and two children to maintain,' he told Mr Paget in court). Paget saw it as the 'greatest mercy' to hand down maximum prison sentences of two months with hard labour to every pilferer brought before him. It was the only way, he insisted, that others would be deterred from ruining their families' lives.[48] He stuck to this position even when the employers pleaded for leniency. Joseph Gulliford was a master carpenter who had worked on the West India Dock for a dozen years. A bandmaster of a volunteer corps, his record was impeccable; at one time £62 had been entrusted to his care and 'not a farthing had been missed'. Several 'gentlemen' came to Thames to vouch for him; he was a family man, an honest worker of 'irreproachable character'. Nevertheless, he had been caught with a pint of overproof rum and his explanation, that he thought it was a bottle of oil, was flimsy and beside the point. Despite the reality that this man would lose his employment and his good name, Paget sent him to gaol for two months.[49]

The poor wages of dockers and the casualization system that required so many of them to compete for work daily were triggers for the 1889 Dock Strike. In that year Mr Lushington was magistrate at Thames and not known for leniency. William Barnes was accused of pilfering from a ship unloading at the Millwall Dock. The second mate discovered that one of the 118 bales of tobacco the ship had transported was missing. Once located it was found to be short by about 9 kilograms (20 lb). The men working in the area were searched and a small amount was found on Barnes. He said he had found it, but Lushington sentenced him to fourteen days' imprisonment with hard labour.[50] Pilfering small amounts like this was commonplace, despite the best efforts of the dock police and the Thames magistrates to prevent or deter it. This was how it had always been on the docks, seen as a 'customary right', a perk of the job, a way to supplement very low wages. Closely linked to this was another activity that has also been considered as a 'social crime' by historians, smuggling.

Throughout the century the Thames was crammed with shipping. Merchant vessels brought goods in and out of the London Docks from all over the world. Given the huge amount of goods coming in and out of the docks pilfering, embezzlement and other forms of theft were a constant problem for the warehouse owners and shipping companies. The state also found it hard to stop individuals or companies from avoiding the tax levied on certain imported goods like alcohol or tobacco and in May 1840 the issue of smuggling came to the Thames Police court. John Rutherford, a ship's carpenter on an East India ship, was charged with having 12 kilograms (27 lb) of tobacco on which tax had not been paid. Faced with a possible penalty of £100, Rutherford pleaded 'not guilty'. Unfortunately for him a customs officer had boarded the ship, searched his cabin and found the walls had been adapted with false panels for concealing goods. The carpenter's berth on deck had also been customized, and here the stash of tobacco was revealed, along with a quantity of cheroots and cigars, all 'liable to a duty of 9 shillings in the pound'. This was not the end of the discoveries. The ship's cook, William Wilson, was also accused. The customs officer searched his berth and found tobacco, cigars and cheroots. The officer said that he could have charged the entire crew with smuggling but chose only to make examples of the worst offenders. Rutherford and Wilson were ordered to pay the duty owning and were locked up in the meantime. It was Rutherford's second conviction, which suggests that smuggling was profitable enough to accept the risks of being caught.[51]

An alert policeman was watching as a cab pulled up outside 33 Flower & Dean Street very early one December morning in 1852. Two men got out and one threw a bundle into a nearby passageway. As Sergeant Aram approached the man took flight, as did his companion, each running in opposite directions. The officer instructed the cab driver to follow one of the passengers while he chased the other. The discarded package contained 213 pouches of tobacco with a street value in 1852 of £50. Both men were eventually arrested but only one was prosecuted. His name was William Watchem (aka 'the Captain'), a known smuggler at the docks. Watchem was fined £100, twice the value of the tobacco. Given that this was an almost impossible sum to find he went to gaol for six months.[52] The case is instructive because it is very likely that Sergeant

Aram was tipped off about the drop in Flower & Dean Street. The smuggler had been under observation by the police, the investigation being led by H Division's Inspector White. Flower & Dean Street was an ideal location for a drop such as this; the area was a dense rookery of alleys and courts, full of lodging houses and workshops that represented a 'no go' zone for the police. The other man may have been a police informant, which may be why he was not presented in court. Issuing fines for non-payment of duty was a standard practice in the Metropolitan Police courts of the late 1800s. Given how hard some forms of theft were to prove, the fact that a person was found in possession of imported goods for which they struggled to provide a legitimate explanation, charging them for the duty was possibly an effective strategy, especially when the accused was unable to pay (as Watchem was).

Cases like these were predicated on the profits to be made by individuals evading excise duty on popular imported consumables (notably tobacco, but also alcohol, tea, sugar and so on). Such a vast volume of these luxuries arrived in London that there was money to be made and it must be the case that the authorities prosecuted only a tiny proportion of the smuggling taking place. The police may have concentrated efforts on known smugglers and smuggling gangs, or groups of criminals engaged in widespread pilfering and smuggling. The seventeen cases of smuggling included in the 1881 sample from Thames Police court lack detail, but they do provide some useful information nevertheless.

Henry Taylor was brought in by Sergeant William Horlock from Thames Criminal Investigation Department (CID) and convicted of smuggling. He paid a fine of £1 6s 8d plus the value of the unidentified goods he had failed to pay duty on. Robert Ling, Alphie Dowlas and George Brown also paid to avoid gaol. Walter Edwards was convicted of smuggling and fined £1 12s or fourteen days, which he paid, as did Johannes Euspheau, a 24-year-old foreign sailor or migrant. Whether his fee was higher because of

his offence or his nationality is unknown, but his bill was £3 2s 6d.
Horlock also prosecuted Alfred Valentine and George Brown
(again) for smuggling, and Lushington handed down fines of 10s
8d each. Phillip Browse paid £2 5s 6d for his offending in July 1881
and two days later John Mitchell, unable to find a similar amount,
went to prison for a month. Horlock was back in court that summer
to bring charges against Gert Manba, another overseas visitor,
who was fined 11s 6d. Most of those prosecuted were men, but not
all. Augusta de Grotte, who may have been German, Dutch or
American, was brought in by Inspector Read and fined £3 4s. De
Grotte could pay, but Caroline Benson could not and went to gaol
for a month. Read also prosecuted Sarah Baker, who was imprisoned
for a month for smuggling because she did not have the £2 15s 4d
needed to avoid it. It may well be that women were less able to afford
fines, but this is too small a sample to draw conclusions from.[53]

Smuggling was a problem for the customs and police, especially when it exceeded the endemic small-scale profiteering that
might be expected to exist in a society where a premium was
earned from luxury items that had become part and parcel of
everyday life. Smuggling and pilferage was hard to prevent, as
excise men, police and merchants had found for centuries. There
was a ready market for 'duty free' merchandise, and smuggling
items through customs was considered to be hardly a crime at all.
Moreover, when smuggling was carried out by organized criminal
networks, there was little incentive to risk intimidation and violence by tipping off the authorities. While it was rarely a 'victimless
crime', that is probably the way many of those involved understood it. That is certainly not how society viewed the next type of
property offending; that perpetrated by swindlers and con men.

Fraud and false pretences

Plenty of fraud cases came before the Metropolitan Police courts in the Victorian period. Some involved elaborate ruses, but William Jewell and Joseph Richards simply relied on talking fast and confusing victims. Jewell was a 38-year-old waterside labourer from Bethnal Green while Richards hailed from nearby Mile End. In September 1895 both were charged at North London Police court with attempting to defraud tradesmen. Jewell was the main player, Jackson his accomplice. Jewell had entered Henry Amos's confectionary shop, placed a sixpence on the counter, and asked Amos's wife for a pennyworth of sweets. Taking the sixpence, she handed over the sweets and placed five pennies change on the counter. This is where the attempt to confuse began. Jewell took a penny from his pocket, added it to the pile and asked her to swap the coins for a sixpence. Before she had time to scoop up the pennies and make the exchange Jewell interrupted, saying 'Give me a shilling instead of the sixpence and the coppers.' He was aiming to confuse and may have succeeded in gaining an extra sixpence had her husband not been listening. When he came in Jewell scarpered. Having been unsuccessful in their attempt at Amos's, the pair tried the same ruse at Mrs Muffett's newsagents in Hackney Wick. Again, Jewell engaged the shopkeeper in conversation. He asked for the evening paper (which cost a halfpenny) and put a shilling on the counter. The newsagent gave him 'eleven pence halfpenny change'. He then asked for his shilling back and Mrs Muffett obliged, assuming he had found a halfpenny in his pocket. But Jewell pushed the money back over to her and asked her to change it for a florin (a two-shilling piece). She told him she did not have a florin to make the exchange. 'Then I have to give you a halfpenny,' he replied. 'No, you have to give me a shilling,' she said. His attempt failed, but probably worked on other occasions. Muffett called the police and with Amos's help the two men were picked out of a police identification parade. There was insufficient evidence to prosecute Jackson as charged, but the magistrate decided there was ample proof of intent and sent him to prison for three months at hard labour.[54] Frauds like this were direct, in that they involved contact with the victim and so a certain degree of immediate personal risk to the perpetrator. Other frauds were much less direct, being carried out at a distance using the relatively new technology of the post and exploiting the growing ubiquity of newspapers.

The case of John Major, convicted in 1880, was a clear example of obtaining money by false pretences. Major, who gave an address in Bermondsey, was brought before the magistrate at Southwark in April. The self-declared print seller was accused of 'obtaining sums of money from various persons in different parts of the country, by pretending to tell their fortunes'. In his correspondence and printed advertising he styled himself 'Methveston, the Great Seer, Philosopher and Astrologer', who promised to 'reveal your future complete, with fate and marriage, family, friends, etc.; what part to travel or voyage to, and other particulars to buyers of three prints, [price] 31 stamps.' Major also advertised 'Talismanic charms' at seventeen stamps, and 'Direction for making a red magnetic present, causing the visit of lovers' for 31 stamps. It was quite a comprehensive service, and it is likely that there were plenty of people gullible enough to believe that a love charm or a promise of a fortune being told was worth sending a parcel of postage stamps. Some of those duped complained directly to Scotland Yard. Since Major had included his address on his adverts the police were able to trace him, and Detective Inspector Fox set a trap. Sergeant Wells sent Methveston 31 stamps and received 'three worthless prints of his "Nativity", all of which were false and complete rubbish'. The police searched his rooms at Ambrose Street where they found 'nearly a cartload' of 'Books of Futurity' and evidence that he had spent almost £30 buying advertising space in regional newspapers. This was no small sum of money in 1880 and testified to the fact that

Major was able to earn a living from his fraudulent activity. His lawyer, Mr Ody, claimed that his client 'was no fraud' and only sold prints. The court hearing was staggered over several weeks as the police requested and were granted time to bring several witnesses to London. Major was remanded and brought back up to court periodically before he was back in court to face his accusers on 24 April.

More details emerged of the material he was selling. Sergeant Wells received 'a letter containing three pictures, telling him he would get married to a rich woman, and lead a happy life, etc.' Inspector Fox's men removed boxes of 'circulars, books, and papers' from Ambrose Street, which they brought to court. These included papers 'inscribed with texts from the Bible, 9,000 handbills, post-cards, and letters addressed to various people in the country', and 'fortune-telling books'. A police inspector from Northampton testi-fied to knowing the man as a convicted rogue and vagabond who had been given a month at hard labour by a Daventry magistrate in 1870. Major had also been convicted in London some years earlier and sentenced to eighteen months for obtaining money by false pretences. The duty magistrate at Southwark committed Major to take his trial at the Surrey Quarter Sessions as a rogue and vagabond.[55]

Using the newspapers and postal system to trick vulnerable readers into parting with money came in different forms in the 1800s. In the early 1890s John George Binet set up his 'National Detective Agency' to investigate a range of private matters including unpaid bills, unfaithful spouses and missing persons. In July 1893 Binet found himself on the wrong side of the law when he stood in the Bow Street dock accused of obtaining money by false pretences. He was charged with placing adverts in the papers for men and women to join his agency. Interested parties were required to send a postal order for 10*s* 6*d* for which, the advert stated, they would obtain a certificate authenticating the holder's position as a detective in the

NDA and details of cases to investigate. In effect he was franchising private detection across the country. Binet was quite successful, and several people sent him money and waited for the work to roll in. Very few, if any, got anything more than a certificate, and some did not even get that. The supposed fraud made the pages of *Tit Bits* and *The Truth*, two of the better-selling periodicals of the day, which hopefully deterred some from parting with their cash. Mr Vaughan committed Binet to take his trial at the Central Criminal Court later that month.[56]

On 24 July John George Binet was tried and found guilty.[57] A Birmingham grocer said he parted with the fee because he believed the letters from Binet were genuine. Another witness, Frederick Selling from Gravesend, said he 'got nothing for my money'. Annabella Jones, a labourer's wife from Billinghurst, said that when no work materialized she made her way to London to see Binet, who explained that 'he gave his London work to the men at Scotland Yard.' Two men from Leicester also paid but got no work, despite Binet's advert specially stating that it was the increase in demand that necessitated the recruitment of more private detectives. The defence argued that Binet was good at being a private detective and that his clients were happy with the work they had commissioned. That Binet and his star employee Mrs J Gray, 'the celebrated lady detective', were competent investigators was somewhat beside the point. The court was told they were in debt and behind with their rent. Perhaps that pushed Binet to try and raise money by using a postal fraud. Binet had tried to evade the law once summonses had been issued. He had been arrested at Victoria railway station, where he was attempting to catch a train out of the capital disguised as a sea captain. Mrs Gray and another of Binet's detectives, 'Chief Inspector' Godfrey, were more successful in escaping, having vanished before the police could catch up with them. The judge sent Binet to prison for a year with hard labour.[58]

Binet's fraud was predicated on the desire of people to find work, or perhaps an aspiration to rise above the drudgery of everyday life to pursue a more exciting existence. John Major profited by selling ephemera associated with society's fascination with what might broadly be termed the occult. This has always been an open door for fraudsters. The reality is that many people would like to know what the future holds even if they are a bit sceptical of the authenticity or reliability of the sources of information (be that newspaper astrologers, fairground Gypsies or anything else). Fortune tellers have always existed, from the ancients to the present, but while in modern society we tend to regard them as mostly

Fortune telling, *c.* 1865, photograph.

purveyors of harmless fun, in the distant past they were sometimes seen as witches and charlatans. In 1735 the laws that allowed for the hanging of people for witchcraft were repealed but it remained a crime to try and trick others into believing you had magical powers. The Witchcraft Act of 1735 remained on the statute until 1951, when the Fraudulent Mediums Act, which allowed for the prosecution of individuals who claimed to be psychic, replaced it.[59] While magistrates and the police rarely turned to the Witchcraft Act as a means of prosecution, they did deploy the Vagrancy Act (1824). This act allowed the police to prosecute pretty much anyone found in a public place asking for money without good cause, the relevant clause being: 'Every person pretending of professing to tell fortunes, or using any subtle craft, means, or device, by palmistry or otherwise, to deceive and impose on anyone, may be treated as a rogue and vagabond, and sentenced to imprisonment with hard labour.'[60]

Fraudulent fortune tellers could also be prosecuted under laws that prohibited the selling of goods or the obtaining of money by false pretences. In late July 1883 it was this activity that brought Charlotte Elizabeth Priscilla Veasey before Mr D'Eyncourt at Westminster Police court. Veasey, aged 68, was accused of obtaining money by pretending to 'tell fortunes'. Several women had complained about her behaviour to the police, who set up an investigation that involved the planting of police witnesses. Detectives Scott and Wilson set up surveillance on Veasey's house in White Lion Street, Chelsea. They also employed an out-of-work serving girl named Reed and the widow of a policeman (Mrs Gregory) to act as supposed clients. As they staked out the house the detectives saw thirteen women come and go during just two hours. On the same day a further five clients called at the house in the afternoon. Mrs Gregory and Miss Reed were questioned. Reed said she been told by Veasey that 'she would have five sweethearts, none of whom would marry her – and that a very "nice young gentleman" had honourable intentions, and would ask [her] out on evening walks.' She paid sixpence for this information and much of the material told to her was vague and commonplace, as many predictions are. In her defence Veasey, known as the 'wise woman from Leicester', insisted that she did no harm and always gave 'good advice', never charging a fixed sum for her services. While it is possible simply to see Veasey as an elderly woman who mixed homespun advice with a bit of smoke and mirrors and charged a not unreasonable amount for reassuring people that everything would be well, D'Eyncourt did not see it that way. He told her that she 'got her living by cheating credulous young women' and sent her to prison for three weeks at hard labour, not even countenancing the alternative of a fine.[61]

Other attempts at defrauding victims involved what is commonly termed the 'confidence trick'. In 1882 Daniel Risbey was in East London to visit his wife, who was undergoing treatment at the London Hospital on Whitechapel Road. The fifty-year-old fisherman from Essex was unfamiliar with the capital and certainly a stranger to the dodges and pitfalls that often befell the unwary. Like many occasional or first-time visitors, he must have stuck out like a sore thumb. As he left the hospital and made his way along Mile End Road a man stopped and started talking to him. As they conversed, he noticed another person just ahead had stopped, having apparently dropped some pieces of paper on the street. The first man, who had introduced himself as Thomas Windsor, picked them up and showed them to Risbey. 'Why', Windsor declared, 'these are £5 notes!' and he called the other man back. He now joined them, said his name was George Boyce and that he had recently come into £300 following a pay-out for an incident on the railway. Boyce declared that 'he meant to do some good with the money and would lend to any deserving man.' What a stroke of luck it was for Risbey to run into two such generous chaps on his visit to London. The pair declared that despite having just met him they trusted him enough to have some of the money up front while they sorted out the 'usual arrangements' of a loan and suggested he wait in a local pub while they did so. This proved that they had confidence in him, they explained.

To further demonstrate that he was worthy of that confidence they asked him to hand over his purse and money while they sorted things out. He now had several £5 notes; they had his money – which only amounted to about 5s anyway. The fisherman took out a few pennies for a beer, handed over his purse and walked over to the nearest pub to wait. Having waited for an hour, with no sign of them, he was making ready to leave when a police sergeant appeared and asked him to accompany him to the station. When he got there Boyce and Windsor were in custody and Sergeant Rolfe explained the situation. The officer had seen the two men talking to Risbey, and since he knew them as 'sharpers' (slang for confidence trick-sters) he decided to watch them. He followed them after they left Risbey and arrested them. When searched they had just threepence, some more of the alleged windfall notes, a few Hanoverian medals, and the Essex man's purse. Both were charged with theft and pre-sented at Worship Street on the following morning, 6 July 1882. The notes were fake – from the 'Bank of Engraving', as Sergeant Rolfe explained. The medals were used to represent sovereign coins (many people would not necessarily have noticed the difference, at least not without careful examination) and the two men were well known to the police. On this occasion Daniel Risbey was rela-tively fortunate and was reunited with his depleted purse having mostly just been made to feel rather foolish. The two 'sharpers' were committed for trial.[62]

The most sophisticated version of fraud required organization and was popularly termed a 'long firm' scam. This is associated in the public mind with criminal gangs (or networks) such as those run by Ronald and Reginald Kray in the 1960s.[63] The term has much deeper roots, however, dating to the late 1800s, well before the twins came to public attention. A simple definition (from J. C. Hotten's *The Slang Dictionary*, first published in 1859) is 'a gang of swindlers who obtain goods by false pretences'.[64] The fraud usually involved the setting up of a supposedly legitimate business to develop a credit history before suppliers were systematically defrauded. The following case, from the 1880s, gives a sense of this form of criminality. Charles John Holmes (aka 'Frederick Jackson') was described at Southwark Police court as a 41-year-old baker, although it is doubtful that he did any baking at all. Holmes opened a shop at 91 Long Lane, Bermondsey, and an account with the London & South Western Bank, which helped to establish his trading credibility. Acting on complaints, police began an investigation headed by Inspector Matthew Fox of the CID. Having obtained a search warrant the inspector turned up at Jackson's shop in May 1880. Inspector Fox reported that:

The shop had the appearance to an ordinary observer of being well stocked. On the shelves were a large number of kegs and cheese boxes, but on inspection they were all found to be empty, and with the exception of some loaves of bread and two sacks of flour, there was not a single article in the shop that the prisoner purported to deal in.

In other words, the shop was a front or a scam, and when he looked further Inspector Fox found the evidence he needed to arrest Holmes. Several letters from suppliers were discovered, along with a blank chequebook and some other paperwork ('40 or 50 County Court summonses and judgments') that showed what he had been up to. Holmes (aka Jackson) had been carefully contacting suppliers all over the country, ordering samples, paying for small orders of goods that he then disposed of quickly, before placing larger orders for goods he had no intention of paying for. He used the bank account to draw cheques 'payable to himself', which, Fox's report continued, 'he passed away in payment of goods, thereby leaving an impression that he was carrying on a genuine trading business.' When it came before the magistrate at Southwark one witness (Edward Ellaby, a starch manufacturer from Battersea) testified that he had received a letter of introduction from C. J. Holmes of Bermondsey, written on a 'bill-head on which the words "Established 25 years" were printed'. Soon afterwards he received an order for 11 kilograms (25 lb) weight of starch. This was never paid for and when another order arrived he 'declined' it and sued for debt.

Ellaby was not the only victim; there were at least 68 other suppliers in London owed money, and a further 40 'in the country'.[65] In May 1880 Holmes was remanded in custody for another week and in August he appeared at the Central Criminal Court charged, alongside others, with fraud. Several other businessmen gave evidence against him here. Stephen Hawtret, a tea dealer in business with his brother and another partner, told the court that 'I supposed we were dealing with genuine traders, and on that belief furnished the goods.' His company was obliged to pay import duty on orders placed by Holmes for which payment never materialized. George Jenkinson, a harness maker based on London Wall, was also taken in by the fraud. He supplied harnesses worth nearly £30 but never received payment. There was a long list of victims, and the amount of this fraud was considerable. Holmes was found convicted of obtaining goods by fraudulent means and conspiracy and sentenced to five years' penal servitude. Three others were similarly convicted but received shorter sentences of eighteen months, and four men were acquitted.[66]

The long firm swindle did not have to involve criminal gangs but was often a conspiracy of more than one individual given that the frauds sometimes involved quite complicated business arrangements. As many of the examples detailed in this chapter indicate, organized crimes like the long firm scam were not the norm in Victorian London. The reality was that most theft was opportunistic and involved single operators chancing their luck. The penalties for getting caught if convicted were severe, but many would have weighed these up against the risks of getting caught in the first place, or the opportunity to wriggle out of a charge for lack of evidence, or to suffer just a short prison term if convicted before a magistrate (from the 1850s at least). Protecting property remained central to the criminal justice system in the 1800s, as it had in the 1700s, but we can see that plenty of those who fell victims to thefts in the Victorian period were small businessmen and women, who were much less able to sustain depredations than the rich and powerful elites that have often been characterized as the architects of a class-based justice system by historians of crime. The police courts reveal the reality of most property crime in nineteenth-century London, which was that those with little or nothing stole from those who had more, but not necessarily considerably more. The next chapter will look at the role of the summary courts and the wider justice system in dealing with a form of crime that ostensibly made no differentiation based on social class – violence.

4

VIOLENCE AND HOMICIDE

C riminal violence covered a wide range of offences in the nineteenth century, from the most serious crimes of murder, manslaughter and rape, to non-indictable instances of assault. The London police courts were frequent witnesses to complaints of assault, many of which were the result of everyday squabbles and the tensions caused by a crowded urban environment and the easy supply of cheap alcohol. Magistrates settled most assault complaints, selecting fines as a suitable punishment in many cases, with imprisonment used either in default of an ability to pay or being reserved for more serious offenders. This was how magistrates had dealt with non-lethal violence in the previous century, as largely a civil matter brought before an ostensibly criminal court.[1] With the introduction of professional policing in 1829 and, as has already been discussed, the impact of this on communities that had not experienced such close control over their work and leisure practices previously, a rise in assault prosecutions might seem inevitable. In what is still one of the most important studies of long-term trends in criminal prosecution for the nineteenth centuries, Vic Gatrell concluded that while rates of violence began at a high in the first half of the century thereafter they fell steadily and significantly.[2] Understanding that fall is more complicated than identifying it, and subsequent work has tried to explain evolving attitudes to violence and changing patterns of prosecution and punishment.[3] What is clear is that the police courts were the starting point for prosecutions for both petty and serious violence, including fatal assaults. This presents an opportunity to see how the summary process interlinked with the jury courts of the capital, most notably the Central Criminal Court, in bringing murderers to justice. Homicide occupied public attention in the second half of the nineteenth century, especially as public executions declined, and hangings were carried out behind prison walls after 1868. After 1842 (when rape was removed from the list of capital crimes) murder was effectively the only crime for which offenders would still hang, and for that reason, plus its capacity to excite emotions like no other form of offending, it fascinated Victorians.[4]

The decline of homicide and the rise of assault

Most researchers would agree that homicide rates began to decline from the late medieval period and that this decline accelerated in the seventeenth and eighteenth centuries. Homicide (murder and manslaughter) rates are usually measured per 100,000 of the population, allowing comparison across time. As Victoria ascended the throne in 1837 rates in England were around 1.7 per 100,000; by her death in 1901 they had fallen to 0.7.[5] Several explanations have been offered for the long-term fall in homicide rates, which need not detain us unduly here. It is perhaps sufficient to say that historians have not achieved consensus beyond recognizing that the causal factors are probably multiple and overlapping, and that statistics are perhaps not as reliable as Lawrence Stone initially claimed them to be.[6] The reliability of police and coroners' decision-making in the Victorian period is brought into sharp focus by recent work that has suggested it is far from certain that all homicides were prosecuted as such, despite it being widely accepted to be the most heinous of crimes.[7] Reflecting on the decline-of-homicide debate, we might ask whether homicide can be seen as an indicator of wider patterns of declining violence in society. Stone certainly believed this was the case,[8] but given the continued presence of violence in the courts of nineteenth-century England as well as in so many forms of popular culture and entertainment, it seems doubtful at best. As we will see, homicide cases often came before the police courts for an initial hearing. Magistrates would normally assess whether a defendant should be committed for trial by jury and the evidence presented by police and medical witnesses was crucial. Sometimes a violent assault was so severe that the victim was unable to attend court and so proceedings were suspended and (most) defendants remanded until they were fit enough to testify. If a victim succumbed to their injuries and died, then a murder charge would follow along with a committal for jury trial.[9] What follows then is an exploration of the sorts of violent incidents that came before the police courts and made the pages of the London press.

Non-fatal violence: assault

Assault was one of the most common charges to be heard before the police courts of nineteenth-century London. Assaults varied, however, and the definition in the Police Code book allowed for a considerable amount of discretion on the part of the victim, police or the courts. Assault could mean something as minor as a shove or a threat, but it could also involve a real attempt to harm. Witness the entry in the Police Code for 1889, which referred to legislation passed in 1861.[10] 'A common assault is the beating, or it may be only the striking, or touching, of a person. Police should never apprehend in such cases, unless they see the offence committed, but leave the party injured to summon the aggressor.'[11]

Assault was a crime that was affected both by prevailing attitudes towards violence and by police practice and legal definitions. If it were adjudged that an assault was accompanied by an attempt at theft, for example, then that might push it to be an indictable offence. If it involved the use of a weapon, or caused actual physical injury, or was perpetrated against a police officer, then again it might be elevated to a more serious crime. Moreover, in periods of public concern about violence or disorder, or when the newspapers had focused on violence at home, the consequences for offenders may have been more severe.[12] Finally, it needs to be acknowledged that while there is a 'dark figure of unreported crime', which arguably obscures any chance we have to understand levels of crime in the past (or indeed the present), this is especially true for non-lethal violence.

The Offences Against the Person Act of 1861 enshrined in law the forms of violence that are prosecuted today, such as grievous bodily harm (GBH), actual bodily harm (ABH) and wounding. All of these could be prosecuted at a higher jury court while the magistracy routinely dealt with common assault with the use of recognizances, small fines or short spells of imprisonment. Common assault covered almost anything that the police or courts defined it as, and it is far from clear what pushed it towards aggravated assault, although the Police Code suggests that this had to involve 'corroborative evidence of wounds'.[13] Prior to this the courts made use of legislation passed in 1828 that increased penalties for some forms of assault, and made it easier to prosecute cases of domestic violence.[14] It was still the case that the police would not routinely prosecute assault cases given the difficulty of proving wrongdoing or apportioning blame, especially in domestic contexts. Barry Godfrey has argued that in the nineteenth century police often chose to avoid prosecutions.[15] Nevertheless the police courts were arenas for all levels of society to complain about acts of violence perpetrated against them and in an urban centre as large as London opportunities for interpersonal disputes were frequent.

In March 1883 a dispute between Daniel Skelton and Frederick Flint about money ended in violence. It was about eleven o'clock at night and they had been drinking in Drummond Street. They divested themselves of their jackets and a so-called 'fair fight' began. According to witnesses the pair sparred for 'several rounds' before 'both men fell'. Flint got up to continue the fight, but Skelton was unable to, having broken his leg. At this point the fight ended because, as Clive Emsley has observed, rules of honour prevented working-class men from 'taking advantage' of an incapacitated opponent.[16] The injured man was carried to nearby University College Hospital and Flint was arrested. The next day Flint was hauled before the magistrate at Marylebone Police court and charged with assault. Flint explained that Skelton was his friend and admitted they had both been 'the worse for drink'. No harm was intended, however, and he said that Skelton had accepted that he was as much to blame for his injury. The court was told that Skelton would be laid up for five or six weeks as a result. The policeman that arrested him challenged Flint's narrative and requested a remand until Skelton was fit enough to present his own version of events. The magistrate agreed but said he was prepared to release Flint if he could find 'substantial bail'.[17]

Whether he made bail or not remains unknown; as with so many of the examples lifted from late Victorian newspaper sources, we can only speculate on possible outcomes. Very many assaults went unreported and unpunished, a fact that is generally accepted by historians. Assault was one of the most frequently prosecuted offences at summary level in the police courts of London, as it was in all the studies we have to date on the activities of justices of the peace in England and Wales throughout the eighteenth and nineteenth centuries. Magistrates in the City of London in the second half of the 1700s spent just under a third of their time hearing individual complaints of assault, most of which ended in a settlement between the warring parties, often brokered by the justice.[18]

Violent offending hearings before the Thames Police court 1881

	MALE	%	FEMALE	%	TOTAL
Assault	289	79	77	21	366
Violent assault	50	87.7	7	12.3	57
Rescue prisoner (and attempted)	17	47.2	19	52.8	36
Assault with felony	15	88.2	2	11.8	17
Causing death	12	85.7	2	14.3	14
Indecent assault	10	100	0	0	10
Assault with wilful damage	7	77.8	2	22.2	9
Cutting and wounding	9	100	0	100	9
Threatening behaviour	5	71.4	2	28.6	7
Assault on police	3	60	2	40	5
Shooting (and attempted)	2	66.7	1	33.3	3
Rape (and attempted)	3	100	0	100	3
	422	78.7	114	21.3	536

(March/May/July/September/November) counting by hearing

Assault was also an overwhelmingly male offence or, perhaps more accurately, men were much more likely to be prosecuted for it. Nearly 70 per cent of the prosecutions (366) in 1881 brought before the Thames court magistrates were simply recorded as 'assault'. Just three men and two women were explicitly charged with assaulting police officers, although some of the other assault cases may well have involved assaults on the police. Richard Martin and Thomas James were both gaoled for two months for assaulting

PC Underwood, while James Bush was sent to prison for a week for his assault on George Brewster (a reserve officer in H Division).[19] Unfortunately the records do not make it easy to understand who the victims were, although sometimes this can be inferred. Nevertheless, there are 115 hearings where we can be fairly sure that the victim of the assault was female and so this allows the following table to be created.

Male on male*	271 (70.2%)
Male on female	45 (11.6%)
Domestic violence (presumed by shared surname)	36 (9.3%)
Female on female	34 (8.8%)
Total	386 (99.9%)

* This is presumption

What the data reveals is that men were overwhelmingly responsible for violence in the homes, workplaces and streets served by the Thames court. They were also the highest category of victims of assault, although a significant proportion, 30 per cent, were women. The number, if not the proportion, of female victims is likely to have been much higher, especially with regards to assaults in domestic contexts. For all sorts of reasons women were reluctant to prosecute their husbands and partners and many only took out a warrant for assault after suffering many instances of abuse, often over several months or years. What the data above shows then is likely to be the tip of a much bigger and darker reality.

Violence between women was rare but not unknown. The 34 hearings here represent approximately one case coming to court per week. Given the 'dark figure of unrecorded crime' this suggests that female/female disputes were fairly common in the East End (and probably elsewhere). Most were dismissed by magistrates who treated them as petty and inconsequential unless injury was caused. Mr Lushington discharged Ann Kavanagh and Johanna Callaghan, two women in their fifties, who charged each other with assault. Cecilia Keffe was given a 20s fine for assaulting Ellen Leahy, which she paid, thereby avoiding fourteen days' imprisonment. Norah Leary was not given the option of a fine when she was convicted of assaulting Mary Cahill, so she went to prison for a fortnight with hard labour.[20]

It has been suggested that the nineteenth-century state increasingly intervened in what had been a largely 'civil' prosecution process for assault, to assert society's growing distaste for interpersonal violence.[21] The 1828 and 1861 acts would certainly support a thesis that the courts were prepared to deal with violent men (and some women) when cases were brought. Whether that reflects a growing distaste for interpersonal violence, however, is moot. Violence remained a prominent feature of everyday life, especially in the poorer areas of London. In March 1867 John Angus, a 'young man' who lived in a court off Windmill Street, near King's Cross, was charged with attacking and wounding Randell Payne, a local bricklayer. Payne, who also lived on Windmill Street, had come out of his house to remonstrate with a group of youths who were making a noise. He told the magistrate at Marlborough Street that:

> he was much annoyed by a number of boys at night in the court he lived in, and requested they go away. They refused to do so, and he then took hold of one boy and pushed him to get him away, when the prisoner [Angus] came and struck him two violent blows on the head with something sharp he had in his hand, inflicting two severe wounds.

Angus admitted striking the bricklayer but denied using a weapon. He justified his action on the grounds that Payne was 'ill-using his brother'. With doubt as to whether a sharp-edged weapon had been used Angus was remanded until medical evidence could be produced. Dr Peter Duncan testified later that he had examined Payne's wounds some 48 hours after the incident had occurred and said that while he had found two contused wounds, which were certainly serious, they were caused by a sharp weapon. The magistrate (Mr Knox) warned the accused that while he would not be prosecuted for wounding, he had 'struck harder than he should have done', and convicted him of common assault. He was fined £5 or a month in prison.[22]

Wounding was a felony under the 1861 act and required a jury trial. Of the 1,888 prosecutions for those convicted of wounding at the Central Criminal Court between January 1862 and the end of December 1900, almost half (49.3 per cent) resulted in sentences of penal servitude or hard labour.[23] Penal servitude – imprisonment in a national prison, accompanied by some form of additional laborious punishment, such as the crank or treadwheel – had replaced transportation to Australia as a sentence from 1857. The period of incarceration was dependent on the severity of the violence used and the discretion of the judge, and within the statistics cited from 1862 to 1900 there are sentences ranging from three years to life. Knox chose not to send his prisoner to the Sessions, perhaps because the use of a weapon was not established beyond doubt, but he ensured Angus was punished, albeit relatively leniently by comparison. This pattern of the use of judicial discretion is consistent with the treatment of low-level violence in the previous centuries and so does not obviously support a thesis of a growing intolerance to violence in Victorian Britain.

The dispute that had led to blows between workmates and had ended with one man in hospital with a broken leg was an example of what is often dubbed a 'fair fight'. The concept of the fair fight was enshrined in a sense of Englishness that was entwined with a widespread tolerance of violence among the elite and working classes in Victorian Britain. Contemporaries lauded the martial spirit of the English working man, and the fistfight was held up as a noble practice that epitomized the English belief in fair play. This manifested itself in the sport of pugilism or bare-knuckle boxing that was so popular in late Hanoverian England. There was money to be made from boxing, as prizes for fighters as well as gamblers and those organizing bouts. However, by the last quarter of the 1800s pugilism was nowhere near as popular as it had been in the decades before the 1820s and even a brief revival following the Crimean War (among concern about the level of fitness of British soldiers) could not overcome developing misgivings about the suitability of the sport, given its propensity to draw large crowds and encourage gambling among the so-called lower orders. Bare-knuckle fighting was not illegal per se, but prizefights (that is, fights for money) were.

In October 1888 Inspector Joseph Capp was on watch outside 30 East Road, near the City Road in the east of the capital, with several uniformed constables. He was acting on information that the address, home to a German club called The Morning Star, was hosting an illegal prizefight. Capp and his men knocked on the door of the club, but no one answered. He tried again with no more success, and so attempted to gain access from above. Inspector Capp climbed onto the roof of the club via an adjoining house and tried to peer in through a skylight, but the glass was cloudy and he was unable to see what was going on below. But he could hear the sounds of a crowd, the sounds of blows and of someone shouting 'time!' Convinced that a bare-knuckle prizefight was underway he instructed his men to move in. As his officers forced their way inside there was a rush of people as the audience tried to escape. When the police broke through, they discovered around two to three hundred people inside. There was a 'ring made of ropes and stakes in the centre of the hall', and two boxers squaring up to each other. The boxers were quickly arrested and removed to the nearest station house. At Worship Street Mr Montagu Williams was told that the police had found tickets for a 'dancing ball' on the floor of the hall, the ruse that the organizers had chosen to cover their illegal event. A poster outside promised that 'dancing' would start at 8.30 p.m., but in reality the only dancing that transpired was around the ring. During the raid the police seized 'gloves, towels, ropes, etc.', all evidence that a fight was underway. Both the men in the dock were bruised and bloodied, so it was clear that when the police had arrived and stopped the fight, it had been going on for some time. One of the pair, Charles Smith, a twenty-year-old bookmaker from Whitechapel, was bleeding from his ear and vomited when he was arrested. The divisional surgeon patched him up so that he was fit enough to attend court. Both he and the other fighter, Arthur Wilkinson (a fish-fryer from King's Cross, also aged twenty), were bailed to appear at a later date. When they reappeared a week later both were fully committed for trial.

On 22 November Smith and Wilkinson appeared before a jury at the Middlesex Sessions of the Peace, charged with 'inflicting grievous bodily harm and conspiring together to commit a breach of the peace by engaging in a prizefight'.[24] The defence was that this was 'nothing but a glove fight', but Inspector Capp was sure the blows he had heard were not muffled by gloves. Gloves were found but they were still tied to the ring posts, perhaps to be hastily put on had the police not been able to gain access so quickly. A man named Marks, who was described as a 'commission agent', claimed he had tied the gloves on the hands of the fighters, so the men's defence rested on whom the jury believed. The pair were convicted and initially fined £10 each plus costs, but the case was also adjourned for a month while the organization of the fight was investigated. It was estimated that the event had generated taxable profits, which also required an additional fine to be paid. However, there was a desire that neither of the men should be sent to gaol and that the persons responsible for organizing the fight should be forced to pay the bulk of the £36 17s that was deemed to be owed in tax. As a result enquiries continued, Smith and Wilkinson's fines were reduced to just £2 each and they were given more time to pay. Wilkinson was still in prison in early January 1889, which suggests he was unable to pay even this. He was also instructed to keep the peace for six months, which presumably entailed refraining from bare-knuckle fighting.[25] In 1897 the Queensbury Rules were adopted in an attempt to clean up the sport and bring it respectability. The Marquess of Queensbury had first published his rules to govern boxing in 1867 (although previous attempts to regulate the sport had been tried in 1838 and even earlier, in the eighteenth century). But illegal prizefights, and the gambling associated with them, continued.

Illegal fights were hard to stop; they took place at night in out-of-the-way places and news of them was spread by word of mouth to avoid police informers. Despite this, in November 1888 Inspector Alcock and his men successfully raided a premises in Dalston and arrested several of those taking part. Thomas Avis and Thomas Porter, labourers at the small arms factory at Enfield, and John Hicks, a carriage builder from Mile End, were charged at Dalston Police court with 'being unlawfully concerned in a prize fight'. The raid had taken place on the Havelock Gymnasium, attached to the Havelock Tavern on Albion Road. Avis and Porter had been in the ring fighting while a crowd watched, but the case turned on whether this was merely practice (sparring) or an actual fight. The men had excellent characters, and a future fight had been arranged and was waiting for official approval. The police had a spy in the gym; a former detective named Rolfe was embedded and keeping an eye on proceedings. The court was told he was ready to give evidence if required but he was not called. The Enfield men were defended by Mr C. V. Young, who explained that they headed up 'rival gymnasiums and were only trying conclusions in a friendly manner'. The magistrate, Mr Bros, was content that nothing illegal had occurred, or at least nothing that could be conclusively proven.

'The evidence shows', he explained, 'that the men were engaged with boxing gloves of the ordinary character and in an ordinary boxing match, which is no offence in law. The lowering of the gas, however, gave the affair a suspicious aspect, which was intensified by the rush of the people.' In other words, while they had been doing nothing that was technically illegal, they were sailing fairly close to the wind and ought in future to ensure they observed both the letter and spirit of the law. Damage had been caused to the property, which had been attributed to the large numbers of spectators and punters who wanted to get in to see the fight, but it was accepted that this had been the result of the police raid itself. All the defendants were dismissed to go back to their places of work and training for the main event.[26] On this occasion the police were unable to secure a conviction, which helps illustrate how difficult it was to prevent these popular manifestations of the fair fight.

While these sorts of prosecutions were newsworthy and not atypical, they do offer a perspective on attitudes towards male versus male violence. Where violence did not involve weapons, magistrates were unlikely to take much action unless there was an exacerbating factor (such as an assault on a police officer, a felony, or particularly drunken or disorderly behaviour). When Lushington sentenced William Clark to six months at hard labour it was in part for his attempted robbery of a sailor in St George's Street, as well as for kicking and punching the policeman that tried to arrest him.[27] In most cases a stand-up fistfight was acceptable and did not warrant prosecution, let alone punishment. John Robinson was fined 20s plus 2s costs for his assault, but he was drunk and the costs were awarded for damage he had caused to Sarah Ann Bruce's property. It is possible that his victim was a shopkeeper or publican who objected to Robinson's drunkenness.[28] Magistrates at Thames used fines or short periods of imprisonment, as well as recognizances to deal with assault. The latter, which was to become one of the 'most frequent outcomes of assault cases',[29] served the purpose of ensuring that offenders did not repeat their violence by 'keeping the peace' towards the wronged party for a set period. How effective this was is difficult to judge. The other tactic, used for all sorts of offending, not just assault, was to remand abusers in custody for a few days. This allowed things to cool off but also enabled magistrates to impose a summary punishment of imprisonment without having to prove wrongdoing. This might have acted as a deterrent against future acts of violence. In reality controlling violence, petty or otherwise, was almost impossible and justices must have recognized that. They imposed penalties where they could and periodically probably resorted to a more punitive action to send a message. The papers acted as a vehicle to ensure such attempts at deterrence had a wider reach. Most obviously magistrates (and the newspapers, by proxy) intervened where the police would not, such as in spousal abuse where it was clear who the victim was and where the fault lay.

Domestic violence

Domestic assault was endemic in late Victorian London. The police magistrate courts bore daily witness to men being prosecuted by their wives or partners for acts of violence. One magistrate, Montague Williams at Lambeth, reportedly said: 'If I were to sit here from Monday morning till Saturday to protect women that had got drunken and brutal husbands, I should not get through half of them.'[30] In many cases the victim stopped short of following through with the prosecution, to the evident frustration of the magistracy, preferring instead to bring her errant husband to be admonished and made to cease his violence, but not to have him sent to gaol or fined. She knew that doing so would have repercussions for her and any children she had. In some instances, the woman's motivation may have been to gain a legal separation; divorce was difficult and expensive and effectively out of the question for the working classes. The alternative was a judicial separation, which, it was widely believed at least, was at the gift of the magistracy. This was probably an erroneous belief. Until the passing of the Summary Jurisdiction (Married Women) Act in 1895, magistrates did not have any legal power to order couples to part. It seems they may have exercised some discretionary power nevertheless, and perhaps, as with many changes to English law, the 1895 act partially legalized something that was already being practised, at least for working-class marriages. For example, in March 1881 Ferdinand Kirsch appeared before Mr Saunders at Thames accused of assaulting his wife, Emma. He was also charged with a violent attack on the police officer who intervened. The magistrate did not commit Kirsch to trial by jury, so either feared a jury would not convict or deemed the violence used was not felonious, but he did send Kirsch to prison for four months (two months for the attack on Emma followed by two for that on the officer). He also ordered Kirsch to pay his wife 10s a week in maintenance.[31] This may reflect the reality that Kirsch had thrown his wife out of the marital home or that it had become impossible for Emma to inhabit it because of Ferdinand's violence. This made it a legal necessity for the husband to pay maintenance and may help explain why women believed magistrates had the power to order separations and to compel abusive partners to continue to support their wives.[32] This chapter will explore the circumstances of domestic abuse and the effectiveness of the summary process for women caught up in it.

Here are two cases of domestic abuse from 1875, which are revealing of contemporary attitudes. In the first, Daniel Lambert was complained about by his wife, Amelia. Lambert had previously owned a pub, but his business had failed and he had been forced to sell up and move to a house in Notting Hill. He blamed his wife for their joint misfortune and consoled himself by going out and getting drunk. One evening he returned home to find Amelia waiting outside. She launched into a probably well-rehearsed diatribe about his drinking. He told her to go inside and when she ignored his instruction he threatened to 'kick her to pieces'. Amelia gave in and went upstairs. Lambert followed her to their rooms and beat her anyway. The couple ended up in court at Hammersmith before Mr Ingham. Lambert was still solvent enough to be able to afford legal representation and his lawyer argued that his client had acted under provocation.

'So [the magistrate asked her], you abused him . . . you answered him back, and used your tongue pretty freely?' 'No, sir' [she responded]. He struck me, pinched me, and kicked me . . . I got away from him and called a constable, but he would not take him, as he did not see any blow struck.'[33]

The police were reluctant to interfere in domestic incidents like these unless they saw clear evidence of violence. Indeed the guidance they received explicitly cautioned against it.[34] The policeman who attended refused to examine her either, because the bruises she had were under her clothes and he said he could not see them without a doctor being present. This drew laughter in the court, as did the remarks about Amelia using 'her tongue pretty freely'. Despite being ridiculed by a male-dominated court, Amelia did have one ally, the landlady who ran their house. She told the court that Mrs Lambert was a 'most sedate woman' and not the monster that Lambert and his lawyer were clearly attempting to describe her as. Daniel Lambert said she had sold all his goods when the business failed and had threatened to poison him, but there was no evidence for any of this. In the end Ingham ruled that Lambert would have to find two sureties at £20 each to ensure he behaved himself, but only for two months. It was a very lenient punishment and reflected the reality that the magistrate thought that Amelia was to blame for her husband's violence. It hardly protected her and perhaps even exposed her to the risk of worse abuse in the future.[35]

On the same day as the Lambert case, newspapers reported another case of domestic violence, this time heard before Mr Cooke at Clerkenwell. On Friday, 16 July, Mrs Badcock was making breakfast and getting her children ready for school. She picked up a pair of her husband's trousers and heard money rattling in a pocket. The children had no shoes and Benjamin Badcock was lazy and reluctant to go out to work. The family was in poverty and Mrs Badcock suggested that since her husband had boots on his feet he might go out and earn some money, so his children might have some on theirs. It was a provocative statement, however reasonable the request that underpinned it. Predictably it sent the 47-year-old casual labourer into a rage and he turned on his wife, hitting her and throwing her onto the bed. He seized the knife she was using to make breakfast and threatened her with it. The couple's eldest daughter, sixteen-year-old Mary Ann, rushed between them fearing that he would harm her mother. Badcock switched his anger to his daughter, punching her in the face several times before running out of the house. When he had gone mother and daughter left the house and applied for a warrant to bring him before a magistrate. When the case came to court Badcock denied the assault, merely claiming that he had 'slapped' his daughter's face for insubordination, as he was entitled to. Mr Cooke required Badcock to find two sureties for £25 each to keep the peace towards his wife and daughter for six months.[36] In both cases a man had been found guilty of violent abuse, but the sanction imposed was relatively minor. Perhaps this discouraged other women from using the courts, given that what they risked was worse abuse. Possibly magistrates, recognizing that imprisoning the head of the household or imposing financial penalties in the form of fines, which had to be paid (unlike sureties, which were intended as a guarantee against future violence, and not a fine as such), would only add to the struggles of working families, impacting the wife and children most directly.

Charities existed to help victims of abuse in the nineteenth century, one of which was the Associate Institute for Enforcing the Laws for the Protection of Women and Children (AIELPWC). The AIELPWC was run by Henry Newman and based at 30 Cockspur Street, near Trafalgar Square. In September 1869 William Moore, a member of the charity, followed a case that was of interest to them at the Worship Street Police court. Benjamin Briggat, a looking-glass frame maker from Mile End, was in court accused of a violent assault on his wife. Mrs Briggat appeared in the witness box swathed in bandages. She was able to give the magistrates a

Paying a fine at Great Marlborough Street, from 'Sketches at the London Police-Courts', *The Graphic*, 27 August 1887.

very full account of her husband's serial abuse of her in the five years they had been married. Many women suffered for months or years before they built up the courage to take their spouse before a magistrate as Mrs Briggat had done. It took determination and resignation in equal measure, as the outcomes were rarely positive. Mrs Briggat told the bench what had happened on the previous Saturday when Benjamin had come home late from work, clearly 'three sheets to the wind' (that is, drunk). She had made him some stew, but he said he did not want it. They argued and he started to kick at her as she was bent over the stove. When she tried to get away Briggat 'seized the iron pot off the fire and beat her about the head with it'. There was more: 'She was soon covered with blood and fell to the floor. The prisoner again kicked her repeatedly while she was down. He also got the poker from the fire-place, and struck her over the back and arms with it, saying he would have her life.' She must have been terrified, and with good reason; most homicide victims in the nineteenth century were wives, children or in some other way a relative or friend of their killers. Her neighbours were too scared of Benjamin to come to her aid, but they did call for the police and she was then able to escape from the room. Her husband's last act was to throw a pail of water over her as she ran out of their home. It took a policeman a long time to contain Briggat and get him to the station. It took Mr Newton just a few moments to send him to gaol for four months at hard labour.[37]

In July 1881 Mr Chance chose to bind Henry Colwell over in an attempt to prevent him assaulting his wife Mary again. She had complained that he had threatened to murder her, seizing her by the throat and coming at her with a kitchen knife. When he was drunk he 'acted like a madman', Chance was told, and she had only escaped physical harm because the couple's landlord had stopped Colwell from throwing her over the bannisters in his drunken rage. None of this was new: Colwell had already been to prison four times for acts of violence towards Mary, so maybe the magistrate thought that by insisting he find two sureties who would vouch for him for three months would be more effective than another period of incarceration.[38]

Many of the cases that came before the Thames magistrates ended without a conviction for the assailant. Ellen Harvey brought a prosecution against her husband John but did not appear to press the charge and so Harvey was released.[39] This was a common enough outcome for assault hearings at Thames; a warrant or summons was applied for, the accused was set in the dock, but no complainant would appear. This occurred in many assault contexts, not simply those that can be clearly identified as domestic. In those, however, this tactic served a multiple purpose. It created a temporary firebreak, halting spousal abuse and, importantly, highlighting it to a wider community. It served as a warning to the abuser of the potential consequences of repeat actions. And in doing so it gave the victim back some agency and leverage while also allowing for reconciliation if both sides were prepared to accept this.

Of course, not all victims of domestic violence in the 1800s were women. Women assaulted their husbands and not always in self-defence. It was rare by comparison but probably more common than court records suggest. If women were reluctant to prosecute their spouses, then men had even more to lose, most obviously their reputations. A man who had to resort to the law to control his wife in the nineteenth century was no man at all.

However, this is exactly the situation in which John Spurgin found himself in late July 1886. Spurgin and his wife ran two oyster stalls, one on Portobello Road and another close by at Westbourne Park. When Harriett Spurgin announced suddenly that she was leaving him to live with another man a row ensued. They may well have come to blows that night, as Harriett ended up with a black eye, which she later claimed had come from John. Whatever happened it ended with Mrs Spurgin leaving the marital home at three o'clock in the morning. She left her clothes and other belongings behind; believing he had rights to these under law, John Spurgin now regarded them as his. Harriett thought differently, and a few days later she turned up at his oyster stall and demanded the return of her effects. He refused, they argued, and she threw a large oyster and then a vinegar bottle at him. As he struggled with her she kicked him in the groin and declared she would 'ruin him' and that one or both of them would find themselves in a police cell that night. Spurgin called a policeman over but because the officer had not seen what happened he refused to intervene. Harriett retreated but returned a little later to continue to upbraid her husband. She hit and kicked him, drawing blood from a wound to his head. This time a constable did see the fracas and intervened. Harriett was taken into custody and the next day she was brought before Mr Cook at Marylebone Police court. She protested her innocence, claimed that John had started it, and explained that he was with-holding her property from her. All she wanted 'was a separation order and her clothes'. Not surprisingly the magistrate sided with the man. Telling her that she was 'a malicious and vindictive woman', Cook sent her to prison for seven weeks with hard labour.[40]

Violence by female spouses may have prompted more serious punishment from the male magistracy since it upset the patriarchal order. Another example, also from the 1880s, was at Thames, where Ada Goodchild, 45, was accused of cutting and wounding her 77-year-old husband John. According to the report there was a history of abuse in the marriage. John Goodchild stood in court, his head bandaged, to testify that Ada had assaulted him a few days previously with a candlestick, adding that he had forgiven her and she had promised never to do it again. Her promise only lasted a couple of days. On the following Saturday night she had come home drunk, 'dragged him out of bed, and [had] pelted him with every conceivable item she could lay her hands on'. Ada attacked him with a knife, cutting him just above his right eye. Bleeding and battered, Goodchild staggered out of their house to find a policeman. Ada was arrested and brought before Mr Saunders at Thames on the Monday morning, having spent a couple of nights locked up. The magistrate upbraided her and said that if she carried on like this she would end up hanging for the murder of her spouse. For wounding John she was sentenced to two months' imprisonment with hard labour.[41] We have no idea what caused the rift between Ada and her husband. The age gap was considerable and perhaps that was an issue: John maybe expected his wife to stay at home, while she sought company and perhaps extramarital relations with men younger than her husband. We can try and imagine her motives, but it may be as simple as her being unable to control her temper when she was drunk. Whatever the case, for the next two months John would have to cope without his wife at home. Just as female survivors of domestic violence often had to weigh up the consequences of prosecuting their abusers, Goodchild's decision to go to law may have given him temporary peace, but he would have to make his own supper and wash his own clothes while she was incarcerated, and then face Ada's possible wrath when she returned.

What is unusual here in both cases is that the abusers were female and the victims male. It is likely that 'husband beaters' were more common than records suggest; the pressures of conventional ideas of masculinity are likely to have put off some men from reporting incidents where their partners had beaten them. It is also notable that the Thames magistrate deemed it appropriate to try the case summarily, despite wounding being a felony. This is a reminder that the generally well-preserved records of the sessions and assizes might overlook more cases of violence in England that were dealt with at a lower, summary level, where comprehensive records have rarely survived.

The table on p. 158 revealed that in the space of the five months of recorded cases at Thames Police court there were 36 hearings where the victim and assailant shared a common surname and so might be presumed to be married (whether legally or in 'common law'). Of those magistrates who have left memoirs or whose comments were recorded by the newspapers, several voiced their frustration that wives tended to take out a warrant against their partners only to forgive the accused once it came to court. Whether this was a strategy or was occasioned by fear of reprisal – or indeed loss of the family's key breadwinner or imposition of a fine that would have a similar effect – is very hard to establish. The reality of this is borne out by the small number of records contained in the Thames register. Most cases where a woman brought an accusation of assault against a man (related or otherwise) were either dismissed or discharged because no prosecutor appeared. In a handful of cases, however, real consequences did follow from the court hearing. For example, Mr Saunders committed Jeremiah McCarthy to the Middlesex Sessions for his alleged assault on his wife, Ellen. The 21-year-old labourer was tried on 4 October 1881 on a charge of malicious wounding but was acquitted by the jury.[42] In another case, 22-year-old Walter Fuller did not get the opportunity to go before an all-male jury and hope they saw his side of his argument with his wife Caroline. Perhaps because the case was brought by Inspector Hildy of CID, Mr Chance was persuaded to hand Fuller a custodial sentence. Fuller was sent to prison for two weeks and further required to provide two sureties of £10 each to insure his good behaviour towards his spouse for three months on his release. Michael Hurley was sent to gaol for three months for an aggravated assault on his spouse Margaret.[43]

'Serving out a copper': assaults on the police

In October 1865 Mary McGrath was charged at Thames Police court with being drunk and disorderly and punching a policeman. Mary was about thirty years old and had a baby with her in court. PC John Mansfield testified that on the previous afternoon he had seen Mary rolling about, quite drunk, on the East India Dock Road. She was carrying her infant and staggering about so badly that she kept banging into the nearby 'walls and houses', which hurt the child and caused it to scream 'fearfully'. All the while McGrath kept up a stream of unpleasant language, so disgusting that several onlookers complained to him about it. Eventually she fell heavily, and a man rushed up to save the child while a police sergeant arrived to help Mansfield take her to the station house. Undeterred by her arrest McGrath lashed out at the constable, blackening his eye. In court the magistrate condemned McGrath's actions and asked if she had a husband. 'No sir, my husband died seven years ago,' she replied. This meant that her baby, which had now been forcibly removed to a workhouse, was illegitimate; presumably the product of a new relationship or casual encounter, and no father was present in court. Drunk, riotous and promiscuous, Mary McGrath did not fit the stereotype of a suitable object of pity. In reality of course McGrath's life became that much more difficult when her husband had passed away. She had been too drunk to recall what had happened the previous day, and what led her to wander the streets in such distress. She had previously been inside a workhouse, but had left. 'I was there long enough,' she explained, and 'I was half starved' and 'discharged myself. I took a drop [of alcohol] and lost myself.' In her version of events she had been so malnourished in the workhouse that a small amount of drink had affected her much more than it would normally. It was a common claim, one that Tottie Fay often resorted to when she imbibed alcohol after release from a period of incarceration. However, instead of opting to find her some help in the form of money, food and shelter Mr Paget sent her to prison for a month at hard labour for the assault on the constable and resisting arrest. As for the child, Paget decided it needed to stay with its mother, so it was sent to gaol with her.[44] Mary McGrath's assault on a policeman in the course of his duty was probably quite commonplace. Thomas Brassington was fined

10s for grappling with police when his twelve-year-old son was arrested for letting off fireworks three days before Bonfire Night in 1881. Richard Martin and Thomas James, two men in their early twenties, were gaoled for two months for assaulting PC Underwood the same year. James Bush got a week for a similar offence.[45]

In the previous two cases it is impossible to know what the circumstances are because the court records are so brief, but four decades earlier an incident in the general area covered by Thames gives a sense of how assaults on officers happened. Rosemary Lane had earned a reputation for criminality throughout the eighteenth and nineteenth centuries. The street was one of several in Whitechapel where the police were cautious about patrolling at night. In October 1847 constable 180H was passing nearby when he heard a commotion emanating from the lane and decided to investigate. He soon found almost two dozen young boys gathered together to form some sort of impromptu orchestra, some banging pots and pans, others clashing knives and cleavers together; even bones were being used to pound out a rhythm on kettles and saucepans. They were making an awful racket. The policeman waded in and tried to disperse the lads. The boys were in high spirits and in no mood to listen. That day there had been a wedding – a Jewish marine store dealer, unpopular in the neighbourhood, had married and the reaction of the boys might have represented some sort of youthful communal protest. From the early modern period right up to the early twentieth century it was not uncommon for communities to express their displeasure or antipathy towards those they disliked or disapproved of by way of a charivari or skimmington. This was an old folk custom involving a mock parade with discordant (or 'rough') music. As the policeman tried to break up the crowd of boys, several attacked him. One in particular hit him over the head with a kettle, knocking his hat into the gutter. He managed to seize the boy, but the others ran away. On the following day the boy (Isaac Gardiner) was brought before Mr Yardley at Thames charged with assaulting a policeman. He was so small his face could hardly be seen as he stood in the dock. When the magistrate was told that the boy had uttered the words 'take that blue bottle!' as he aimed a blow at the constable there was laughter in court. Isaac denied the charge: 'It was a bigger boy, sir,' he said. 'How could I reach up to a tall policeman's head?' Yardley was in no mood to have his court descend into comedy nor was he about to condone bad behaviour by 'street urchins'. Telling the child that 'boys must be taught to conduct themselves properly,' he fined him 5*s*. Since the boy had no money he was sent to prison for three days. The lad was led away whimpering that it was unfair and he 'didn't see much harm in having a lark on a weddin'-day'.[46] The attack on this officer was in all probability simply a reaction to his attempt to curtail their fun but there was certainly a deep-seated resentment towards the New Police among working-class communities. The police patrolled the streets and interfered with working-class life in ways that brought them into daily conflict with youths, gamblers, drunks, prostitutes and street vendors. Costermongers particularly disliked the police, as one of them explained to Henry Mayhew:

> As regards the police, the hatred of a costermonger to a 'peeler' is intense, and with their opinion of the police, all the more ignorant unite that of the governing power. 'Can you wonder at it, sir,' said a costermonger to me, 'that I hate the police? They drive us about, we must move on, we can't stand here, and we can't pitch there.'[47]

In late 1887 James Mask was brought before the magistrate at Marlborough Street accused of assaulting PC Palk. The attack had occurred on 6 October, but the policeman was so badly injured that he was unable to attend for over a week. Mask was described by his lawyer as a 'hard-working man', a costermonger with a large family. As a result of the policeman's actions in moving him on and impounding his barrow he 'had lost his stock of fruit and suffered in other respects'. However, he was 'penitent and sorry for what he had done' and begged for leniency. The magistrate Mr Mansfield was told that three men had set upon the constable, who had been hit on the head 'with a weight'. Mansfield said it 'was a cowardly thing for three men to set upon one', but accepted that the officer might have 'acted indiscreetly in interfering with the men'. He fined Mask 20s, which, while it was a hefty amount to find, was at least preferable to imprisonment.[48]

Homicide: manslaughter and murder

On 15 May 1859 Ann Fadden was standing outside her front door at one o'clock in the morning when her brother, Jeremiah Coghlan, came by with a friend whom he shared lodgings with. Jeremiah was drunk and an argument broke out. Truth is always hard to discern where accusations of 'he said, she said' are thrown about, but it seems that Coghlan and Ann's husband, James Fadden, had sustained an antipathy over many years, which manifested itself in outbreaks of petty violence and name calling. At some point Ann and her brother Jeremiah started grappling with each other and she called him names, later admitting to shouting: 'Go along, you long-nosed vagabond and look out, he is down the street, and if he hits you he will give you something.' She was referring to the fact that her spouse, James, was visiting friends just a little way off ('listening to the newspaper being read') and she was expecting him to return home soon. In fact, James had heard the shouting and was already on his way. When he saw Coghlan fighting with his wife he intervened, telling his brother-in-law to go home. When the young man refused, Fadden threatened him. Ann tried to stop things escalating, warning him against picking a fight with a stronger man, but Fadden was not in the mood to be talked down. According to John Coghlan, brother to both, he was in a belligerent mood and growled, 'I will give him a blow that he won't be able to hit me.' With that he shoved his sister out of the way and rushed at Fadden. Coghlan threw a punch and Fadden fell to the ground, where he lay senseless for several minutes. As soon as everyone recovered their wits, they realized that James was bleeding from a cut to his neck, and he was taken to Guy's Hospital. The house surgeon at Guy's, Mr James Wood, treated him but the bleeding could not be stopped and on 3 June James Fadden died. Jeremiah Coghlan had been arrested the morning following the assault and Fadden's hospitalization, and at this point his brother-in-law was still alive. Coghlan was still angry when PC George Vellacott arrested him and was showing no signs of remorse for his actions. As the policeman led him away he declared: 'If I am given in charge I shall do for the b—; if I get over this I shall do for him.' A knife was found at his lodgings and the police took it as evidence. Having been remanded several times by the magistrates at Southwark Police court, on 11 June 1859 he was fully committed for trial.[49] Jeremiah Coghlan appeared at the Old Bailey on 13 June, accused of 'wilful murder'. Both his sister and his brother gave damning evidence against him in court. Nevertheless, the jury only found him guilty of manslaughter, so he avoided the possibility of hanging for his crime.[50] Instead he was transported to Australia for a period of twenty years.[51]

As we have seen, the summary courts were often the first port of call for women who had experienced violence at the hands of their husbands or partners. Most cases did not make their way to court and in very many of those that did the victim either withdrew her complaint at the last minute or simply refused to give evidence against her assailant. Women's motives for this were mixed but partly driven by an often-misplaced belief that their partner would behave better in the future. Women frequently excused abuse on the grounds that the perpetrator was only violent when he had been drinking; he was a 'good man' at other times. The problem with this strategy was that violence often begat violence and excusing it could store up unresolved conflicts for the future. Domestic violence might begin as low-level abuse but end up being life threatening, or worse.

John Wicks and his wife, Elizabeth, had both been drinking on 14 April 1877. John had earned a reputation in the community for violence when under the influence of alcohol. Elizabeth was also known to resort to violence when her temper flared. The couple lived in Kensal New Town in northwest London and Wicks earned his income as a chimney sweep. When John came home that evening an argument flared about money. He was drunk and Elizabeth had shared two or three pints with a friend, so was not sober either. Wicks complained that he had no money left and demanded she hand over the cash that she had sewn into the pocket of her skirt for safe keeping. When she refused they came to blows. The reports of the fight are fraught with conflicting evidence from Wicks, his mother-in-law and other witnesses. Domestic struggles like this were quite often public affairs, given the crowded accommodation of late Victorian London. It is possible that in order to defend herself Elizabeth picked up the fender from the fire and threatened her husband with it. When he pulled a knife she threw the fender at him and he retreated from the room. His wife then seized the next available weapon she could find, a large spoon, and came after him. The pair ended up in the garden, which was where George Abbott, a van boy who lived opposite, saw them. Abbott was drawn to the quarrel by the noise, as was Henry Stacey, and both saw Elizabeth strike John with the spoon. Stacey later testified that Elizabeth was in a rage and was shouting 'stab me you b—— if you are a man, stab me, stab me.' Soon afterwards the sweep aimed a blow at her neck and when his hand came away blood spurted from the wound. Wicks had stabbed his wife. He was arrested and she was taken to hospital where, despite the best efforts of the surgeons at St Mary's, Paddington, she died ten days later. The court was told that 'Inflammation of the throat' had 'set in the same night as she was stabbed, and she was unable to swallow anything except iced water'. She died as a result of 'exhaustion caused through not taking food and inflammation of the lungs'. It must have been a terrible and extremely distressing way to die. On 23 May, after several appearances before him while Elizabeth's life lay in the balance, Mr D'Eyncourt formally committed Wicks to trial for murder at the Central Criminal Court.[52] He had pleaded not guilty and claimed that she must 'have fallen against the knife'. He admitted being drunk and offered that in mitigation. The police detective who interviewed Elizabeth in hospital confirmed the pattern of events as she described them, but added that she had at the last described her husband as a gentle man when he was sober. 'There is not a kinder man or a better husband,' she had insisted, reiterating the defence that so many wives offered their abusive partners. The house surgeon at St Mary's was questioned at the Old Bailey as to whether the wound could have been caused by accident: 'It is unusual to get such a wound in that way, but it might be [possible],' he observed. That was enough for the all-male jury. Despite evidence that John Wicks had killed his wife in a drunken rage while he was holding a sharpened knife in his hands, the jury acquitted him of all charges, manslaughter included.[53] He walked free from the Old Bailey exonerated by men who clearly believed that he was provoked and that his incapacitation due to alcohol absolved him of the responsibility for his wife's death.

In December 1891 James Muir, a 39-year-old shoemaker, was accused of the murder of Abigail Sullivan, with whom he 'at times' cohabited in Shoreditch. It seems the couple had a tempestuous relationship and drunken arguments were frequent. At some point the pair separated, with a suggestion that Muir had been seeing someone else, a lodger at the house in Old Nichol Street where Sullivan had lived with him. This woman was Selina Lewis, and she was present when the fatal attack occurred. Selina Lewis told Mr Rose, the Worship Street magistrate, that Abigail Sullivan had been speaking with Muir in her room when things became heated. Muir hit Sullivan and she fell down. Muir then made to leave, saying he was off to get a drink. Selina also left but returned a few minutes later with a boy. Since Abigail was still lying prone on the floor, Selina told the lad to fetch over a lamp so she could examine her. When he did so they discovered blood flowing from a wound in her chest and within moments realized that Sullivan was dead. The police were called and the body assessed by Percy Clark, an assistant to Dr Bagster Phillips, the police surgeon. Clark testified that Abigail had suffered a fatal wound that had 'penetrated the lung and divided the aorta. The cause of death was syncope [loss of consciousness] and loss of blood'. The weapon was produced in court, a 'thin-bladed butchering knife', and the police inspector present said it must have been wielded with 'considerable force'. Selina admitted that the quarrel had been about her relationship with Muir. The knife was also hers, but she had not seen Muir use it. There was little doubt that Muir had stabbed his former lover because as he was arrested outside he tried to throw the knife away. Muir was remanded in custody again so that the Treasury solicitor could summon five more witnesses for the prosecution.[54] It took until early February for the case to make it to the Central Criminal Court at the Old Bailey, where Muir was found guilty of murder. One witness who knew the pair well was Caroline Hall, who told the Old Bailey court: 'I have heard him threaten her – I heard him say that he would give her a good hiding some night, and that he would swing for her.'[55] James Muir did 'swing for her' on 1 March 1892 at Newgate Prison, where he was hanged by James Billington. The motive given for the killing was that, while Muir and Abigail had split up, she 'still pestered him for money', possibly to support the baby girl whom Muir had fathered before he left to start a new relationship with Sullivan.

The front facade of Newgate Prison from the Old Bailey, illustration from Walter Thornbury, *Old and New London* (1873–8).

Both deaths were occasioned by the everyday tensions encountered by couples across the capital and nation, and by the prevailing acceptance of violence in domestic contexts. The presence of alcohol was undoubtedly a factor but not a mitigating one. James Muir was convicted because it was beyond reasonable doubt that he had stabbed Abigail Sullivan. John Wicks was acquitted simply because some doubt of his intention remained. Both women were killed by men unable to control their tempers and who were used to resorting to physical violence. Violence was endemic in the Victorian capital and it suffused society at all levels. The court records and the newspaper columns are indicative of this, but to what extent were the police courts of any real use to those that suffered violence? The 1861 Offences Against the Person Act built on previous legislation that attempted to rationalize and codify the laws concerning

violence, but did this in any way prevent violent acts? Finding
definite answers to either question is problematic since we cannot
know the real level of interpersonal violence in nineteenth-century
London. The 1828 inquiry into policing in the capital was told that
assaults involving drunkenness 'occupied a considerable portion
of the courts' time'. Whether this reflected a real rise in violence
or just 'an increased willingness of the public to employ the courts
instead of resolving disputes on their own' was less clear.[56] The
same might be argued for women taking their husbands to court.
A woman stood in the witness box wreathed in bandages was a
common sight and almost invariably her first prosecution of her
spouse did not dovetail with the first abuse. Many women refrained
from going to law until they had suffered multiple attacks and had
tried all they could to placate or cajole abusers in the hope they
would change. Perhaps it was the realization that the violence was
not going to stop, or a very real fear that it would become worse,
perhaps much worse, that forced them to risk public shame by
airing their dirty laundry in a police court. The risks were great, the
rewards less tangible. So why bother? Presumably they believed
that in so doing they would gain some respect and force a change
in their situation. Does this reflect an acceptance of the role of the
courts as arbiters in working-class marital disputes, perhaps culminating in separation with a guarantee of financial support? In
this period working-class marriage was perhaps less absolute and
more nuanced than modern views of the Victorians suggest. If
Matthew Sweet is correct in suggesting that many working-class
men and women 'took a very equivocal and pragmatic attitude to
marriage and cohabitation', then very many more of the acts of
violence involving men hurting women might highlight domestic
disputes than simply those where couples shared a surname.[57]
The Victorians were fascinated by murder despite its prevalence
being firmly on the decline. The infamous murderers of the nineteenth century – William Corder, put on trial in August 1828 for

the murder of Maria Marten in 1827; the Mannings, executed in November 1849; 22-year-old Lefroy Mapleton, convicted of murder and hanged in 1881; American-born Florence Maybrick, accused of murdering her husband in 1889 and sentenced to life imprisonment; and the unknown perpetrator of the Whitechapel killings in 1888 – prompted a surge in newspaper readership and spawned a true crime publishing industry, which in some cases (notably Corder's) encompassed other forms of material culture.[58] Murder was thankfully rare and very seldom was it as melodramatic as popular culture portrayed it. Most of it was as mundane as the routine day-to-day violence that was the subject of so many hearings at police courts. Most also involved working-class protagonists, once again reinforcing the narrative that crime, violence and immorality were problems to be found among a subsection of society, and not to be associated with those who were deemed to be respectable.

5

JUVENILES IN THE POLICE COURTS

I n the Victorian era the legal age of criminal responsibility was just seven. However, the principle of doli incapax (incapable of evil) meant that in practice it had to be shown that a child up to the age of fourteen understood that what they were accused of doing 'was "seriously wrong" and not merely mischievous'.[1] With the age of criminal responsibility so low, it was inevitable that many children were brought before the criminal justice system at all levels, some to be imprisoned, transported and even sentenced to death and hanged. The vast majority of those aged seven to sixteen would, however, have experienced the system from the dock of a police court rather than being arraigned before a jury at the Old Bailey or quarter sessions, a point that has perhaps been neglected in previous studies on youth and crime.

Until the late eighteenth and early nineteenth centuries there was no real mechanism to deal with juvenile offenders differently to adults. Certainly youth was more likely to work in the favour of those accused of thefts punishable by death in the 1700s, and there was a general tendency to leniency for juveniles (at least until they reached their teens, when contemporary concerns began to work against them).[2] But children were hanged and many others transported to Australia, so we should not downplay the reality that a harsh penal system considered youth no barrier to responsibility and punishment. Attitudes towards young offenders began to change in the aftermath of the French and Napoleonic Wars

(1798–1815). The years of war had ravaged Europe and Britain, and in emerging from conflict England experienced quite considerable social upheaval. With rapidly expanding urban centres like Birmingham and Manchester alongside more established cities like London, and a gradual move from an agrarian to an industrial economy, the spotlight of attention focused on the urban environment. Commentators in the capital drew attention to the 'alarming increase' in juvenile crime in London and a committee was established. The inquiry concluded that parental neglect, a lack of education and suitable employment, as well as poor habits and immorality were to blame for a rapid rise in youth crime.[3] The creation of the Metropolitan Police in 1829 may also help explain a rise in numbers of youths being prosecuted as many of the offences that they were typically charged with were those that involved the street or public spaces where the New Police were determined to establish their authority.[4] Thereafter young offenders were routinely considered as part of a discourse about the emergence of a 'criminal class' in the early Victorian period.[5] Young 'delinquents' graduated to become fully fledged members of the 'swell mob'.

Victorians fretted about a youth culture that was fuelled by earnings. Independent earning meant that children as young as eleven or twelve were becoming economic adults. Commentators were concerned at the way in which they chose to spend this money – on drink and gambling and in congregating in groups outside the supervision of adults where they could stray into 'music halls or worse and thereby [sink] into corruption and vice'.[6] Henry Mayhew interviewed youths waiting outside dance halls and was disgusted at the way in which young girls cavorted openly in the streets. The implication was that the morality of young people was at risk and commentators were quick to relate this to promiscuity. Victorians also worried about what impressionable young people were reading. Sensational cheap fiction was frequently blamed for juvenile crime. The epithet of 'penny dreadful' was applied in the

1870s to emphasize that these publications represented the ultimate in bad taste. As Francis Hitchman, a literary critic, complained in 1890, 'when it is remembered that this foul and filthy trash circulates by thousands and tens of thousands week by week amongst lads who are at the most impressionable period of their lives, it is not surprising that the authorities have come to lament the prevalence of juvenile crime.'[7]

The popularity of plays based on the lives of criminals and the use of such material by youths was almost evidence itself of criminality, as John Springhall observes. One lad purportedly told the arresting policeman, 'I was tempted to do this by reading the tales.'[8] Much of this concern with youth and delinquency, drunkenness, immorality and crime was also tied up with middle-class concern about the underclass, about poverty and about the good health of the nation. Desires to reform young offenders in this period and earlier were accompanied by a wider social policy of wishing to improve the character of the poorer classes.

With the concept of the juvenile offender (or delinquent) established, by the 1820s individuals, organizations and the state began to develop mechanisms to deal with young offenders differently, or separately. While this was not achieved until well into the twentieth century, we can see the seeds of this in the nineteenth. Youth offenders were gradually moved to separate institutions (dedicated prison hulks, for example, or Parkhurst Prison, which opened in 1838). In the 1850s the reformatory movement created a series of local institutions nationally to deal with the problems associated with 'delinquent' youth. Legislation in 1847 and 1850 enabled petty crime by those aged fourteen to sixteen or under to be prosecuted at a police court, greatly reducing the number of young prisoners taken before a judge and jury and limiting the numbers that could be given substantial prison terms as a consequence. Before we explore this in more detail, let us begin with the idea of the young offender.

The image of the juvenile criminal that most of us will have is that of the Artful Dodger and his fellow pickpockets, described by Dickens so vividly in *Oliver Twist* (1838). Dickens wrote this while living at 48 Doughty Street in Bloomsbury, and he used his own experiences and observations to create his characters. In 1835 Dickens had worked as a reporter for the *Morning Chronicle* and often attended the nearby Marlborough Street Police court, writing up cases for the *Chronicle* and another London paper, the *British Press*.[9] It is likely that the central characters of Dodger, Fagin, Nancy and Bill Sikes were all based, however loosely, on individuals or types that Dickens encountered or had described to him. Fagin in some ways resembles Ikey Solomons, the so-called 'prince of fences' who operated as a thief and receiver of stolen goods from the early 1800s until his death in Van Diemen's Land (Tasmania) in 1850.[10] William 'Bill' Sheen, a notorious criminal who came to the attention of the press and parliament in the mid-1830s (at just the time Dickens was preparing to write *Oliver Twist*), might actually be a better fit. Heather Shore speculates that Dickens may have taken the character and criminal activities of Sheen, who was Welsh, and transposed them onto a Jewish Fagin.[11] And when we look at the pages of the newspapers for the 1820s it is possible to see the sketchy beginnings of the Artful Dodger and his crew in a case from 1823.

Three boys, all fourteen years of age, were brought before the City magistrate at the Guildhall. James Morgan, Henry Moir and George Singleton were jointly accused of stealing handkerchiefs in St Swithin's Lane. Mr Sandford, who was walking up the lane, noticed that his handkerchief was missing and on turning around saw a small boy (named Davison), who informed him that some other lads had been attempting to pick his pocket. Sandford followed the boy to Lombard Street, where he pointed out one of the culprits (Morgan), who was wearing a brown coat. A constable was summoned and Morgan was taken to Giltspur Street, the City's holding gaol. Morgan loudly declared his innocence despite his face being well known to the City watch and constables. While he continued to protest, saying he had 'never been in custody before', Singleton arrived with a black coat over his arm that he said he had brought along because it belonged to his chum Morgan. If his intention was to demonstrate that Morgan was the victim of mistaken identity then the stratagem failed. The officer he spoke to was suspicious. On surveying the room, he noticed another smaller boy (Moir), who had no coat. Moir was recognized as being released from Newgate prison only the day before, having 'had the good fortune to be acquitted on an indictment for picking pockets'. Davison now swore that he had also seen Moir with Morgan in St Swithin's Lane, so Moir and Singleton were swiftly arrested. Moir's parents (both 'respectable working people') appeared in court at Guildhall and lamented the fact that they could do nothing to keep their son on the straight and narrow. They told the magistrate that 'they were desirous that he might be disposed of in any way that might prevent his destruction'. No one appeared for Morgan, his friends having 'given him up as incorrigible'; Singleton said he had an employer who would speak for him. All three lads were remanded for re-examination at a later date, when Sandford could appear to prosecute them.[12]

A Henry Moir was prosecuted at the Old Bailey in May 1823 for attempting to pick a man's pocket in St James's Park. He was found not guilty.[13] A year later a sixteen-year-old Henry Moir was sentenced to fourteen years' transportation for stealing a handkerchief. Moir appealed against the sentence in 1825, but unsuccessfully, and was shipped off to New South Wales on the *Albion*; by this time he was eighteen.[14] James Morgan met a similar fate. In June 1823 James Morgan and Edward Pettifer were tried at the Old Bailey accused of stealing a handkerchief 'privately from the person' of John Radford. Radford had been out in the City walking on Long Lane by Smithfield when he felt something by his pocket. He saw his handkerchief fall and caught it, noticing two lads pass either side of him. A City constable who had been watching for thieves near the market moved in to help arrest them. Morgan gave his age as fourteen, Pettifer said he was fifteen; both were convicted and transported for life.[15]

The interviews that William Augustus Miles conducted with juvenile felons being held on the prison hulk *Euryalus* reveal the reality of young lives caught up in criminal activity of exactly the sort described in the case of Moir, Morgan and Singleton. Miles saw these children as part of a 'criminal class' in early Victorian Britain and his writing reflects a widespread anxiety about criminality, and youth crime in particular.[16] His interviews, albeit formulaic and filtered through Miles's own prejudiced viewpoint, are enlightening. Anderson, 'a Whitechapel thief', told Miles he was fifteen years old, his mother was a 'drunkard', and his father was dead or had left home. He and two brothers supported the family, his sisters having left to get married. Like many of the boys Miles spoke to, Anderson said he could read but not write, suggesting a very basic education. He stole in company with a second boy (as Morgan and Pettifer operated) and considered twelve handkerchiefs a day an 'average' haul. He had been sentenced to seven years' transportation.[17] Another lad, Hickman, had already earned a significant criminal record by the time he was sent to the *Euryalus* at the age of sixteen. He told Miles he had been to the house of correction in Coldbath Fields four times, both the New Prison at Clerkenwell and Newgate twice, and once to Brixton. He admitted to being a thief 'on the town' for three years and progressed to theft from gambling at 'heads & tails' in the street. He operated with a fellow accomplice and 'generally had thirty shillings a day' to show for it. Even if we can expect some level of boasting, this suggests that picking pockets on the capital's busy streets was profitable, so long as you avoided getting caught.[18]

Temptation was everywhere for children and teenagers in London. When Louis Perry sent his errand boy off to deliver some work for him, he gave him strict instructions. Lipman Forkell was to deliver some boots to his customer using a barrow, and then drop the barrow off at the hire place. The lad was told not to forget to collect the 10*d* change due from his deposit. However, Lipman, a twelve-year-old from Whitechapel, failed to return Perry's money. This was a second chance for Lipman; he had been accused of stealing money before but had been let off with a warning. He did not get a third chance. On Thursday, 7 August 1879, the boy was brought before Mr Bushby at Worship Street and formally charged with stealing 10*d* in silver coins. The magistrate told him that to have taken to stealing at such a young age was very serious and he would be punished for it. On top of sending him to prison for three days, Bushby ordered that the boy be given 'twelve strokes of the birch rod', to be administered by a police sergeant.[19]

The registers for Thames show several children sentenced to a birching. Charles Marsh (10) received five strokes for 'a felony'; Edward Lewis (12) eight, while Arthur Symons (13) and Arthur Brown (12) got ten, all for a similar crime. William George (13) was birched for embezzlement.[20] Throughout the century children were flogged by prison officers or the police for all sorts of petty crime. The amount of punishment varied, from twelve to twenty lashes using a birch rod, to extremes of sixty 'lashes of the cat' (whipping) on offenders as young as ten. On occasions there was public outcry as the screams of children were heard emanating from within Bow Street magistrates' court and other places, and crowds would sometimes intervene. Many policemen were reluctant to carry out floggings and some magistrates prided themselves on not handing down sentences of whippings on youngsters. Nevertheless, the whipping of juveniles was retained until well into the twentieth century. It was finally removed from the disciplinary armoury of the criminal justice system in 1948.[21] Lipman's case does reveal the change that had happened in the second half of the century in respect of juvenile offenders. Unlike the young men on board the

Euryalus, he was not facing a year or more on a prison hulk and a long sea voyage to Van Diemen's Land. Transportation to Australia had wound down in the 1850s and was formally ended in 1867.

Street arabs

The police courts of late Victorian London fairly regularly witnessed prosecutions of fathers who were accused of allowing their children to play truant. In the civil registers of the Thames court for 1885 the single most numerous complaint was for infringements of the Education Act (1876), accounting for 31 per cent of hearings.[22] Fines were handed down that did little to help, because in some instances parents needed the children at home to help either with piecework or, more often, to care for infants or elderly relatives while they went out to work. The alternative to a fine, if the parents could convince a magistrate that they had tried to ensure their offspring attended school, was to send the child to an industrial day school, where discipline was stricter.[23] The act also imposed tough financial penalties on employers who employed children under ten years of age, another disincentive to interfering with children's education. Some tried very hard to ensure their offspring gained an education, but this could be hard when the kids did not have boots or decent clothes to go to school in. Pride existed in working-class communities and maintaining an image of respect-ability was every bit as important to them as it was to the middle classes with whom it is often more associated.

There was tremendous poverty in 1880s London but that did not prevent families striving to keep standards up. Mrs Rochford and her neighbours appeared to be fighting a losing battle with their collective brood of five youngsters, however. Walter Rochford (11) and his brother James (10) appeared in court at Marlborough Street alongside Ernest Flowers (10), Albert Carey (11) and Thomas Copeland, who was just 8. The 'interesting youthful quintet' had been picked up by the police because they were begging in Wardour Street. Four of them had no boots and yet they had walked from Hammersmith, several miles away. Their mothers were in court to answer for them and to listen to the story they gave Mr De Rutzen. The boys said that they often played truant from Board school, preferring instead to hide their boots in an empty house in Shepherd's Bush to go begging house to house or in the streets. They slept in empty properties, or tramcars, and even a dog kennel. Some of them had been absent from home for a week and so sending them to Board school was clearly pointless. The magistrate decided to use his powers under the act to send them to an industrial school. It would probably mean the five would be broken up and would be separated from their families. Until places were secured for them the five were dispatched to the workhouse while the industrial school officer was sent for to determine their fates.[24]

Begging was just one mischief truants got up to, another was gambling. In 1881 dozens of young men and children were brought before the magistrates at Thames charged with gambling in the street. Lushington and Saunders typically handed down fines of anything from 1s to 10s. In the case of James Darby (18), Thomas Munday (19) and Henry Shore (18) the Vagrancy Act was specifically mentioned in the ledger: in the hundred or so other examples the clerk merely recorded the sentence (usually a fine with three to seven days' imprisonment for those unable to pay).[25] Daniel Lay was just eleven and was discharged by Saunders, as was twelve-year-old George Ingram. But age was no barrier to punishment, as Charles Davis discovered when he was fined 2s 6d for gambling, with the threat of three days inside if he (or more likely his parents) failed to cough up. The fine was paid and Charles released.[26] In July 1877 a small group of lads had gathered to try their luck tossing halfpennies at the end of Gas Factory Lane while two younger boys kept lookout. Unfortunately for the eight or nine players the police were too quick for them. Most scattered before PC Ward was able to nab them, but Henry Mitchell was carted off to face the music. Charged with gambling on a Sunday, and in possession of 21*s* of silver coin and another 3*s* 6*d* in bronze, he was fined £1 or fourteen days behind bars.[27]

We can get some clarity on the grounds for prosecution from a case reported in October 1869 in the East End. Seven youths, aged fourteen to eighteen, were charged at Worship Street with gambling in the street and on a Sunday. They were all fined between 3*s* and 7*s* 6*d*, but one, Timothy Casey (16), decided to mount his own defence. He argued that since they were playing in Victoria Park and not in the street, they 'could not possibly cause an obstruction'. Mr Newton warned him this was a 'dangerous objection to take'. Cases like this were, he explained:

> generally disposed of under the laws relating to street
> obstructions, the provision of which enabled a magistrate
> to give the accused the option of paying a fine. But when it
> was proved that a prisoner had been gambling on a park
> or common, the magistrate had no alternative but to send
> him to prison at once.

The lad withdrew his objection, and they accepted their fines.[28] This is indicative of the nature of prosecuting street-based offences in the nineteenth century and the flexibility that the law provided. David Churchill has argued that once the police established itself as a force, all sorts of individuals and groups 'came to understand that the street was the domain of the police'. Churchill terms this 'police-consciousness', defined as 'an awareness that one's everyday conduct in public space was subject to sanction according to pre-scribed notions of good order'.[29] It was the police who enforced what was deemed to be 'good' conduct, even if they did not write the laws that they used to prosecute 'bad' conduct. Or tried to enforce it, of course. Much has been written about the role of the New Police as 'missionaries' among the working class, as the vanguard of middle-class morality bringing an enlightened sensibility and order to fast-growing urban spaces.[30] The reality was, as Churchill notes, that the forms of popular culture that some in authority deemed unsavoury or unsuited to a modern city – such as gambling or drinking – survived and persisted despite periodic crackdowns and the baleful glare of the Bobby on the beat.[31]

Victorian concerns about youth did not end with children playing truant or 'street arabs'.[32] In the last decades of the century a more threatening image of youth emerged, the hooligan. In early January 1877 Joseph Allen was walking out with his 'sweetheart' on Kingsland Road, Dalston. It was just after midnight when the couple found their route barred by as many as twenty youths. The youths were 'occupying the breadth of the pavement ... pushing all persons into the road'. This is a fairly typical report of youth group behaviour for the late nineteenth century. In the 1870s and '80s they were usually referred to as 'roughs' (although that term was also applied to agitators in political crowds and other unruly elements of society). From the late 1890s the word 'hooligan' was adopted, having been immortalized by 'Alf' from Lambeth, in Clarence Rook's *Hooligan Nights*.[33] As the gang of youths reached Allen and his girl, they pushed him about as they had done everyone else. When he objected, he was surrounded, beaten about the head and knocked to the ground. As he attempted to 'fight his way out' one of the group, nineteen-year-old Thomas Robson, 'rushed upon him and struck him two blows on the left side of the head above the temple', cutting him badly. Robson ran away but Allen chased and wrestled him to the ground. Robson was handed over to a nearby policeman who took him into custody, resulting in a hearing at Worship Street. In front of the magistrate Robson challenged Allen's version of events. He suggested instead that Allen had sustained his wounds in a 'fair fight' and called witnesses to back him up. The magistrate chose to believe his victim, who appeared with his head heavily bandaged, and committed Robson to trial by jury.[34] Tried at the Middlesex Sessions on 8 January, Thomas Robson was convicted of wounding and sentenced to nine months' imprisonment.[35] The Allen/Robson case has echoes of a murder that made headline news in 1888, a year dominated by the actions of a serial killer in the east of the capital.

The late 1800s saw the emergence of regular 'moral panics' about youth and youth violence.[36] Gangs of young men (and women) appeared in many of Britain's major cities and made the pages of local and national newspapers as a result of real and imagined fears about their anti-social behaviour. In cities like Liverpool and Manchester historians have drawn a link between declining industry and violence in working-class culture.[37] These 'gangs' adopted a uniform dress style and a loose organization based around the control of territory, with associations to petty crime and prostitution. Salford's 'scuttlers', Birmingham's 'Peaky Blinders' and London's 'Hooligans' all sported contemporary fashions but with adjustments that made them identifiable as belonging to a particular group.[38] Moral panics about gang crime occurred at several points in the late 1800s as the newspapers focused attention on youth. One correspondent to a local West London paper, who signed himself 'Boffin', wrote: 'I was speaking to a police inspector on this subject recently. His words were "Ten years ago this juvenile gang crime was unknown beyond the East End; now they are all round us."'[39]

The 'bandit gangs of London' featured as a part of the *Pall Mall Gazette*'s critique of policing in the capital in 1888, at the height of the Whitechapel (or 'Jack the Ripper') murders. The paper reported that several gangs, with names reflecting the territory they claimed sovereignty over, were 'infesting' the capital. The 'Fitzroy Place gang' and the 'New Cut gang' were joined by others who had adopted titles drawn from popular print culture. These included the 'Monkey Parade gang', the 'Jovial Thirty-Two' and the 'Gang of Roughs'.[40] In 1882 a prosecutor at Worship Street commented that London 'was infested . . . by gangs of men who appeared to be banded together for the purpose of fighting other gangs, and using the most lawless violence, not only to those they called their enemies, but to the public.'[41] This violence is evident in the wounding of Joseph Allen in 1877, who narrowly escaped a worse fate.

Joseph Rumbold was not so fortunate, dying in his girlfriend's arms just outside the gates of Regent's Park in May 1888. Rumbold's death was the consequence of an incident that echoed the assault on Allen. On 23 May a young couple, Frank Cole and his sweetheart Louisa 'Cissy' Chapman, were walking along the Marylebone Road close to Madame Tussauds waxworks when they were challenged by two youths who asked if they knew 'the Fitzroy Place lads'. A failure to respond prompted the boys to summon a larger group of youths who, having determined that Frank was a member of a rival gang, attacked him and Louisa. Frank escaped with a beating, but when he met up with his pals they swore revenge. The following evening the 'Tottenham Court lads' set off for Regent's Park to look for suitable targets. One of them, George Galletly, the youngest of the gang, was carrying a large knife, quite possibly because he felt obliged to establish his position among his peers. As the gang traversed the Outer Circle of the park they ran into a young printer's machinist – Rumbold – who was walking out with his girl, her sister and another young man. Rumbold was challenged, as Cole had been, and when his answer failed to satisfy his interrogators, he was chased and set upon. Rumbold was stabbed by Galletly and died on his way to hospital. In the aftermath several arrests were made and many of the gang members appeared before a police court, where the case was sent for trial.[42] The trial took place on 30 July 1888 at the Old Bailey, where, of the eight young men arraigned, only Galletly was convicted.[43] The judge, Justice Hawkins, condemned the 'cowardly nature of [the gang's] conduct' and sentenced Galletly to death.[44] Immediately appeals for clemency were made and he was reprieved on account of his age, with five hundred people signing a petition to save him from the noose.[45] Galletly remained in prison until July 1898, when he was discharged, aged 27, as a habitual criminal.[46]

Reforming children: Mary Carpenter and the Reformatory movement

In 1854, following a campaign by Mary Carpenter and others, parliament passed the Reformatory Schools Act.[47] This legislation allowed magistrates to send children (up to the age of sixteen) to a state-certified reformatory school for a period of two to five years. Carpenter and her colleagues believed that juvenile offenders needed to be removed from bad influences and environments and given an opportunity for an education and training for a new life. Giving evidence to a parliamentary committee in 1852, Carpenter expressed her horror at finding children as young as seven and eight in London's Millbank Penitentiary.[48] She argued that sending small children to prison was 'worse than useless'.[49] Alongside her collaborator, Russell Scott, she had pioneered their reforms in Kingswood from 1852. The Reformatory Schools Act was a worthy innovation, but it was undermined by a lack of money and the imperative that all juvenile convicts should spend time in a prison first (usually two to four weeks). Without proper state funding the number of reformatories established was limited and the levels of staffing always lacking. While the state made a contribution, parents were compelled to pay a fee of up to 5s a week.[50] Without the space to hold juveniles, many were simply returned to their parents once they had served their initial sentences and those in care were not always given the education promised because there were insufficient staff to supervise them adequately.

The Reformatory Schools Act was followed in 1857 by the Industrial Schools Act. While the former was intended to provide an alternative, more clearly reformative punishment for juvenile criminals, the Industrial Schools Act aimed at preventing children from becoming criminal in the first place.[51] These might be those identified by the courts as suitable objects for reform, but parents could also ask a magistrate to commit their child to an industrial school. Children found begging on the streets could be sent to an industrial school, as could orphans, those found living in brothels and the offspring of parents deemed unfit (through criminal activity or drunkenness) to look after them.[52] Truants were also sent to industrial schools, as we saw earlier. The Police Court Missionary Thomas Holmes condemned the 'wicked indifference' of parents who allowed or even pushed their children into criminality, adding that '[no] one knows better than the magistrate that undisciplined idleness is the ruin of growing boys.'[53] If parents could be identified the court could, as with reformatories, order them to pay towards their child's upkeep. Thus parents were held to account for the behaviour of their children and obliged to pay towards their 'reformation', while also risking losing all rights over them to the state.

Eliza Wood, Emma Major and Margaret Hawkins are just three examples of the problems the reformatory movement encountered in its early years. In the spring of 1860 the three girls, with an average age of ten, had been convicted of stealing at Lambeth police court. When it was explained to Mr Norton, the magistrate, that the girls' mothers were 'drunken and dissipated women' living in an area around Kent Street (a district notorious for crime and prostitution), he decided to use the new option allowed by law and sentenced them to three weeks in prison to be followed by four years in a certified reformatory. The girls were taken to the Wandsworth house of correction but at the end of their term the prison governor wrote to Norton. He apologized but said it was impossible for him to send the girls on to a reformatory because there was nowhere that could take them. The only certified school in London was at Hampstead, and that was full. He explained they had already turned away another child that Norton had sent their way. The governor had been trying to place the trio at a reformatory 'in the country' but without success. There was nothing he could do but send them back to Lambeth to the care of their parents.[54] It seems that the new legislation was the victim of its own success; so keen were magistrates to use the option of sending children away that the reformatories simply could not cope with the numbers. Intervening in the lives of these three girls in an attempt to reset them and steer them away from a life of crime reflects popular concerns that seem to have been borne out by recent research into the criminal histories of women in nineteenth-century Liverpool and London: 46 per cent of women convicted of offences in Liverpool in the period 1853 to 1887 had started offending aged ten to sixteen; in London the figure is slightly lower (at 30 per cent) but still significant.[55] For many girls (and boys) an early brush with the law was sufficient to deter them but serious recidivism often started young.[56]

As noted earlier, the creation of the Metropolitan Police meant that there was a more regularized police presence on the capital's streets, which directly impacted juveniles. The police, under pressure to justify the rates spent on them, focused on easy targets to boost arrest figures, and these were often the 'street arabs' or 'urchins' that 'infested' the city's streets. Charles Nye (14) and William Pincombe (13) were just such a pair of delinquents and in January 1878 they were set in the dock at Clerkenwell Police court accused of stealing sixpence from a five-year-old boy, simply named as 'Hunt'. The thieves were already 'known' offenders and were under police surveillance. Two detectives from N Division named Vincent and Armstrong had been following them at a distance for an hour and a half, watching carefully as they approached, stopped and chatted to several children. They stopped to talk in a friendly way to the little boy called Hunt, then suddenly snatched the bag he was holding and ran away. Police soon caught the pair, but Detective Armstrong saw Pincombe discard a sixpence as he fled. In court the police told Mr Hosack that the lads were suspected of committing a string of robberies and had previously been birched and sent to prison for six weeks. The magistrate was loath to send them to gaol, saying they 'were too young to undergo a long term of imprisonment'. Instead he decided that they should go to a reformatory where they might stand some small chance of being rehabilitated. The court clerk made some enquiries and later that day Mr Wills, an Industrial Schools officer, appeared in court to say that there were some vacancies on the *Cornwall* Reformatory Training ship. Happy with this option, Mr Hosack sentenced each lad to fourteen days' hard labour in prison; thereafter they were to be sent to the *Cornwall* for two years.[57] Magistrates handing down a reformatory sentence had to include a period of hard labour, to soften up defendants and remind them that they were being given a chance at reform. Mary Carpenter had argued against sending children to prison but society demanded that they were punished as a form of deterrence.

As a crowd of shoppers were peering through the windows of the London Stereoscopic Company in Regent Street, looking at the display of photographs within, two young thieves were hard at work behind them. John Thompson (16) and Catherine Hayes (12) were busy 'dipping' pockets to see what valuables they could steal. Unfortunately for the pair they were also being observed: PC Tiernan had spotted them. He knew Thompson and so the lad was arrested and escorted to a nearby police station. Once he had deposited Thompson he returned and, finding Hayes putting her hand in a lady's pocket, the constable quickly apprehended the girl. The lady was not inclined to prosecute as she had no desire to be seen at such a common place as a police station house, but she did tell the officer that her purse contained seven sovereigns, so Catherine's intent was proven. The two would-be felons were brought before Mr Knox at Marlborough Street Police court where they were accused of attempting to pick pockets.

Thompson had been 'known' to police 'for some time', having previously been convicted of shoplifting. Since his arrest he had

Last remains of the Fleet Prison with advertising, illustration
from Walter Thornbury, *Old and New London* (1873–8).

been identified as wanted for the theft of a gold watch valued at
£15. Constable Tiernan had investigated the character of Catherine
Hayes and found that it was 'very indifferent'. She had been expelled
from school on more than one occasion under suspicion of stealing
property that had gone missing. Knox sent Thompson to gaol for
three months as a 'rogue and vagabond', a useful catch-all term that
meant that no offence of stealing had to be proven against him;
merely being on the street as a person known to the authorities and
without being able to give a good account of himself was enough
to allow the law to punish him. As for Hayes, the law now had a
supportive alternative to prison or transportation and so she was
sent to Mill Hill Industrial School, where she was to reside until

she reached sixteen years of age. There she would learn useful skills such as needlework and laundry, which, it was hoped, might help her secure a job when she got out. Girls like Hayes would be taught with a heavy helping of discipline and morality, in the hope that this might correct and improve their characters.[58]

Hayes's experience was now much more typical for young people caught up in crime or, through poverty, parental neglect or abuse, deemed 'suitable objects' for removal to an industrial school. By the 1870s there were over 8,000 children in such institutions and that figure would continue to rise until the end of the century.[59] In 1886 the home secretary, Sir William Harcourt, was concerned with the ill effect of imprisoning juveniles and began an enquiry. The Howard Association pointed to the example of practice in Massachusetts, which had pioneered the use of probation. This led to the 1887 Probation of First Offenders Act,[60] but, as Dorothy Bochel notes, it 'added virtually nothing to the existing methods of dealing with young and minor offenders'.[61] A welfare approach to the treatment of juvenile offenders would have to wait for a new century.

Child exploitation and abuse

The police courts may have served a disciplinary function for a society determined to guide the development of working-class children in a positive, productive direction. The records, however, also reveal children as the victims of adult exploitation and abuse. From the 1820s onwards a steady stream of migrants arrived in London from Italy, many of them young boys who had been trafficked. At mid-century Henry Mayhew estimated that there were around 1,000 street musicians in London, many of them young Italians from Parma. The children brought over were attached to masters (or 'padrones') who supplied them with instruments and animals and sent them out to beg. These child musicians were expected to earn money for their masters, rather like the relationship between a prostitute and her 'bully' or pimp. As John Zucchi describes, the masters supplied the boys with animals ('monkeys, mice, and squirrels [and] also dogs, tortoises, and even porcupines'). These were rented to the boys for a price that ranged between 1s 6d for a 'box of white mice' to 2s 6d for the much rarer porcupine: 'for 4s a boy could also rent a barrel-organ. The dancing dogs came to 5s a day, but for that price the boy got four dogs in dresses, along with a spinning wheel, pipe, and tabor.'[62]

In the 1860s a campaign to restrict street musicians was led by Michael Thomas Bass and the inventor Charles Babbage, who published a book of complaints and other evidence gathered from interviews and letters from the public, many of whom wrote to support Bass's efforts as an MP to introduce a ban on street organs.[63] Among those names supporting Bass's campaign were Charles Dickens, John Everett Millais, W. Holman Hunt and Wilkie Collins. His pamphlet also included reports of hearings at the police courts, which demonstrated that the existing law was ineffective in curtailing what the *Examiner* described as 'The Grinding Oppression'.[64] Given that the padrones swiftly paid any fines imposed, the impotence of the law was self-evident. Bass's Bill for the Better Regulation of Street Music within the Metropolitan Police District was passed into law in late July 1864.[65] Bass had success in some small way by removing the need for complainants to cite illness as a factor in requesting musicians to move on and that from then on itinerant musicians ('buskers') could be charged under the Vagrancy Act (1824) if they were presumed to be begging.[66] It did not stop the exploitation of children however.

The children trafficked as musicians were relatively fortunate compared to some victims of abuse in Victorian London. On 11 October 1870 Margaret Waters was hanged for the murder of more than a dozen infant children, all of whom had been given into her care. Waters was the most notorious 'baby farmer' of the

Victorian age. Many children suffered or died at the hands of neglectful or inept baby farmers and after Waters's conviction parliament acted to protect children from this abuse, passing the Infant Life Protection Act of 1872.[67] Baby farming was a form of early fostering, but one that lacked checks and controls. The mothers of illegitimate children (or poor women unable to cope with bringing up a child while working) were able to place their offspring with a baby farmer to raise. They would pay a small weekly fee and in return the newborn child would be nursed by someone else. Often the money was simply not enough and farmers struggled to keep the children properly nourished. Illness followed malnutrition and death came soon after. Waters deliberately allowed her charges to wither and die, but very many infants simply died of unintentional neglect.

The Infant Life Protection Act required foster carers to register with the parish authorities and represents the first attempt to regulate baby farming. In August 1872 Annie Wheeler was brought to Hammersmith to answer for the death of a five-week-old baby in her care, Sarah Ann Nash. Wheeler, dressed in mourning, was represented by a solicitor, Mr Claydon. She was charged with manslaughter. Dr William Henry Harvey testified to visiting Wheeler's house in Fulham where he examined the child. The female baby had died of 'exhaustion for the want of nourishment', he stated, and it was not the first death at Wheeler's home. A few weeks earlier he had pronounced death on another infant who had died similarly of malnutrition and diarrhoea. Detective Manley also testified that while he was investigating Sarah Nash's death, he noticed another child who was 'very thin, and apparently dying'. He took this child away and placed it with the Fulham workhouse authorities. Wheeler explained that little Sarah had been in her care for just three weeks. She had been paid £4 and was to be paid 7s 6d a week thereafter.

Wheeler was fostering children but two at least had died in her care, and another was now in the workhouse infirmary in a very weak state. Infant mortality was high in the Victorian period, so the death of a child, especially an infant in its first year, was not at all unusual. The question here was whether Sarah's death was caused by neglect, which was manslaughter, or was simply unavoidable. Wheeler was remanded in custody and set for trial later that summer. However, the case against her was weak and did not get past the grand jury at the Old Bailey. There was insufficient evidence to proceed, the prosecution barrister told the judge. Wheeler was released and able to return to 'caring' for little children. If this was an early test for the Infant Life Protection Act, then it failed rather badly.[68]

The Society for the Prevention of Cruelty to Children (spcc) was founded in 1884. The cruelty that was most difficult to detect then remains true today: that perpetrated by parents or other relatives of children, because it is often hidden within the family. This was the case with Ethel Newberry, a child of ten who was abused and half-starved by her father and aunt at the family home in Sydenham in May 1889. The case came to the attention of the spcc, who brought a prosecution at Greenwich Police court. In the dock were Phillip Newberry, the child's father, and Mary Phillips, her aunt. Ethel had been beaten on her back by her father with a cane on numerous occasions. When examined by a doctor the extent of her injuries was considerable, with several scars and abrasions. Her aunt had hit her over the head with a copper stick and smacked her wrists with a cane. The abuse alerted neighbours, who had complained to the local Poor Law relieving officers, who visited the house. Ethel was found to be almost emaciated, weighing just 13 kilograms (30 lb) when she should have been at least 22–27 kilograms (50–60 lb) at her age.

The child was taken to the local workhouse, where she was treated for her injuries and properly fed. When she was well enough the case came before Mr Marsham, who quizzed the father and aunt about their treatment of Ethel. The court also heard from Ethel herself. The whole episode revolved around food. The doctor who checked her over at the workhouse could find no explanation for her emaciation that suggested a disease, concluding that the family had not been giving her enough to eat. This may have been an attempt on their behalf to discipline the child for behaving badly, but if it was it only made things worse. In desperation Ethel began to steal food. She admitted to the magistrate that she had taken cakes from a shop, and this was why her aunt had 'whacked' her. The justice decided that while there was little evidence to prove that Mary Phillips had done more than was deemed normal in terms of chastisement, the cruelty of the father was excessive and so he was committed for trial at the Old Bailey.[69] However, this is where this case disappears. There are no records of a Phillip Newberry standing trial at the Old Bailey or appearing in the prison system.

The London SPCC was successful in petitioning parliament for a change in the law to protect children from abuse. The Prevention of Cruelty to Children Act was passed in 1889 and with it police were authorized to remove a child from its parents if cruelty was suspected and give it into the care of the parish. On conviction for cruelty, anyone 'who wilfully treats or neglects any boy under fourteen years of age, or any girls under sixteen, in a manner likely to cause unnecessary suffering' was liable to a £50 fine or three months in prison.[70] Organizations like the SPCC and the RSPCA, founded in 1824, frequently used the summary courts to bring prosecutions and to observe hearings to gather evidence in support of their campaigns. They, like the officers of the Society for the Suppression of Mendicity, which had been founded to stop begging in London, recognized the importance of the police courts as arenas of negotiation, discipline and control, and as the places where most Londoners experienced 'justice'.

6

PROSTITUTION AND THE POLICE COURTS

Among almost 3,000 entries in the Thames Police court register for 1881 there are only three recorded uses of the word 'prostitute'. Lydia Butler, a 24-year-old woman, was brought before Mr Lushington as a 'riotous prostitute' and released on her own recognizances. Alice Turner was charged with being a 'disorderly prostitute' and was sent to prison for a fortnight under the terms of the Vagrancy Act. Mary Smith (22) avoided gaol by paying a 10s fine for being riotous and using obscene language to the officer who arrested her.[1] The apparent absence of prostitutes from the court is a reminder that prostitution was not an offence in law in the 1800s. Notwithstanding this, many of the women brought into court charged with being disorderly, for drink-related offences, and some of those charged as petty thieves, may well have sold sex at certain points in their lives (as the life of the notorious Tottie Fay reveals), but they were rarely prosecuted as sex workers.

To gather data for his report on prostitution in Victorian London, published in 1857, William Acton used statistics from the Metropolitan Police, which recorded 8,600 prostitutes operating in the capital. It was also noted that there were 2,825 brothels. The women were subdivided into three categories: 'Well dressed, living in brothels', 'Well dressed, walking the streets', and 'Low, infesting low neighbourhoods'. Acton recognized that the figures, particularly for women selling sex on the street, were approximate and probably conservative.[2] They are, however, much lower than the wild estimations of 80,000 or more made by Henry Mayhew and Bracebridge Hemyng in 1861.[3] In reality it was probably impossible to measure the exact numbers of prostitutes operating in the capital at any one time or indeed to determine what defined a person as a prostitute. In recent years we have been asked to reconsider whether it is appropriate or accurate to describe the canonical 'five' victims of the Whitechapel murderer as prostitutes.[4] Some Victorian commentators struggled or simply avoided attempts at definition. William Tait, who treated prostitutes admitted to the Edinburgh Lock Hospital, defined the prostitute on moral terms, writing about women who had chosen a 'life of impurity and licentiousness'.[5] Mayhew and Bracebridge wrote at length about the long history of prostitution and classified the women by the men they associated with ('sailors' women', 'soldiers' women' or 'thieves' women'). Prostitution was firmly linked to the notion that a criminal class operated in mid-Victorian London. Mayhew emphasizes this by presenting his readers with the statistics of women prosecuted for picking pockets over a decade, even though by his own admission relatively few were convicted. He attributes this to an understandable reluctance on the part of male victims to come to press charges in court.[6]

Demonized as the 'Great Social Evil' (the 'public symbol of public vice', as Judith Walkowitz dubbed her), the prostitute occupied a prominent position in the minds of Victorian moralists. Yet attitudes towards prostitutes and prostitution fluctuated, with depictions of the women involved ranging from those who were seen as dangerously undermining the sanctity of marriage and disease spreaders to those who were unfortunate victims of male exploitation and lust. The Victorian prostitute was also intertwined with the urban environment, the growth of which in the industrial age was itself a cause of concern for some contemporaries.[7] Some even went so far as to grudgingly accept prostitution as a 'necessary evil', its existence preventing the corruption of thousands of 'innocent' women and girls by men unable to control their lustful urges. Concerns about the danger posed by sexually transmitted diseases brought about the passing of laws in the 1860s that attempted to regulate the sex trade. Prostitution was not made illegal, but the authorities were empowered by legislation that allowed women to be taken off the streets, and forcibly examined to establish if they were carrying a sexually transmitted infection such as syphilis or gonorrhoea. Those deemed infectious were then locked up in a hospital until they were deemed 'clean', placed on a register of 'common prostitutes', and released. At any point those registered could be re-examined. The legislation – the Contagious Diseases (CD) Acts – passed in 1864, 1866 and 1869 came out of concerns expressed in the aftermath of the Crimean War about the health of men serving in the armed forces.[8] The CD Acts were only applied to garrison and port towns and only applied to women. Soldiers and sailors were encouraged, but not required, to subject themselves to examination. The CD Acts prompted outrage from some, in part because they were seen as legitimizing prostitution.[9] Others saw them as an attack on women and provoked a campaign led by Josephine Butler to repeal the acts. In 1886 the Ladies National Association for the Repeal of the Contagious Diseases Acts finally achieved its aim of having the legislation struck from the statute book.

Identifying sex workers in the police courts

For all sorts of reasons identifying prostitutes in the police courts is problematic. As noted above, prostitution was not a criminal offence in law. The associated offences of disorderly conduct, drunkenness and antisocial behaviours were generally dealt with by police using the catch-all Vagrancy Act (1824).[10] The Metropolitan Police Act of 1839 made soliciting an offence, but this proved hard to apply in practice.[11] A woman had to be identified as a 'common prostitute' (therefore one with a record of offending behaviour, known to the police and courts).[12] In addition police had to show that she was walking the streets with the intention of soliciting custom, and that she was causing an annoyance to other street users. Given that magistrates were reluctant to accept the uncorroborated word of a constable and witnesses were often unwilling to go to court to be associated with prostitution, very many women avoided court altogether. There may have been another reason why prostitutes were able to avoid a court appearance. Women selling sex were vulnerable to unscrupulous police constables who recognized an opportunity to extort money or services from them. Reminiscing about his experiences in the early 1900s, Hugh Gamon wrote:

> Prostitutes can be blackmailed. They will say that they need never go to the police-court if only they have money. No doubt this is untrue, but there is a grain of truth at least in it. There are police who are not ashamed to take from these outcasts and pariahs of society something of their illicit earnings, as the price of forbearance.[13]

Gamon was not alone in criticizing the police. Horace Cox, while assured that most officers were honest and trustworthy, reflected that the police had considerable discretionary powers when it came to enforcing the vagrancy laws, choosing whom to arrest or to let off with a warning. Magistrates were also, by the last decades of the century at least, much more likely to accept the word of a constable over the person occupying the dock, especially if she was a working-class woman of dubious morality.[14]

For an example of how difficult prosecutions were, consider the case of a man who reported being robbed in the late 1850s. On Saturday, 13 November 1858, Mr Chamberlain had been out late in Bridgewater Gardens in the City and was making his way home. He had had a lot to drink when two women approached him on the street and asked him if he would like to 'treat them to some gin'. This was a common enough solicitation by prostitutes and there is little doubt that Chamberlain, a musician by trade, understood this. He took them up on the offer and the trio headed to a public house where they drank together. Some time afterwards they all left, and the women allegedly dragged him reluctantly across the square for the purpose of sex. However, having got their 'mark' into a dark corner of the gardens the women stood aside as two men rushed up and robbed him. Chamberlain claimed that he tried to resist but one of the women hit him in the face and knocked him down. He lost a fob watch in the process. This was the story he told the Guildhall Police court magistrate Alderman Lawrence. Only one defendant was in court to hear the charge: Mary Blake had been picked up by police at a pub in Goswell Street the following day but denied any knowledge of the crime. Her lawyer said it was a case of mistaken identity and Chamberlain, who was by his admission drunk at the time, was an unreliable witness. The alderman was inclined to agree but, given that Blake was a 'bad character' and reportedly ran a brothel, he decided to remand her in custody to see if more evidence could be found in the meantime. No such evidence materialized. This is hardly surprising; this sort of encounter was common and very hard to prosecute successfully. Without the watch being found on Mary, with the victim effectively admitting he had chosen to go for a drink with known prostitutes, and his drunken state (which impaired both his judgement and his ability to make a clear identification of the culprits), few juries would have convicted her.[15]

Many of the women brought before Thames court in 1881 or any of the other London courts throughout the century as 'drunk and disorderly' (or one of its variants) may have been prostitutes (however that was defined), but since they were not prosecuted for selling sex the court registers, and even the newspaper reporters, do not always make that explicit association. The Mendicity Society

Entrance to the Clerkenwell tunnel from Farringdon Street, illustration from
Walter Thornbury, *Old and New London* (1873–8).

would regularly prosecute street beggars, among whom were 'unhappy young girls' who prostituted themselves, perhaps as many as sixty a day according to one author writing at mid-century.[16] Much of the prostitution in the capital has to be seen as a product of endemic poverty or, at best, as a temporary and strategic life choice for some young women who rejected both the moral constraints of Victorian society and a life of drudgery.[17] There must have been plenty of women like Bridget Lacking, an Irish prostitute identified by Lucy Williams as someone who had racked up more than forty convictions for drunkenness, disorderly behaviour and petty violence. She regularly used a false name, adopting those of housemates or a male partner or pimp.[18] An ever-changing name would have made Lacking harder to track through the courts and was a strategy adopted by many repeat offenders, as we saw with Tottie Fay, but her history also reminds us how difficult it is to identify prostitutes in the record.

Any woman the police believed to be a 'common prostitute' or 'night walker' could be arrested for soliciting or for loitering for the purposes of soliciting business, but police were advised to exercise 'great tact and patience' in dealing with them.[19] That tact was stretched to the limit when police or members of the public were assaulted by prostitutes and their pimps or friends. PC George Stancombe was on duty on the Euston Road, an area synonymous with prostitution and crime in the 1800s, when he observed a group of young women and men harassing pedestrians. At least one of the girls was soliciting prostitution and one man was clearly uninterested and pushed her away. This prompted the others to grab handfuls of mud from the street and pelt him with it. The man was then punched in the face before the constable intervened. Mary Ann Paul and James Madden were arrested and charged at Marylebone with soliciting and assault, respectively. The case was initially adjourned because the 'gentleman' that PC Stancombe alleged Madden had punched was not in court, despite signing the charge sheet at the station, which required him to be present. Madden and Paul denied everything but were unable to bring witnesses to back up their version of events. Crucially the gentleman, Charles Thomas, made a late appearance to confirm the policeman's story. The magistrate was told that Paul was frequently seen on the Euston Road 'annoying' passers-by and that couples like her and Madden preyed on the unwary, robbing them when distracted. Paul, just seventeen years old, was sent to prison for a month; Madden got two months and was led away shouting his defiance.[20]

Kate Berry was described as a 'very disreputable prostitute' when she appeared at Westminster charged with refusing to quit licensed premises and with assault. The assault was on a potman who was trying to get her to leave the Coach and Horses pub in Chelsea, a place from which she had already been banned on several occasions. She had been barred from the premises for using bad language and stealing sips from customers' drinks. Whether this was part of her method of soliciting, which would seem possible,

White Hart tavern, Bishopsgate Street, 1810, illustration
from Walter Thornbury, *Old and New London* (1873–8).

or a reflection of her lack of funds, Mr Poole (the proprietor) did not want her in his establishment because he feared it would give it a bad reputation. The magistrate sympathized but without any evidence of the assault or of the accusation that Berry was 'riotous' until she was manhandled out of the building, he discharged her with a warning not to return.[21]

If common prostitutes were considered a perennial problem but one that society could, on the whole, live with, child prostitution was another thing entirely. In February 1886 a 21-year-old woman named Louisa Hart appeared at Marylebone Police court charged with 'unlawfully procuring' two young girls for 'immoral purposes'. The girls in question – Rosie Shires (12) and Florence Richardson (13) – were both present to testify that they had more than once been taken to Hart's home to have 'intercourse . . . with old men'. They were paid 10s each and sent home in a hansom cab.[22] Both girls lived on St Thomas's Road, Finsbury Park. About six months previously Shires had shown her friend a calling card with the name 'Louisa Hart' and an address – 43 Markham Square, Chelsea – and Rosie asked Florence if she would accompany her there to visit Mrs Hart for 'tea'. In December the pair went to the address, where Florence noticed a lady in riding habit get off a horse and enter the house. A few minutes later the pair were invited into the drawing room, where the lady in equestrian garb introduced herself as Louisa Hart. She welcomed Rosie and said: 'Oh, I am glad you have brought someone with you.' Florence waited while Hart and Rosie left briefly, apparently going downstairs to the parlour. They then had tea together before the door opened and an elderly man entered the room.[23]

The children's testimony revealed that this was not a one-off incident; Rosie Shires had been induced to go to Hart's house on more than one occasion and had been paid to have sex with men. Initially Florence said nothing about her experience and spent the money she received on 'sweets and cake'. However, she later discovered that Rosie had also been 'ruined' by the old man and that her mother (Mrs Shires) had found out and was angry. At this point the police were informed and Hart was arrested. She claimed that the girls had told her they were over sixteen and her lawyer asked for bail, which was refused.[24] Hart was charged under the recently enacted Criminal Law Amendment Act (1885), which had been passed in the wake of the 'Maiden Tribute' scandal.[25] The 'Maiden Tribute of Modern Babylon' was a series of articles published in the *Pall Mall Gazette* over the week beginning 4 July 1885. Authored by the paper's firebrand editor William T. Stead, it was an exposé of child prostitution in the capital of empire.[26] Stead, a pioneer of 'New Journalism', went undercover and employed a retired prostitute and procuress named Rebecca Jarrett to demonstrate how easy it was to buy a child of thirteen for sex. The victim, Eliza Armstrong, was inveigled away from her mother, who was assumed to either believe her child was to be placed in service or was in fact well aware that she would be sexually exploited. Either way Mrs Armstrong accepted £5 for her daughter, who was taken away to be examined to determine her sexual innocence. Eliza was then placed in a hotel room, drugged unconscious so that Stead could act out (up to a point) the defilement that she might have been subject to had he been a genuine client. The child was then spirited away to be cared for by the Salvation Army while Stead wrote up his article as part of his campaign to force the passage of the Criminal Law Amendment Act, which had stalled in the House of Lords. The article caused a sensation, drew brickbats of criticism hurled at Stead and Mrs Armstrong, but achieved the goal of changing the law and raising the age of consent. Stead, Jarrett and some others involved ended up before a jury at the Old Bailey and he and the former procuress were sent to prison for short terms.[27]

Understandably, given its context, the case of Louisa Hart occupied the papers from the first report of her appearance at Marylebone through to her eventual trial by jury. Hart was back in the dock on 16 February, when the Treasury case against her began in earnest. Florence Richardson repeated her evidence with a little more detail and was cross-examined by Hart's counsel. He asked questions about her father and her siblings that she refused to answer, merely saying they were 'respectable'. The line of questioning seems to have been intended to portray Richardson and Shires as far-from-innocent victims and this continued when Mrs Shires came to the witness box. She had not allowed her daughter to come to court, seemingly trying to protect her from the unfolding scandal. Unfortunately the magistrate, Mr De Rutzen, insisted that Rosie attend the next hearing and remanded Hart once again.[28] Shires kept her daughter away from the next hearing, but was warned to produce her next time or a warrant for her arrest would be issued.[29] By the end of February the *Pall Mall Gazette* was referring to Hart as the keeper of 'a child's brothel', but also reflected on a suggestion that she was herself the victim of child sexual exploitation. Emma Barker, a female searcher at Paddington police station, testified that Hart had told her that she had been married at fifteen to a man who had coerced her into the offences that she was charged with. Hart had said 'she had had six years at the same sort of life [as she was inflicting on Florence and Rosie], and she seemed to be in great distress of mind'. Barker added that Hart described the girls as 'prostitutes', was told by them that they were sixteen (or even eighteen, as was later stated in Hart's trial),[30] and that they were fully aware of what was being asked of them.[31] The *Gazette* asked why Mr Hart was not being held up to the scrutiny of the law.[32] It continued its criticism a week later, noting that Mr Ben Hart was attending court, assisting the defence of his wife, and was clearly 'the real keeper of the house'. It also wanted to know the identity of the 'old gentleman' (the 'chief criminal') who had paid to have sex with the two underage girls.[33]

Rosie Shires finally returned to give evidence on 8 March, by which time Mrs Hart had acquired a new lawyer. The press had reported that her previous counsel, Mr Dutton, had been growing increasingly anxious as the case against his client unfolded, so perhaps he stepped away. Or maybe the Harts decided they needed fresh eyes on the case. Whatever the truth, Mr Boardman took over and cross-examined Rosie in the witness box. She admitted that she had been to Mrs Hart's as many as ten times, but she had no idea what sort of house it was. She knew the word 'prostitute' but not what it meant; she had no idea what a brothel was when she first went to 35 Albany Street (Hart's address). Other addresses in Albany Street were cited, as were the names of a Mrs Bedford and a Mrs Shaw, either or both of whom seemed to have had an unstated connection with the Harts. Boardman's intention was presumably to attempt to inject some doubt into Mr Rutzen's mind that Rosie Shires was entirely innocent of what she was being asked to do, and to infer that her mother was knowingly involved (echoing the criticism levelled at Mrs Armstrong for 'selling' her child to Rebecca Jarrett). He also pressed the child to admit that she had appeared on stage and to tell the court where. Rosie refused until the magistrate accepted it was a valid question and insisted on an answer. Rosie Shires told the court that she had appeared at Ramsgate when she was about six and more recently in London at the Park and Standard Theatres.[34] On this occasion the *Pall Mall Gazette* printed a wood engraving of Louisa Hart that showed her as both respectable and fashionable, sporting a dark hat and veil.[35] The case for the prosecution was concluded on 9 March and Hart was committed for trial at the Central Criminal Court, bail being set at £500.[36]

This was an early test for the Criminal Law Amendment Act that Stead's *Gazette* had done so much to get passed into law. The trial began on 8 April 1886 before Justice Wills. Hart was charged with aiding and abetting assaults on Richardson and Shires and with 'inducing the girls to frequent her house'. Hart pleaded not guilty. The entry in the Proceedings of the Old Bailey is scant: it merely lists the charge, the names of the defendant, Shires, and the legal teams before recording verdict and sentence.[37] This is because the content of the case was deemed salacious, and the Old Bailey Sessions Paper had a policy of not printing material that might corrupt the morals of the reader. Given that the press widely reported much of what was said in court, we might observe that the practice was somewhat pointless. The jury heard over the course of several visits how the girls were told to undress and that they were exposed to 'immorality and indecency', before on the final occasion Shires was 'ruined'. She was examined by a surgeon, who confirmed that she had been violated.[38] The judge intervened when the defence's cross-examination reduced the two young witnesses to tears. Justice Wills described Richardson and Shires as 'unhappy children, who were on the borderlands of respectability, and were always in danger of being shoved over', adding that it was inevitable with witnesses 'in these cases'. He urged Mr Rowland to exercise 'great care'.

Inspector Morgan, the detective who arrested Hart, provided one of the most damning pieces of evidence. He revealed that in a search of the property at Markham Square he had found a cork stopping up a hole that allowed the user a view of the adjacent bedroom. A similar hole was found at Fulham Place where Hart had been arrested. It suggested that Hart was, or had, been using several locations for the purpose of child sexual exploitation.[39] The judge's summing up reminded the jury of how 'wicked' the charges were but also warned them that young girls were apt to tell lies. The jury accepted that Hart had been misled as to Richardson's age but not Shires, finding Hart guilty on one count only. The judge was scathing in his condemnation of Louisa Hart, describing her as callous and cruel in her treatment of both children. He sentenced her to five years' penal servitude.[40] The *Gazette* reflected that the sentence was a heavy one to impose on such a young woman, if 'not undeserved'. It described Hart as 'more sinned against than sinning', however, now connecting the case to Rebecca Hart, a notorious procuress. Louisa had (in modern parlance) been 'groomed' and then had been coerced into grooming other girls just like her. The real culprits were men like Ben Hart, the *Gazette* argued, and those 'old gentle-men' who paid for sex with children. 'The scenes of debauchery described yesterday', the paper continued at the close of its coverage of the case, 'confirm only too terribly the worst passages of the "Maiden Tribute".'[41] This was one of a number of prosecutions under the new legislation that the press published as part of its coverage of 'everyday crime' reportage.[42] Hart was imprisoned in Woking Gaol until her release on licence in August 1889 into the care of the Royal Society for the Assistance of Discharged Prisoners. She gave her occupation as 'actress', a reminder of the close association in the public consciousness between the women who acted a role on the stage and those who sold sex.[43]

Prostitution was not a crime in Victorian England, but many working-class women were arrested and dragged before magistrates to be admonished, fined or locked up for being part of a criminal class. They were prosecuted for summary offences that required little proof beyond the word of a policeman and were judged on their reputations as much as on the evidence of any wrongdoing. That plenty of these women were arrested when they were on the streets and often having consumed alcohol was, in the eyes of contemporary society, proof that they were not respectable. Magistrates and police did not always see eye-to-eye, but when it came to prostitution they were much closer in outlook. Prostitution was considered to be a threat to a stable and ordered society. The women who chose or were forced (by 'bullies', 'pimps' or poverty) into prostitution were rejecting the role laid out for them – that is, to be obedient wives and doting mothers. They were an offence to the state and that could not be ignored. The reality was, however, that many if not most of these women were the victims of society, every bit as much as Eliza Armstrong, Florence Robinson or Rosie Shires were victims. The courts rarely if ever dealt with the underlying causes of prostitution or the men and women who ran the trade. Instead they settled for the easy targets and allowed the exploitation to continue.

John Thomson, *The 'Crawlers'*, 1877, photomechanical print.

7

POVERTY AND HOMELESSNESS

On 29 September 1888 *Punch* published a cartoon by John Tenniel alongside an article on East End slums. Tenniel's iconic image of the 'Nemesis of Neglect' was published at the height of the Whitechapel (or 'Jack the Ripper') murders as London reeled from the terror created by a serial killer the police seemed unable to catch. Tenniel's cartoon and its accompanying text suggested the murderer was a product of the degraded environment in which his victims lived and died. There were numerous warnings about the risks associated with ignoring the state of the poor in late Victorian London. In 1883 the Reverend Andrew Mearns attempted to shock a largely middle-class readership out of any comfortable sense of complacency with first-hand descriptions of the squalid conditions the poor inhabited. He suggested that their cramped living quarters were a breeding ground for immorality where 'incest is common'.[1] Two years earlier George Sims had written: 'This mighty mob of famished, diseased and filthy helots is getting dangerous: physically, politically and morally dangerous. The barriers which have kept it back are rotten and giving way [and] it may do the state a mischief if it be not looked to in time.'[2]

In February 1888, before serial murder dominated all other news, a 76-year-old man appeared at Westminster Police court to ask for a summons against an officer at St Luke's workhouse, Chelsea. The elderly man moved slowly and spoke with difficulty, clearly suffering with injuries. He explained that he had sustained these when a workhouse attendant turfed him out of his bed at 6.45 in the morning, as punishment for being fifteen minutes late getting up. He had only just got to sleep, he said, having been kept awake by others' coughing and by cramp in his legs. 'I am so badly bruised that I have not been able to walk upright since,' he complained. The man had no family or friends and had been an inmate of the workhouse for six years. Mr D'Eyncourt granted his summons and excused him the fee.[3]

There is no record of the outcome of this complaint, but it reiterates the role of the police courts as arenas in which even the poorest could seek support or guidance. On the same day across the Thames at Southwark Sarah Ann Davis stood in the dock, cradling her baby. She was accused of begging in London Road. She denied this, arguing that she 'was selling some pins to get some food for her children'. Her husband was in prison, having been locked up for begging. The magistrate (Mr Slade) asked her why she had not taken herself and her children to the workhouse. 'I don't want to break up the home while my husband is away,' she said. Her husband was an out-of-work carpenter who was willing to do any job he could get, she declared, but work was in limited supply. The year 1888 was when the word 'unemployment' entered the dictionary; for the previous few years large numbers of unemployed men and women had gathered in Trafalgar Square to listen to socialists and free traders bemoan the state of the economy and the capitalist system that had seemingly failed so many.[4] There were plenty of people in Sarah Ann Davis's situation but not all of them were as fortunate in court as she was. Her landlord told the court that she and her family were respectable and quiet tenants, but were two weeks behind with their rent. 'You are not going to turn them out?' the magistrate asked. 'On no, sir, certainly not. What would become of the little children?' he replied. 'Very well, I will discharge her now,' the justice concluded. 'You can go now, Mrs Davis,' he added. 'You will receive some coal and bread tickets from the Poor-box Fund, and you had better apply to the Relieving Officer for some out-door relief.' He warned her against begging in future and she left, with applause ringing out in court.[5] Individual acts of decency were not enough to mitigate the realities of abject poverty, however. On another day Sarah might have gone to prison and had her children taken away or been forced into the workhouse, where the family would have been broken up.

Prison was where Priscilla Herman was sent after ending up before a magistrate at Worship Street in 1865. Priscilla, just fifteen, was an inmate of Bethnal Green workhouse and was charged with criminal damage. The court heard that Priscilla, described as 'placid' but displaying 'features indicative of . . . abandoned and vicious conduct', had smashed five panes of glass and verbally abused a female staff member. Ann Summers testified that when she had been asked to do some cleaning Herman had refused and threatened 'to beat my _____ old head in'. The workhouse staff had found her work in domestic service, but her behaviour kept getting her dismissed. It seems Priscilla had anger management problems and her language was often 'most shameful and disgusting'. The police constable said that she had admitted breaking windows, but no one knew why. The magistrate asked the girl why she had left her last placement, but she remained mute. A further question about her behaviour was also met with silence, until the magistrate asked, 'Where are your father and mother?' At this Herman broke down and started sobbing. 'I haven't any,' she cried. She then apologized and promised to 'be a good girl' if she were given another chance. She did not get that chance; the nature of her crimes (threats of violence, damage and bad language) required punishment in the magistrate's view, and he sent her to gaol for three weeks, effectively undermining any chance of her finding an honest living in the near future.[6]

Between 1886 and 1889 Charles Booth applied social science principles to challenge a socialist claim that 25 per cent of Londoners lived in poverty. He mapped poverty across the capital by systematically surveying London street by street. In 1889 he published his *Descriptive Map of London Poverty* as sixty sheets of hand-coloured maps, illustrating poverty levels with a simple colour code. The wealthiest streets were highlighted in yellow (or gold), the poorest ('semi-criminal') in black. In all Booth found that Henry Hyndman, the leader of the Social Democratic Federation, had actually underestimated the problem. Instead of 25 per cent of Londoners living in poverty, the reality was more like 35 per cent. Booth not only mapped poverty, he investigated the causes, concluding that 'casual work', 'low pay' and 'irregular earnings' were the main causal factors.[7] London's population had grown during the century and overcrowding and competition for work ensured many lived in squalid conditions on meagre wages. Hundreds died every year from malnutrition, homelessness was endemic, and levels of infant mortality were high. In St Giles, one of the capital's poorest districts, 187 of every 1,000 children did not make it to their first birthday; in Whitechapel the figure was 184 out of 1,000. Disease killed many in the 1800s, and not just children. Cholera struck in 1832, 1849 and 1854, killing thousands, but tuberculosis, bronchitis and smallpox were among the most virulent and consistent killers across the nineteenth century.[8] These illnesses also affected those who were able to afford medical help, however ineffectual, but ravaged the poorest communities where weakened constitutions were so much more exposed to sickness.

The Victorian Poor Law

Those out of work or in need had few options beyond turning to the parish for help. After 1834 this meant the workhouse, as both Priscilla Herman and the unnamed elderly gentleman who came to the Westminster Police court discovered. The Poor Law Amendment Act (1834) was intended to force anyone seeking poor relief to enter the workhouse, instead of being relieved 'outdoors' (by providing parish funds to supplement or replace loss of earnings). Families were separated – husbands from wives, mothers from children – and paupers were set to work in conditions little better than prison. The workhouse 'test' ensured that those seeking relief were genuinely in need and prepared to accept whatever rules the workhouse applied in return for a roof over their heads and sustenance. Moreover, the principle of 'less eligibility' meant that the experience of paupers had to be worse than that of those who were gainfully employed and, given that the labouring poor of Victorian London generally eked out a low-paid existence, this necessitated workhouse conditions that deterred shirkers from seeking help. Workhouses served each of London's parishes, with casual wards (for the 'destitute wayfarers, wanderers, and foundlings') established from 1864. From 1867 a single set poor rate was levied across London as part of legislation intended to separate the Poor Law's obligation to provide poor relief from its role as a provider of medical help to the poorest. The Metropolitan Poor Act (1867) also enabled the creation of asylums for the sick poor following criticism of workhouse conditions in *The Lancet* and by Florence Nightingale.[9]

The workhouse system was punitive and the occasional scandal (such as that at Andover in 1849, which exposed the local union as cruel in its mistreatment of paupers) merely highlighted the prevailing ideology of the British state, which saw pauperism as a character flaw. Those seeking relief were dubbed 'undeserving' if they were fit and able to work and took no account of the failure of capitalism to ensure work was plentiful, regular and properly remunerated. Dock labourers were just one group of workers who suffered from highly competitive seasonal employment, which drove down wages and forced thousands to turn to the parish or

Applicants queue for poor relief at Thames Police court, from
'Sketches at the London Police-Courts', *The Graphic*, 27 August 1887.

charity when times were hardest. Others were forced to beg,
prostitute themselves or steal. Poverty brought many Londoners
before the police courts: some, like Priscilla Herman, to be chastised as ungrateful and others, like the elderly victim of abuse, to
seek justice.

The police courts served as arenas for the negotiation of all
manner of things in the 1800s. They were much more than simply
courts focused on crime, punishment and maintaining order. However, a skewed view is often reinforced by the newspapers' selection
of cases to bring to the attention of their readers. They often chose
outrageous, amusing, shocking and heart-wringing stories, or
examples that reminded the public that working-class men were

brutal, that theft was common and that fraudsters might entrap the unwary. When Ellen Potts came to the Guildhall Police court to ask for Alderman Moon's help it gave the court reporter of the *Morning Post* the perfect opportunity to highlight another perennial theme of Victorian popular culture: the misuse of authority by a lowly public servant. The press, led by *The Times*, was frequently critical of the New Poor Law in the early decades of its implementation, with 'penny-pinching officials' held up as examples of maladministration and cruelty.[10] It probably helped the narrative here that Potts was 'a good-looking girl of about eighteen' and her oppressor had garnered a local reputation for meanness. This story had a melodramatic narrative that readers could easily understand and identify with, having as it did a villain (in the form of petty officialdom) and a damsel in distress. Ellen Potts explained that she had been thrown out of her home after a row with her mother 'over a shawl'. Such mundane things could easily spark conflict in working-class families, for whom possessions, few as there were, were highly prized. With nowhere to go Ellen knocked on the door of the West London Union workhouse in the City.[11] The relieving officer, a man named Miller, refused her entry on the grounds that her mother took in lodgers at her house on nearby Cloth Fair and so was perfectly capable of supporting her daughter. Alderman Moon was angry with the officer, whose only defence was to claim he was following the policy of the Union. The alderman quickly established that Mrs Potts herself was in receipt of poor relief and that Miller was aware of this. 'Then how can she support her daughter?' the magistrate demanded to know. 'You have discretionary power', he continued, '[a]nd I think it is a most cruel act of a man to refuse shelter to a girl under such circumstances, and your conduct is most disgraceful.'

When Miller tried once more to say that Ellen was her mother's responsibility rather than the parish's, the alderman silenced him:

You may be a good badger for the guardians, but at the same time a disgrace to human nature. No wonder, when females are thus cruelly refused an asylum, so many should become prostitutes for the sake of obtaining that relief for which the ratepayers are rated so heavily. There are constant complaints of your hard-hearted conduct, which is a disgrace to your nature.

This brought cries of 'hear, hear' in court, which reinforced the narrative that Miller was the villain and Potts his unfortunate victim. The chief clerk advised the alderman that Miller was liable to a £5 fine for his actions in disobeying the general rule that 'relief shall be given to all persons in urgent distress'. After one more forlorn attempt to shift responsibility from himself to the guardians, the relieving officer finally acknowledged what was required of him. 'Is it your wish she be taken into the house?' he asked the alderman. 'If so I will do it willingly.' Miller avoided a fine and Potts was admitted to the workhouse, so that she was no longer at any immediate risk of falling into an even worse fate.[12] This case reflects the fact that magistrates like Moon had the authority to challenge decisions made by relieving officers and force them to support paupers. They could also directly help by distributing money from the poor box and some were quite happy to do so. In 1844 Marlborough Street magistrates paid out '£355 to 903 applicants', most of whom had been refused support by the parish. At Greenwich the average given was 4s 10d per person, a sum David Green describes as 'relatively generous'.[13] It probably was generous, for on the occasions when outdoor relief was given it rarely exceeded 2s 6d a week.[14]

The stipulation from 1864 was that all workhouses provide a casual ward for the situation Ellen Potts found herself in. Casual wards were not welcoming places. In 1866 the journalist James Greenwood spent a night in one and described the process of being admitted, separated from his possessions (in case they were stolen) and directed to sleep in a room 'thirty feet by thirty' that 'reeked' from the thirty or so men and boys already admitted. The workhouse woke sleepers at seven o'clock in the morning, Greenwood was reunited with his own clothes before a dismal breakfast was served and the casuals were set to work grinding corn. Greenwood's description of his brief time is powerfully revealing of the desperation of those seeking relief in such a place and he cautions his readers that he had spared them the worst.[15] For all his personal experience in the 1860s Greenwood was still quick to highlight those paupers he saw as undeserving of sympathy later in his writing career. He would have dubbed Edward Crossman, prosecuted at Thames Police court as a refractory pauper, a member of the 'Lazy League'. Crossman, it was claimed, avoided the difficult sections of old rope, preferring the 'tender' sections to the tough bits and refused to touch some lengths claiming they had been 'messed about by other people'. By 1902 Greenwood's view was that the workhouse gave a pauper supper, bed and breakfast, and for those who resented or refused to

Sir Luke Fildes, *Applicants for Admission to a Casual Ward*, 1874, oil on canvas.

perform menial work in return it was the business of the court to discipline them.[16]

Whether Ellen Potts got the support she needed is doubtful. Eight years earlier two women were admitted to the City workhouse having not eaten for several days. Instead of the hot meal they craved all they were given was 'a small bit of dry bread'. Their reaction was to start breaking windows and pulling out the fittings in the hope that they would be convicted of 'wilful damage' and sent to prison. The women's actions were made in desperation, something the alderman magistrate acknowledged. However, while bemoaning the fact that 'a gaol should be sought after as a superior refuge to the workhouse', he still sent them to gaol for two months. The overseer of the poor admitted conditions were bad but said that the workhouse was overwhelmed with paupers seeking shelter at night, with more than fifty asking for relief every evening.[17] It was not uncommon for poor Londoners to damage property to draw attention to their plight. Before 1834 those seeking relief sometimes smashed windows and attacked property in the hope that a magistrate might send them to prison or give them alms from the poor box. Mr Bennett at Thames, giving evidence to the Royal Commission on the Poor Laws in 1834, complained

> of being forced to deal with over 100 applicants a day and, because of the refusal of the Shoreditch overseers to provide relief for the casual poor who applied late at night, it was not unusual for him to have to sit to 10 or 11 p.m. issuing orders for relief.[18]

The principle that a person applying for relief had to be genuinely unable to support themselves through other means may well have led some applicants to hide any 'wealth' they had. In August 1860 an elderly lady went to court to ask the advice of the Lambeth magistrate, Mr Elliot. Mrs Till (who was probably widowed and certainly alone) told the justice that on 4 April she had pledged 8*s* with a pawnbroker for sixpence. The magistrate was puzzled; why would she hand over 8 shillings only to take 6 pennies in return? Till replied: 'The fact was, your Worship, that I was going into the workhouse, and knowing that the money would be taken from me I adopted that manner of securing it.' Rather than pawning her money she had in effect deposited it so that the authorities could not use it to pay for her care. The court usher confirmed the practice, telling the court that when paupers entered the workhouse they were stripped and their clothes washed. Any money found on them was 'appropriated to their support'. Mrs Till said she could hide 6*d* in her mouth so the inspectors would not find it. Having been discharged from the workhouse she was now having trouble getting her money back. The pawnbroker was denying her the money because she could not state exactly which coins constituted those she had pledged. The usher said he was familiar with the pawnbroker, who was a 'respectable' man, and with his Worship's leave he would speak to him and get the money back.[19]

Given the horrors of the workhouse it was seen as a place to be avoided at all costs, even if this meant homelessness and a reliance on begging to survive. Begging was illegal in Victorian Britain under the terms of the 1824 Vagrancy Act, which criminalized begging and homelessness by making it an offence punishable with imprisonment to be found on the streets or in 'any deserted or unoccupied building' and 'not giving a good account of himself or herself'.[20] The police could prosecute anyone apprehended in this way as 'idle and disorderly'. Any resistance would compound their offence and could increase the punishment. The act made it a crime to be poor by stipulating that any able person who 'wilfully' refused work was liable to a month in prison.[21] Beggars and those sleeping rough became a target for the New Police tasked with keeping the streets clear and with imposing the order and discipline that urban improvement demanded. Yet the police were not the only enemies of the poor: independent citizens also took it into their own hands to attempt to remove the problem of begging in London.

Formed in 1818, the Society for the Suppression of Mendicity had a straightforward objective: to prevent people begging. It tried to move beggars off the streets and out of the capital, if possible, by giving them small amounts of charity. The Society preferred not to give money, instead offering tickets that recipients could exchange for an investigation into their circumstances. In 1850 a note explained their methodology:

> The society gives meals and money, supplies, mill and other work to applicants, investigates begging-letter cases, and apprehends vagrants and impostors. Each meal consists of ten ounces of bread, and one pint of good soup, or a quarter of a pound of cheese. The affairs of the Society are administered by a Board of forty-eight managers. The Mendicity Society's tickets, given to a street beggar, will procure for him, if really necessitous, food and work. They are a touch-stone to impostures: the beggar by profession throws them aside.[22]

This was designed to root out those they saw as fraudsters, who would not want to have their case considered. Men like William Horsford worked as Mendicity Society officers, looking out for beggars on the streets and taking them before magistrates to be prosecuted under the Vagrancy Act. In early December 1839 Horsford was following two persons he believed to be 'incorrigible beggars', Edward Johnson (aka Watson) and Mary Carrol. Mary had dressed in widow's weeds to make herself look as desperate as possible in order to attract sympathy from passers-by, while Johnson was described as a 'miserable wretch'. Horsford had spotted the pair in Pall Mall and followed them through St James's

Park to a public house in Pimlico. They left the pub after an hour and moved on to Sloane Square, where they started to knock on doors. At one house, where the lady resident had a reputation for charity, Carrol thrust a letter at the servant who opened the door. When the servant sent them away without accepting it, they tried their luck at a chemist's shop. Horsford entered behind them and, as they tried to extort money, seized them. The pair appeared before Mr Burrell at Queen's Square and the letter was read out. It described Mary as a 'widow afflicted with rheumatism and divers [*sic*] other complaints', adding that she had 'a large family, and that her husband had been killed but a few weeks ago by a gentleman's carriage running over him'. It was signed 'Mr Churton of Ebury Street' and urged the reader to assist Mary in any way they could. Johnson had several other letters on his person, each addressed to a different well-heeled recipient, including the Bishop of London, Marquess of Londonderry and Countess of Ripon, and carrying its own particular tale of 'distressing accidents and dreadful diseases'. Johnson admitted writing the letters and justified it by stating that Mary was a deserving case, and he was only trying to help. The magistrate had no sympathy and sent them to prison for three months.[23]

At the end of June 1886 two individuals were brought up at Lambeth for begging. On the previous evening Joseph Boseley from the Mendicity Society had been watching them in Camberwell. Both appeared to be women and they clutched an open Bible. As passers-by approached they would ask for a donation, which, if forthcoming, was rewarded with a verse of scripture. However, when their requests for alms were ignored or refused, they behaved in ways that led Boseley to suspect they were not as pious as their 'act' suggested. Having been after them for weeks he arrested them for impersonation. Despite outward appearances, one of the pair was actually a man dressed up as a woman, which was presumed by Boseley to be a ruse, as a pair of females asking for charitable donations to a 'good cause' seemed more believable. Mary Ann

Saunders was 55 and her partner, Henry Bennett, ten years younger. Bennett was set in the dock still wearing 'female clothing, with hat and ribbons, and hair hanging down his back'. When questioned he continued to speak in a high-pitched impersonation of a female voice, as he had been doing as he stood beside the road in Camberwell. Boseley told the magistrate, Mr Biron, that there had been multiple complaints about the duo and that they 'were old mendicants'. Saunders could often be seen pushing Bennett around in 'a perambulator', always dressed as a woman and always begging. He saw them as a couple of charlatans entirely undeserving of public sympathy, let alone their money. Biron remanded them for further enquiries.[24] Bennett fainted in the dock, which the papers saw as yet another example of imposture and an opportunity to poke fun at him for the amusement of its readership. On 9 July they were brought up again and the magistrate sent them both to prison for a month for begging, declaring them to be 'rank imposters'. As he was led away Bennett cried out: 'A month, what for? I didn't beg; I only give bits of scripture comfort.'[25]

The newspaper reports reveal that malingerers were brought before the magistracy to be punished for begging with great regularity. Indeed, the frequent reporting of those who were 'shamming' is likely to have reinforced the idea that many of those asking for help did not need or deserve it. The distrust of beggars and those claiming welfare benefits has a long history and persists today.[26] But the courts also helped the poor, handing out small sums of money, and were not averse to taking to task those who abused paupers in their care. In May 1868 the Thames Police court was graced with the presence of the 5th Marquess Townshend, the former Liberal MP for Tamworth, who enjoyed a reputation as 'the pauper's friend'. Townshend was a reforming politician who made it his business to know what was happening in the capital's workhouses. He was in court in 1868 to point out the mistreatment of a young lad in the casual ward of the Ratcliffe workhouse in Stepney,

East London. The anonymous young man had been released onto the streets wearing a rough canvas suit of clothes that was printed with the following text: 'Jack from the country' on the back of the jacket and 'Lazy scamp' on one trouser leg. The intention was clear: after leaving the ward he would be exposed to ridicule in the streets, presumably deliberately to deter him from ever seeking asylum there again. Having been presented with this disturbing scene, Mr Paget sent a runner to bring Wilding, the labour master and superintendent of the Ratcliffe workhouse, to answer for himself. Wilding claimed to have followed the rules. The lad had been given food and shelter but had chosen to cut up his own clothes and so had nothing to wear. Consequently he had been provided with a rough canvas suit. He marked the suit accordingly as an appropriate punishent. The pauper explained that the reason he had ripped up his clothes was 'that he could not wear them any longer, [since] they were very dirty and covered with vermin'. Paget sided with the pauper, perhaps out of a genuine sense of 'fair play' or possibly because of the presence of the marquess. He instructed the clerk of the court to send a letter to the Poor Law Board to report the misconduct of the labour master. Lord Townshend said he would also bring the matter up with the board: 'If paupers were thrust into the streets with such extraordinary comments and inscriptions on their garments it would ... give rise to inconvenience and breaches of the peace.' More practically, the marquess also undertook to provide the lad with a new set of clothes and a pair of boots. The canvas suit would be returned to the Ratcliffe workhouse, hopefully for disposal. The watching public gave him a rousing cheer as he left the courtroom; here was one small victory for the ordinary man over the hated keepers of the pauper 'bastilles'.[27]

So far this chapter has focused on the experience of poverty in its physical state. The poorest frequently went without food or had so little that they were malnourished. A lack of food and shelter brought very real and apparent physical problems, rendering those affected more susceptible to disease and early death. But it is very likely to have triggered or worsened mental health problems as well, although given the state of understanding in the Victorian period many sufferers would have received little or no support.

Suicide

For some the constant struggle to survive became all too much and the court records regularly feature those who reached the point of no return. The Thames and its bridges, the canals that criss-crossed the metropolis from east to west, and (from 1863) the newly laid-out underground railway all offered desperate people the opportunity to take their own life. Workplace and domestic poisons and the relatively easy availability of firearms added to the ways in which someone intent on suicide could achieve their aim. For those who failed, however, an appearance at a police court often followed. In many ways, however desperate the stories of these individuals, the tales described in this chapter are of the 'lucky' ones who survived to fight another day.

The act of taking one's own life (suicide) was a crime in both civil and religious law until 1961.[28] However, the law required that a person accused of suicide was committing the action deliberately: *felo de se* in law (felon of him or herself). In medieval law this entailed the forfeiture of property to the monarch and denied the deceased a Christian burial in consecrated ground. However, by the Victorian period the practice of seizing the property of suicides had long disappeared and suicides were almost invariably deemed to be 'of unsound mind' (non compos mentis) by coroners at inquest. The second stipulation regarding suicides, the refusal of a traditional Christian burial, was more relevant for the general population given that only a relative minority had substantive goods that might be forfeited. Until 1823 those taking their own lives could not be buried by a clergyman of the Church of England or interred in a consecrated graveyard. They were, in effect, denied the burial rights that most people believed ensured them the 'sure and certain hope of resurrection'. In practice this meant that suicides were buried outside of graveyards and in some cases at parish boundaries or crossroads, akin to the manner of burial of executed criminals.

One dramatic example of this was the burial of John Williams's body at the junction of Cable Street and Cannon Street Road in 1811. Williams had stood accused of the murder of two households (the Marrs and the Williamsons) twelve nights apart on the Ratcliffe Highway and nearby on New Gravel Lane in one of the most sensational murder cases of the period. Williams, whose guilt was far from established, supposedly took his own life as he awaited trial. His dead body was paraded along the Ratcliffe Highway in Wapping before being buried in a shallow grave with a stake driven through his heart.[29] Williams may have been one of the last individuals to suffer such an ignominy and even by 1811 such burials were extremely rare. In 1823 the law was changed to allow for private burial in a parish burial ground, albeit without Christian rites.[30] It also removed the necessity to drive a stake through the corpse's heart. In 1880 legislation made it possible for suicides to be buried with rites on Church land so long as the service was silent; in 1882 the silent aspect was removed.[31]

Although suicide was a crime for many centuries, the act of attempting to take one's life was not. Action was normally taken to help those who had tried to kill themselves, or at least efforts were made to ensure they could not try again, but it was not an offence in law. Until the 1830s, as MacDonald and Murphy point out, 'arrests for attempted suicide itself seem to have been rare.'[32] It is probably no coincidence that the rate of arrests of those bent on self-destruction rose with the establishment of the New Police.[33] As Olive Anderson writes: 'Only the advent of the new police made it practicable routinely to treat attempted suicide as an offence.'[34] Once arrested by a policeman (who had either seen the attempt, had been alerted to it by a passing 'good Samaritan' or was called to take charge of a rescued attempter), the culprit would be processed at the station house before being taken before a magistrate, usually the following day. They were kept overnight so they could sober up (if they had been drunk) rather than being quickly released (as some other drunks were by City of London police). It is also notable that the police chose to charge them with attempted suicide rather than the more common, and easier to prove, offence of being drunk and disorderly or incapable.

A total of 26 persons are recorded in the Thames register as being brought before the magistrate accused of attempting suicide in the period from March to the middle of November 1881. This represents less than five months (since the register covers just six alternate months), so there were approximately five per month or just over sixty in any given calendar year. Given that this includes only those individuals whom police or others chose to prosecute, or those that were discovered, and only those brought to the Thames Police court, we can be fairly sure that attempted suicide was not uncommon in late Victorian London. As will become clear, the majority of those arrested for attempted suicide were very similar to many others brought before the police courts for other crimes that reflected social problems in the Victorian city. As Anderson comments, 'the petty offenders who were the chief target of the new police overlapped with many of the sorts of people who were prone to make suicide attempts.' We should see these attempts in context, she argues, as often being a by-product of the drunkenness and violence that loomed so large in the street life of early nineteenth-century London. Here too were those who rejected the alternatives offered to them when they had reached the point of absolute despair – the workhouse casual ward or a visit to a parish relieving officer – or, as Anderson argues, 'sometimes they were begging dodges, like the feigned war wounds, dependent families, and other plots used by beggars'.[35]

Of the 26 individuals prosecuted at Thames all but a handful were simply discharged. This is in line with studies of mid-Victorian London, which show that despite a supposed 'crackdown on suicide attempts in public spaces' most police court magistrates took a lenient approach.[36] Very few were sent on to face a trial by jury (despite attempted suicide being an indictable offence that was liable to a maximum sentence of two years in prison).[37] Annie Walker, who was just twelve years of age, was sent to the workhouse for a week, as was Elizabeth Edwards (aged 38).[38] They were probably treated as pauper lunatics in the first instance, the workhouse providing temporary refuge if not much in terms of skilled care. Walker's example echoes that of an eleven-year-old girl called Sarah Gould who was prosecuted in 1849. Gould was seen running down the steps at London Bridge near Fenning's Wharf at five o'clock on 16 July. She jumped into the river and was swept under a passing barge. A policeman saw what happened and managed to get help to drag her to safety. When she finally recovered consciousness, she told the officer that she was driven to the act by the abuse meted out to her by her mother. The Southwark magistrate ordered that she be confined in gaol for 'a few days' so she could be examined by a surgeon and cared for by a 'minister of the Gospel'. He had decided that her mind 'was disordered' and this was the best way to prevent her attempting her life again.[39] No consideration appears to have been given for exploring her reasons for self-destruction. Thomas Bevan, 37, was committed to the Sessions, the only one of the defendants to be sent there.[40] Several of the accused were remanded, most for a week so their circumstances could be checked; invariably they were then released without further action.

Also in 1849, over in Westminster, one defendant – Kate Sliptrott, a 28-year-old tailoress – was detained so that she might 'have the benefit of good advice' from the prison chaplain before being released into the care of her employer. Sliptrott had admitted to taking poison after the death of her common law husband to whom she was 'devoted'.[41] Selina Athaway, 35, was convicted of assault in the course of her arrest, and it was probably this offence (not the attempt on her own life) that brought her a sentence of seven days' hard labour. Eliza Welsh was punished similarly, earning ten days in gaol for being drunk and disorderly and assaulting the officer who arrested her. William Wharron, 23, was convicted of being drunk and attempting suicide and was fined 40s, which he paid. Edward Allen, also 23, was less fortunate: he was unable to pay his fine of 5s for assaulting the person that discovered him attempting suicide and so went to prison for five days instead.[42] Few of these 26 cases made the pages of the newspapers (perhaps itself a reflection of how commonplace attempts like these were), but in early March 1881 (before the register commences) the case of Jane Shipley was reported. Shipley, a young woman who appeared at Thames court looking very unwell, had been seen at two o'clock in the morning running towards a bridge that crossed the Regent's Canal. PC Alexander Harvey saw Shipley turn down Longfellow Road, tear off her bonnet and jump over a wall. He rushed over and found her collapsed on the footpath; she had leapt 4 to 6 metres (15–20 ft) but missed the water. With help he managed to get her to the London Hospital for treatment. The magistrate remanded her to the workhouse 'against her wish', the paper recorded.[43] Elizabeth Jones threw herself into the London Dock in May 1881, claiming she was being followed. The actions of a brave passer-by and PC Curtis of H Division saved her life. Curtis had thrown a rope to the woman, but she refused his help. James Connor snaked down the rope and held her afloat until a police boat arrived to bring her to safety. It was the daring nature of the rescue, and the fact that Connor was so badly injured in the effort that he was laid off work, that rendered this story 'newsworthy'. Jones, described as 'an unfortunate' (a prostitute), claimed that she had been followed by four men and bitten by a large dog, and said she had jumped to escape and would do so again. Mr Lushington ordered that the young woman's mental health be investigated before she was released.[44] The intention of Lushington and his fellow magistrates at Thames would seem to support Anderson's argument that the aim of the authorities of the day was not to punish those attempting suicide. Instead they worked to 'promote public order, and then to identify suicide-prone individuals and channel towards them the attention of the social workers of the day'.[45] How successful that policy was is open to debate.

While it was largely an accepted 'truth' that the 'weakness' of women's minds was more likely to drive them to take their own lives, the reality was that men 'committed' (or attempted) suicide more frequently. However, gendering suicide in this way to make it a 'female malady' (as Elaine Showalter has dubbed madness in the 1800s) fitted contemporary tropes more closely.[46] While men do feature in newspaper reports of attempted suicide, it is more common for the examples to be of young women and for the act to be one of drowning rather than hanging, shooting or other forms of self-harm. Moreover, within the proliferation of popular print culture in the 1800s were very many examples of young women ending or attempting to end their lives by leaping into a canal or river.

In London certain spots were closely associated in the public consciousness with suicide: 'the Regent's Canal, the swing bridges over the Docks, the stretch of the Thames between London and Westminster Bridges, or the Hampstead and Highgate ponds'.[47] When Sarah Keyworth tried to jump off Westminster Bridge she was providing the *Morning Post*'s reporter with exactly the copy he needed to reinforce the weakness of the 'fairer sex' in the minds of his readership. A gentleman named Houghton saw Sarah, 'a respectable-looking young woman', running along Westminster Bridge. Mr Houghton testified at Southwark Police court that the woman was 'calling out in a frantic manner' before she 'suddenly stopped and climbed over the railings of the bridge'. He must have feared that she was about to jump and so grabbed hold of her. She struggled, saying 'let me go, let me go!', but he held on until a policeman arrived to help. Sarah was taken to a police station and brought up before the magistrate in the morning. At her first hearing she was described as 'sullen' and said she had fully intended to have 'destroyed herself and was sorry the gentleman had interfered'. Mr Woolrych remanded her and instructed the prison chaplain to visit her. She was back up in court a week later, and this time her sister was there to support her. Keyworth was repentant, and through floods of tears she said, 'she was very sorry for such an attempt on her life. She knew the wickedness of it and promised never to do it again.' Her sister said she could only imagine she had been driven to it after 'words with her young man'. She promised to look after her and the magistrate admonished Sarah and let her go without any further action.[48] The procedure the magistrate followed here

Paddington Canal, 1820, illustration from Walter Thornbury,
Old and New London (1873–8).

was fairly typical. Keyworth had attempted her life in a moment of
seemingly desperate unhappiness. The Victorians did not understand
mental health as well as twenty-first-century society claims to, but
asking for the chaplain to assess or give succour to someone who
had tried to kill themselves is in keeping with attitudes towards this
manifestation of 'madness'. Those attempting to kill themselves were
sometimes referred for medical assistance and then prosecuted
merely for a misdemeanour. In most cases the accused was
remanded so that enquiries could be made into their mental health
and character with the aim of ensuring that they did not repeat
their actions.

While sex workers were among the most common victims of
suicide, they were not alone in deciding that the world that they
inhabited offered them little hope. As PC 99 of L Division made his
usual patrol by the Surrey side of Blackfriars Bridge, he saw a
woman sitting on the steps by the water. As he approached, he could
see that she was in considerable distress and asked her what she was
up to. Elizabeth Briant, a woman described as 'elderly' by the court
reporter, told the constable that she had been so 'cruelly beaten by
the man whom she had lived with for thirty-eight years that she was
tired of her existence'. When he found her she admitted that she
was working up the courage to throw herself into the river to drown.
Given that attempting suicide was a crime, the policeman arrested
her and the next day she was brought before the magistrate at
Southwark. Elizabeth cut a forlorn figure in the dock, her arms and
face covered with bruises. She told the magistrate that on the previous Saturday her husband had 'knocked her down, kicked her, and
blackened both eyes' before throwing her out to 'starve in the streets'.
The magistrate asked her if she had any children, and she told him
she had eight, 'but only one was living, and she hoped he was serving Her Majesty in India'. She had lost seven sons or daughters
and her only surviving son was thousands of miles away. There was
little the justice could do except order the arrest of the husband

and send the poor woman to the workhouse to be cared for. Once there, she would probably not expect or be able to support herself sufficiently to leave and was therefore effectively being condemned to live out the remainder of her days as an institutional pauper.[49] Elizabeth Briant was rejecting the alternatives society offered women in her situation. Poor, bereaved and without a family to help her, all she could do was turn to the parish for support. She connects with a number of the 'paths to suicide' identified by Anderson among female suicides in mid-Victorian London: 'drink; bodily and mental illness; unemployment and business troubles; public disgrace and private self-reproaches; and family strains, emotional disappointment, and bereavement.'[50] These examples offer glimpses into the lives of others, like Emma Elizabeth Rogers, who tragically succeeded in taking their own lives and who have left us no clear sense of what led them to such desperate action. Roger's body was recovered from the Thames at Stoney Deep, Twickenham. The coroner's jury attributed her death to 'being at the time of the commission of the said act in a state of unsound mind'.[51]

Not all accusations of attempted suicide resulted in convictions, as the majority of the 26 cases at Thames in 1881 show. Of these, nine were discharged once an explanation had been given, while most of the rest were discharged after a short spell on remand or a visit to the workhouse for further examination. Only five resulted in either a committal to a jury court or a form of punishment (a fine or imprisonment). This reflects the probability that in most cases these were desperate acts quickly regretted or cries for help, not serious attempts at self-destruction.

Sections of the London Underground railway have operated since the 1860s and throughout its existence it has been associated with suicide attempts and tragic deaths. According to one piece of research, suicide on the railway increased after 1868 (just five years after the first train ran) when newspapers published details of the methods would-be suicides used, thereby highlighting a form of self-slaughter that may otherwise have remained clandestine.[52] On 27 June 1893 Isaac Shelton, a 63-year-old 'house decorator' who lived on the Edgware Road, was seen entering the tunnel at Baker Street underground station, heading for Edgware Road. It was 5.45 p.m. and a fellow passenger shouted to him but was ignored. As Shelton entered the tunnel a train was arriving in the station. Fortunately, since he had been seen, the driver was alerted and the service detained. The station inspector (a Mr Coleman) was summoned to the platform, while in the meantime a young man named Albert Swift set off in pursuit of Shelton. Directed by the sounds of someone scrambling about, Swift found Shelton 'about 150 yards into the tunnel, lying across the metals of the upline'. He tried to get the man's attention and lift him up, but all he got back was the request to 'Leave me alone, I'm going home.' Coleman and a porter soon arrived to assist and eventually the three of them managed to drag Shelton up and off the tracks and back out to safety. He seemed 'sober, but excited', they later testified. The case came before the Marylebone magistrate, Mr Plowden. Shelton claimed he had no recollection of how he had got where he was. He said he had been having epileptic fits for twenty years and one had come on as he made his way home that evening. His wife appeared and confirmed that her husband suffered from epilepsy and was subject to fits. Shelton may have suffered from epilepsy, but in this scenario it seems much more likely that he was overcome by despair and sought a way out of his misery. It appears that this was also the opinion of the justice, who remanded Shelton in custody to seek a medical opinion on his condition.[53]

Joseph Nadall was an unfortunate person. Having failed to kill himself in March 1866 he found himself in the dock of the Worship Street Police court before Mr Ellison. Nadall, a 35-year-old labourer, was described as being 'without hope'. He had taken poison and when found was taken to the police station, where he was examined by a Portuguese-born surgeon, Mr James Sequir. The doctor found him in a 'very prostrate condition and suffering greatly' and quickly administered an emetic followed by an antidote. When sufficiently recovered Nadall told him he had gone to a rag shop where he had bought a small bottle and 'two pennyworth' of oxalic acid. He took these to a water pump in the street and added some water. Having mixed his potion he 'drank it off'. The magistrate inquired as to exactly how much oxalic acid was required for a dose to be fatal. 'About half an ounce', replied the surgeon, adding that this would cost between a penny and twopence.[54]

The hearing next turned to who had supplied the poison. A teenage lad admitted selling Nadall the acid and told the justice that he was 'in the habit of serving these packets to shoemakers and others, who use it in their trade'. He explained that 'the packets are 1*d* each, and I gave him two of them.' The magistrate was then shown a similar blue packet labelled as 'Shoemaker's poison'. Mr Ellison was surprised and concerned that the young assistant had not asked any questions of Nadall and had not objected to selling him poison when he clearly did not resemble a shoemaker. The lad's master, Mr Blackwell, now felt the full force of the magistrate's anger: 'This boy of yours has acted with great incautiousness – very great ... Poisons should never be sold without at least inquiry being made as to the purpose for which they are wanted.' Blackwell tried to explain that he always told the lad to ask questions before he sold anything, but there was little conviction in his words. He and his boy had not broken any laws and so having been publicly rebuked they were free to go. As for Joseph Nadall, he explained that he was 'impelled to the attempt on his life by reduced circumstances'. In other words, it was poverty and unemployment that had driven him to such drastic action. Mr Ellison had little sympathy. 'You should have applied to the parish,' he told him and remanded him in custody while he decided what to do with him.[55] Once again Anderson's observation that attempted suicide 'expressed dogged resistance to the workhouse system' is evident.[56]

Poison was the method of choice for most men attempting suicide in Southwark in the 1860s and, along with cutting or stabbing themselves, probably offered more chance of intervention than some other forms of self-murder.[57] Those resorting to poison or knives might survive long enough to be taken to hospital, although contemporary medicine might not then be capable of saving their lives. Daniel Davidson did not employ an over-the-counter poison in his attempt to end his life but resorted instead to noxious fumes. The shoemaker was charged at Bow Street in May 1847 after one of his neighbours noticed the smell of smoke emanating from the room above him. When the smell became overpowering the resident ran upstairs and forced his way into Davidson's room. He found the shoemaker struggling for breath, lying on his bed. There was a pile of burning charcoal in a pan in the middle of the room and all the windows were shut. This was not the first time that Davidson had tried to kill himself; the assistant relieving officer from the Strand Union testified to that effect before a medical certificate was secured that declared the poor man to be insane. The parish authorities took him away, presumably to be locked away in an asylum.[58]

In May 1893 the press reported a tragic case from Hackney. Police were alerted when two servant girls ran out of a house in Amhurst Road shouting that 'something was wrong'. A police sergeant from J Division entered the house and soon heard cries of distress emanating from a back room on one of the upper floors. Forcing the door open he discovered a man and a woman in bed. The woman was dead, with an obvious bullet wound to the head. The man was barely alive and was wounded in at least three places, his stomach, groin and thigh. The man was Thomas Morgan and the woman was his wife. A further search found Morgan's fifteen-year-old stepson Arthur Jennings, who had also been shot through the head. His condition suggested he had been shot while he was asleep, having retired to bed early that evening after competing in a running race that day. Thomas Morgan was known to have been suffering from poor mental health brought on by 'sunstroke' and 'paralysis', and he was taken away to the German Hospital in Ritson Road to see if his life could be saved.[59] He died soon afterwards and more information about the incident emerged in the aftermath. The two servant girls, Louisa Woolley and Maud Austin, both seventeen, gave statements that their master and mistress had been on 'bad terms' for some times. The couple hardly spoke to each other anymore, communicating merely 'by signs'. It was Louisa who discovered Arthur's body and raised the alarm having found the door to the bedroom locked.[60] Morgan's wounds were severe and he died in some agony, the press recorded.[61]

The coroner's jury found that Morgan had murdered his wife and stepson and then committed suicide 'whilst temporarily insane'. It seems possible that at some point Thomas Morgan had suffered a stroke that had rendered him partially disabled and affected his mind. The couple had been out during the day of the shootings and Morgan had consumed some alcohol. Whether this provoked an argument that tipped him into such drastic action is impossible to know, but he was a man with a reputation for beating his wife and on this occasion it seems he finally lost any control he had previously possessed. The 'Hackney Tragedy', as it was dubbed, was newsworthy in part because the Morgans were lower middle-class businesspeople, running a coffee shop and living above it. They kept two servants and were to all appearances 'respectable'. Thomas Morgan was not the typical suicide but his violence towards his wife and child were all too common. Had he lived Morgan would probably have avoided trial by virtue of being deemed insane. Most of those making attempts on their lives were treated leniently by the magistracy; from the 1890s they were frequently handed over to the care of the Police Court Missionaries, before the formation in 1907 of the Salvation Army's Anti-Suicide Bureau based at 101 Queen Victoria Street.[62]

Locking up a vulnerable person who had attempted to take their own life in a prison or workhouse for a week or two might seem callous through modern eyes. Anderson, however, points out that it may not have been when seen in the context of available services for those who turned to such a desperate action. 'Safety first' operated, isolating the individual in a secure environment where they might get some sort of expert help (from the prison chaplain and surgeon), while also obtaining a report for the magistrate to help inform what support was available for the person once released from such care. Once again, remand seems to have been the most effective weapon in the armoury of police court magistrates and was something they routinely deployed in dealing with attempted suicides.

Poor mental health impacted individuals in nineteenth-century London for a variety of reasons, not all of which have been included here. There were, for example, suicide attempts by those whose relationships had broken down, or whose love was unrequited. But at the heart of most of these acts was desperation, an inability to cope or a refusal to accept what pauperism meant in the 1800s. The courts frequently bore witness to the devastating impact that poverty had on the lives of those who had committed no crime, but had simply been unable to find work or work that paid enough to put food on the table and a roof over their heads. The poor turned to the courts because they often had nowhere else to go even after 1864, when the casual wards system was supposed to operate more effectively. They clearly believed, perhaps with some justification, that police court magistrates were more likely to help them than poor law officials. Regardless of the efforts of justices who handed out money from the poor box, there was no effective safety net in Victorian London and the prevailing attitude that saw poverty as an individual character flaw to be punished, rather than a social problem to be solved, ensured that any system for properly supporting people would not be created until 1945 and the election of a socialist government. Henry Hyndman may have been inaccurate in his estimations of poverty levels in 1885 but he was not wrong about the cause, which was capitalism.

8

POLITICS, RIOT AND TRADE UNIONISM

Having enjoyed several decades of relative stability following the failure of the Chartist movement to substantially reset the balance of power, the British state was set for a significantly more challenging period in the last quarter of the century. London became a haven for foreign revolutionaries who feared incarceration for their political actions and provided asylum for thousands of Jewish refugees from the Russian Pale of Settlement, many bringing radical political views with them. The British state also had problems much closer to home. The 1880s saw a renewal of the 'dynamite war' as Irish republicans set off bombs in London and other cities in their campaign for an independent Ireland. Chartism may have failed, but economic downturn in the 1880s, unemployment and concomitant increases in poverty and homelessness brought thousands of Londoners onto the streets. Rioting in 1886 led to heavy-handed policing of demonstrations the following year, with multiple injuries and a handful of fatalities. Gareth Stedman Jones has identified this as a period of anxiety for the governing classes.[1]

While in many ways the police courts can be seen as useful arenas of negotiation for working-class people, when it came to protests, rioting and other expressions of political independence the magistracy most often lined up on the side of the state. One obvious example of this was the prosecution of striking workers in the late 1880s as organized labour flexed its muscles. Alongside the more everyday business of the courts – petty crime, drunkenness, assault and standard regulation – there were sporadic moments that reflect the underlying radicalism of some elements of a working class that chafed under the yoke that held it in servitude. The records of business at the police courts reveal a culture of resistance that had deep roots and long traditions.

The Fenian 'dynamiters'

In May 1867 John Jones had been released from imprisonment on a ticket-of-leave and returned to his family in London. His licence required that he report to the police within 48 hours of being released and that he carry his ticket-of-leave on him at all times. Thereafter Jones was required to report monthly to his nearest police station. He was expected always to sleep at his stated address and no other, as the police were supposed to be able to find him if they needed to. This close relationship with the police must have made it difficult for a convicted criminal to return to normal life. The prison stamp would have been on Jones following his release: the deathly pallor, close-cropped hair, poor constitution and sunken eyes, all products of the 'hard labour, hard bed, hard fare' policies of Edmund Du Cane's prison system, would have marked him out as an ex-convict.[2] With little opportunity to re-join 'straight' society Jones would naturally have gravitated back to the 'criminal class' that Mayhew and Binney had described in their writings.[3]

In late November PC Harry Shaw noticed Jones in Golden Lane, Clerkenwell, speaking with a group of men the officer knew to be convicted thieves. According to the officer's testimony at Clerkenwell Police court, Jones had gone to express his sympathy 'with the relatives of three men who had been hanged at Manchester on the previous day'. These were the so-called 'Manchester Martyrs': William Philip Allen, Michael Larkin and Michael O'Brian. All three were members of the Irish Republican Brotherhood and had been part of a crowd of more than thirty who had attacked a police van carrying fellow 'Fenians' to gaol. In the attempt to rescue the prisoners Police Sergeant Charles Brett was killed.[4] Two of the five men convicted of Brett's murder had their death sentences over-turned. Allen, Larkin and O'Brian were not so fortunate and were hanged in front of a huge crowd at Salford Gaol on 23 November 1867. This was one of the very last public hangings to take place in England. Karl Marx remarked that the hangings served the cause of Irish nationalism better than many an act of terrorism because it gave them martyrs to act as inspiration for the next generation of freedom fighters. Understandably though, anyone celebrating those responsible for the death of a fellow police officer was unlikely to earn much sympathy from a serving constable. Jones had joined a procession of men and women who marched from Clerkenwell Green to Hyde Park. PC Shaw followed to keep an eye on them. As he 'dodged' in and out of the crowd the constable suspected he was trying to pick pockets but had no definite proof. In the end he collared Jones and cautioned him, demanding to see his ticket-of-leave. Unable to produce it he was summoned to appear to explain himself.

In early December a 'rough'-looking Jones presented himself before the sitting justice. He said little, as 'it was no use for him to speak, there [being] no justice for a ticket-of-leave man'. The police 'had entered into a conspiracy to injure him, and he could do nothing', he complained. The magistrate asked to see his licence and he was remanded in custody so that one of his friends could fetch it.[5] Within days Clerkenwell itself experienced the full force of Fenian terror as conspirators attempted to break their fellow nationalists out of prison by blowing open the gate of the prison. On 13 December twelve people were killed and more than a hundred were injured in what *The Times* described as 'a crime of unexampled atrocity'. Eight men were charged, two of whom turned Queen's evidence against the others. Two more were acquitted by the Grand jury and in the end only Michael Barrett was held responsible for the bombing. On 26 May 1868 Barrett earned the dubious honour of being the last man to be publicly hanged in England as William Calcraft 'dropped' him outside Newgate Gaol.[6]

In the wake of the bombing at Clerkenwell Marx commented that blowing up innocent civilians in London would not help the cause of Irish nationalism. He suggested rather that it would help the British government. His 1867 comment is eerily prescient to the modern ear: 'The London masses, who have shown great sympathy towards Ireland, will be made wild and driven into the arms of a reactionary government.'[7] In the 1880s the 'war' resulted in several terrorist attacks in the capital, none of which were very successful or had the impact of Clerkenwell. At the end of May 1884 the *Pall Mall Gazette* reported several incidents under the headline: 'Dynamite outrages in London'. Scotland Yard was attacked. A bomb was detonated in a toilet block behind the *Rising Sun* public house, knocking out all the lights in the pub and the nearby police lodgings. Several people were hurt, mostly by flying glass and debris, but no one was killed. The target was presumed to be near the headquarters of the CID or, more likely, the recently inaugurated Special Irish Branch. Almost instantaneously another explosion rocked Pall Mall as a bomb went off outside the Junior Carlton Club, a favourite of London's elite.[8] Nearby were the offices of the Intelligence Department of the War Office, which may have been the real target. Again, there was lots of broken glass and superficial damage but few casualties. A third bomb in St James's Square seems to have had similarly limited effects: several people were treated for cuts, but no one died.

The paper also reported that a terrorist attack on Trafalgar Square had been foiled: 'While all this excitement was going on, some boys, passing close to Nelson's Column, noticed a carpet bag reclining against the base of the pedestal.' The bag was seized by a vigilant policeman who thought the boys were trying to pinch it. He saw one of the boys aim a kick at the bag and probably thought they were about to run off with it. When the bag was examined, it was found to contain 'seventeen and a half cakes of what is believed to be dynamite, and a double fuse'.[9] Earlier that year there had been similar attacks at Victoria Station and other stations on the London Underground and in 1885 bombs were detonated at the Tower of London and Houses of Parliament. In 1884 a gang of Irish republicans blew themselves up on London Bridge while trying to set a fuse, which detonated accidentally.[10] In 1885 some of those responsible for the bomb attacks in London over the previous year were brought to trial at the Old Bailey. James Gilbert (alias Cunningham) and Harry Burton were convicted of treason after a long trial and sentenced to penal servitude for life.[11]

Policing protest: Trafalgar Square

Public demonstrations became commonplace in the 1880s as demands for Irish Home rule, support for socialism, protests against unemployment and declarations both for and against free trade brought thousands of people onto the capital's streets. The 1880s was a turbulent decade for poverty and austerity, and hundreds slept rough in the streets, squares and parks of the capital. Trafalgar Square was a focus for public gatherings from the 1840s, with the Chartists holding a demonstration there in 1848. Police regularly soused the benches in Trafalgar Square in the 1880s to deter the homeless from using them as beds and local residents demanded action to clear the area of the unwanted 'residuum' or 'dangerous classes'.

There were two occasions when the frequent manifestations of public discontent in the square ended in chaotic scenes and bloodletting. The first was the so-called West End riots in February 1886; the second was 'Bloody Sunday' in November 1887. Accounts of

Nelson's Column under construction in
Trafalgar Square, London, 1844, photograph.

both riots are open to interpretation as newspaper bias and the
inherent chaos of public demonstrations that fragment, as these
did, make any analysis problematic. A rally called by the Fair Trade
League in Trafalgar Square faced off against a counter demonstration organized by Henry Hyndman's Social Democratic Federation.
Policing was fairly inept. Since no mounted officers were stationed
in the square and the person in charge, Superintendent Walker,
was all but invisible (dressed as he was in plain clothes rather than
uniform), intelligence was limited at best. As a group of 'roughs'
moved off in the general direction of the West End police efforts
to head them off were undermined by confused instructions.
Reinforcements were sent to the Mall (to protect the Queen) and
not Pall Mall (as required) and so some sections of the crowd ran

riot among the fashionable shops and gentlemen's clubs, causing much damage and unnerving the government. Counter-accusations that members of Pall Mall's illustrious clubs had shouted abuse and provoked the 'mob' were reported but generally given short shrift.

As unemployment grew and London's parks and squares became impromptu hostels for the homeless and impoverished, the newly appointed commissioner of police, Sir Charles Warren, faced a dilemma. Warren took over from Sir Edmund Henderson, who had resigned in the wake of the West End debacle. Warren was determined not to allow such wanton lawlessness on his watch. He ordered his men to break up protests in Trafalgar Square and issued an edict to ban demonstrations there altogether. In doing so he fell foul of those championing the British right to freedom of speech and assembly, but he received plenty of encouragement from the establishment media as well. In the end radicals determined to test Warren's resolve by calling a meeting for 13 November in the square. Warren opted for strength and sent his officers in to break up the demonstration. The result was a pitched battle in Nelson's shadow. Around two hundred people were injured and a handful lost their lives, either immediately or in the aftermath by succumbing to injuries sustained. While *The Times* came out in support of Warren's decisive action, other elements of the press were critical, notably William Stead's *Pall Mall Gazette*. Ultimately the rioting did little or nothing to advance the cause of revolution, but it blighted Warren's stewardship of the Met and probably contributed to considerable press criticism of his approach when the Whitechapel murders terrified Londoners several months later.

The West End riots resulted in several prosecutions for 'breaking windows and rioting', the *Morning Post* reported. Others faced charges relating to looting, adding fuel to arguments at the time that the rioters were members of the criminal class and not politically motivated.[12] Over the course of the next few weeks a handful of individuals were committed for trial at the Surrey Sessions or at the Old Bailey. Frederick Barton and his son Thomas were tried for possession of counterfeit coin after a policeman had searched their premises in St Giles looking for goods stolen in the riots. Both were convicted despite Frederick taking full responsibility and exonerating Thomas, but both escaped gaol and instead were asked to enter into recognizances against their future behaviour.[13] The paucity of evidence of prosecutions in the aftermath of the West End riots suggests that the authorities were simply unable to identify rioters or those committing acts of larceny during the riots.

The capital has a long history of protests and riots. The Gordon Riots in June 1780 perhaps represent the single most destructive week in the city's history, outside of wartime, since the Great Fire of 1666. Protests occurred for all sorts of reasons: economic, religious, social and political. In June 1855 a bill was introduced to Parliament to close shops and suspend public transport on Sundays, to better enforce the observation of the Sabbath. Lord Robert Grosvenor presented the bill and it sparked a series of demonstrations by working-class Londoners, who attacked both the bill and the hypocrisy of the aristocratic class that sought to impose it. Jerry White described the scene of a 'mob' gathering '[a]long the carriage drives between the Serpentine and Kensington Gardens crowds . . . to hoot and hiss the phaetons of the rich and their Sabbath-breaking servants. There were cries of "Go to Church!" and horses were made to shy and bolt.'[14]

The disorder spread and on Sunday, 1 July, around 150,000 people turned out to protest. Lord Grosvenor's house was attacked and his windows smashed. The police eventually restored order after a baton charge but almost fifty constables were injured. In the aftermath of the riots against Lord Grosvenor's Sunday Trading Bill there were dozens of prosecutions before magistrates. On Sunday, 15 July, *Reynolds's Newspaper* reported several examples, including that of Charles Whitehouse, a lad of fourteen, who was present in the crowd gathered outside the peer's London home in Park Street.

The charge of smashing windows and causing criminal damage was brought by Inspector Webb, who described how he had seen the boy throw a stone towards Lord Grosvenor's window and went into the crowd to arrest him. Several of those assembled complained, saying that he had done nothing. As the inspector and a group of constables led Charles away there was a cry of 'Rescue!' and people in the crowd turned their fury on the police, pelting them with stones and anything else they could find. The attack was so violent that the police were forced to take refuge in the Mount Street workhouse. Two officers were so badly hurt they remained unable to return to duty. Webb explained how, while they sheltered in the workhouse,

> the mob became so furious, calling for the release of the boy, otherwise they would pull down the building, that it was thought advisable, to prevent more serious consequences, for the constables to sally out with their prisoners, and literally fight their way through the mob to the lock-up house.

In his defence the lad said that he had been forced to throw a stone by others in the crowd. This made no impression on the Marlborough Street magistrate, Mr Hardwick. Addressing the boy, he declared, 'You must have been very imperfectly educated to have done an act of malice to a person to whom you are a stranger and who never did you the least harm.' His words were aimed at any person present in court who might have been involved and, via the newspaper, the wider reading public. The boy's actions were serious, he said, and rioting, if proven, could result in a sentence of transportation to Australia.[15] If anyone came before him charged with inciting or organizing the rioting and stone throwing, he would commit them for trial. The boy's father appeared in court to see his son fined 40*s* for throwing just one stone. He was mortified, saying he had tried to prevent all three of his children from getting mixed up in the trouble. On the day he had taken two of his boys on a long walk as far away from the crowds as he could but had never thought that Charles was likely to get mixed up in it.[16]

Lord Grosvenor dropped his unpopular Sunday Trading bill and peace returned to the capital's streets. Three years earlier, during the 1852 General Election, Radicals stood candidates against the Whigs and the Tories in the two seats that served the London constituency of Middlesex. The Radicals were a splinter group of the Whigs dedicated to extending the franchise to include the working classes and agitators against the hated Corn Laws, which kept food prices high for the poorest. Middlesex had been a hotbed of radical politics from at least the late 1600s, most famously in 1768 when widespread rioting accompanied the election of John Wilkes. In 1852 there were more political riots there as supporters of the Radical candidate Ralph Bernal Osborne clashed with those of his Tory counterpart, John Spencer-Churchill, Marquess of Blandford, during the campaign to be the constituency's second MP (the Whig candidate was the clear winner in first place). An effigy of the marquess was carried through the streets along with a stuffed fox on a pole labelled 'a Derby puppet'. Lord Derby had become prime minister in February 1852 following the fall of Lord John Russell's Whig ministry. It was a minority government and it too collapsed in December that year. The riots resulted in a series of arrests and led to three men appearing before Mr Paynter at Hammersmith. All were working class. Thomas Hall, 25, was a sweep; Edward Hewett, 33, and William Cook, 19, were labourers. After the poll closed disturbances erupted at Hammersmith and police stationed to keep order were attacked. Some of the police were in plain clothes, watching the crowd, and Hall was seen parading with the stuffed fox. PC John Jones testified to being assaulted by Hall, adding that as he tried to make an arrest a 'mob' closed in on him. PC Petit went to help and was thrown to the ground by Hall and kicked in the face, leaving bruises visible in court. The other two defendants joined in the fracas. PC John Searle was threatened by Cook, who carried a large stick that had been used to display a flag. The police had taken the men into custody after a struggle and at the station the men had bragged that any fine they got would be paid by the candidate they had supported, Ralph Osborne. Gangs of 'roughs' were a feature of election campaigns in the period, and intimidation was common in elections since there were no secret ballots until 1872. The magistrate established that none of the trio was a voter and the police said all were known ruffians who had appeared for assault before. It is possible that the Radicals hired them, as the trio later claimed, although they would undoubtedly have denied this. Even if Osborne had agreed to pay any fines it did not help the men. Paynter told them their behaviour was 'disgraceful' and said they had 'interfered with the freedom of the election' by preventing voters from going to the hustings. He sentenced Cook to a month in gaol and the others to three weeks each.[17]

Trades unions, pickets and industrial disputes

The biggest single industrial dispute of the 1880s was the dock strike that broke out in August 1889. The strike over pay and conditions of working brought the London Docks to a standstill. The workers' demands were far from revolutionary: they demanded sixpence an hour and a guarantee of at least a half day's work (four hours) for those taken on in the morning 'call' at the dock gates, and an end to the 'plus' bonus system, which exploited casual workers via the contract system. The Dock authorities and owners refused all the demands and the dockers, led by John Burns, Ben Tillett and others, and supported by the community, successfully won their dispute later that year. During the strike there were numerous prosecutions of dockers and their supporters as the police tried to prevent secondary picketing and the intimidation of strikebreakers. Moreover, the strike emboldened other workers in the area, just as the 'Match Girls' strike a year previously had inspired the dockers to act.[18]

On 21 August 1889, just a week after Tillett's call for action ignited the strike on the docks, Mark Hacht found himself in front of Mr Saunders at Worship Street charged with assaulting a policeman. Hacht was an eighteen-year-old tailor who lived at Wood Street in Spitalfields. The court was told that a strike was taking place at the factory of a local furrier called Koenigsberg. Hacht was part of the picket gathered outside the factory on Commercial Street where he and others were intent on preventing employees from entering. Hacht had no connection to the furriers nor did he work for Koenigsberg: instead he was, in the words of the prosecution lawyer, 'a paid agitator'. It was alleged that when a worker tried to enter he was threatened by Hacht and struck with an umbrella. This prompted a police constable to intervene. As they struggled a 'mob of Jews' tried to pull the policeman off his prisoner, forcing PC Littlestone to brandish his truncheon to 'hold back the crowd'. There were witnesses who denied Hacht had done anything at all, but the magistrate chose to believe the policeman and the furrier's lawyer. Saunders declared it 'one of the worst cases of the kind he had heard' and 'an offence that must be put down'. With the dock strike occupying so many column inches at the time it was hardly surprising that a representative of middle-class and elite society should choose sides quite so obviously. The young man was sent to prison for three months with hard labour.[19]

In December 1889, some months after the dock strike, Charles Stephens, another 'union man', appeared at Worship Street. A complaint had been brought against Stephens by an unnamed sandwichman, who had been standing outside Shoreditch church when Stephens approached him and enquired as to whether he was a member of a trades union. 'If you don't belong to a Union, I ain't going to let you carry them boards about,' Stephens told the man before wrestling with him and breaking the straps of the boards, which ended up in a heap on the street. Stephens was charged with disorderly conduct and assault. Mr Montagu Williams wanted to know what 'Union man' meant. The sandwich-man professed not to know so Stephens interjected from the dock: 'I asked him if he belonged to the Labourer's Union.' A 'Union for what?' asked Mr Williams. 'To prevent a man working unless he belongs to it,' came Stephens's defiant reply. 'That is a very disgraceful union then,' snapped the magistrate. At this Stephens produced a small booklet from his pocket and handed it to the policeman by the dock. It was entitled 'The Dock, Wharf, and General Labourers Union of Great Britain and Ireland'. It was stamped to show that Stephens was a fully paid-up member. It was the union that Ben Tillett had formed in 1887 as the Tea Operatives and General Labourers' Association and which had more than 30,000 members by the end of 1889. Stephens was part of a growing movement of organized labour and his confidence and bravado in the dock are perhaps indicative of how union members felt in the wake of their victory that year. Montagu Williams, however, was neither impressed nor intimidated:

> You are one of those men that get up these Unions and strikes. You are all talk, and there is no work in you. Well I will teach you, and others like you, that you shall not interfere with men who choose to work. You will go to prison for 21 days.

Stephens was led away, defiantly shouting the odds.[20] The magistrate was reinforcing the power of the state by using his discretion to punish a man severely, not specifically for his offence (assault) but for his challenge to authority and to his position in society. The assault was minor and may easily have been dealt with by a fine, but a prison term, which would entail Stephens being locked up at Christmas, sent a clear message to anyone believing that victory in

John Thomson, *The London Boardman*, 1877, photomechanical print.

the Great Dock Strike would lead to any meaningful change in class hierarchies.

Throughout this book we have seen that working-class Londoners, while clearly disadvantaged by comparison to their wealthier neighbours, did have agency within the police courts. What is harder to determine is whether this agency existed at all times and, most importantly perhaps, when the state and its instruments were facing challenges or feeling the pressure of popular concerns about economic distress. It is arguably easier to dispense justice without fear or favour when society is enjoying stability and when prosperity, however relative, is experienced by the majority. Working-class Londoners were used to being poor in the 1800s, but at particular pinch points the levels of distress reached critical levels and that is when the fabric of society can be seen to have frayed. In these moments some magistrates chose to give alms and succour to those they deemed deserving and to come down particularly hard on anyone who posed a threat to the stability of a Victorian capitalist society riven by class privilege.

CONCLUSION
THE PEOPLE'S COURTS?

This study has built upon the foundations laid by Jennifer Davis's seminal work to firmly establish the centrality of the summary courts to the operation of justice, social control and urban regulation in Victorian London.[1] While this book was in the process of being written we have had another very welcome addition to the history of police courts, which might now receive the attention they deserve.[2] While historians of crime have dabbled with the summary process we still have very few volumes that deal exclusively with the process of justice below the jury courts of assize and quarter sessions.[3] This is despite the reality that the overwhelming majority of those experiencing the law in the past would have done so in a magistrate's parlour, at petty sessions convened in a local inn or at an established police court. If we want to understand both the nature and extent of criminal activity, as well as the reaction of the state and citizens to it, we need to look at where it was most often prosecuted and not just where the harshest punishments were handed down.

Moreover, we need to recognize two further important aspects of the summary process. First, that it was often the starting point (in a legal sense) for prosecutions that played out before a judge and jury. In many of the cases discussed in this book a magistrate chose to send defendants to face a jury trial, and sometimes we have been able to follow these through to conclusion. This demonstrates the importance of summary hearings as a filter for the higher courts.

Many times magistrates were simply applying law to commit the accused, but not always. As had been the case in the previous century, magistrates applied the law with discretion, choosing whom to send for trial. From mid-century the discretionary practice, adopted for more than a century, of dealing with petty property offenders summarily was enshrined in laws that gave magistrates formal powers to deal with first and young offenders, and those accused of committing small value thefts. From 1855 offenders were also given agency to ask for their cases to be dealt with by a magistrate, by admitting guilt and accepting a lesser punishment, and so avoiding the perils of a jury trial and much more punitive treatment.

Second, these courts did so much more than deal with property crime and violence. As we have seen, the police courts helped regulate trade in London, they dealt with a huge amount of antisocial behaviour and drunkenness and were both a haven for the 'deserving' poor and an instrument for control of the 'feckless'. These courts touched everyday lives in ways that the Central Criminal Court at Old Bailey never did. Consequently, they offer an often unseen view of the Victorian capital, of a London that emerges from Dickens's literature but rarely from official sources. For this we have the ubiquity of newspapers to thank, and it is telling that most of the material utilized here comes from the second half of the century. Once Chartism had been defeated, politicians were more comfortable with allowing newspapers to reach a wider, working-class readership. This, combined with technological developments in print and distribution, enabled a popular press to thrive, growing into the behemoth of news and comment it is today. At the heart of this growth was 'crime news', a phenomenon that was far from new in the 1800s, but which formed a staple of daily and weekly news columns, with the 'police intelligence' from the magistrates' courts a key feature and attraction for newspaper circulation figures. Every paper carried this news, in one form or another; even specialist organs like *The Era* which focused on entertainment news. A regular reader of a newspaper in the 1800s could scarcely avoid reading about crime, cruelty, violence, about the impertinence of cab drivers or the mean-spiritedness of parish officers. Drunks, ne'er-do-wells, tramps, prostitutes, mendicants and charlatans were all part of the regular diet of these columns. Alongside were cunning thieves and fraudsters, revealed in all their trickery so readers might be armed against them. Dexterous pickpockets rubbed shoulders with shoplifters practised at distraction; one can almost hear the head of the household reading reports aloud as cautionary tales for the unwary. Dark stories of violent husbands, cruel parents and vicious thugs reminded middle-class readers of the 'barbarity' present in the lower orders. That, and the immorality exposed by contemporary reportage of the poor, reinforced class distinctions and a sense of superiority. And it is evident that familiar themes such as these resurfaced periodically, allowing the papers to feed off one another and respond to or create public concerns and 'moral panics'. Newspapers do not just print the news, they create it. This is not new; the press has been doing this for well over a century and, of course, continues to do so.

So this volume, which grew out of my daily engagement with the columns of the Victorian press, is also a study of how the media of its day chose to frame the problems of its society. Accurate court records of summary proceedings for the nineteenth century are minimal compared with the excellent coverage of jury courts. There is nothing as extensive as the Old Bailey Proceedings for the police courts. But the records that do survive, like those from Thames Police court, show that the papers selected atypical cases to highlight. Literally hundreds of hearings took place at police courts daily, whereas the press picked around a dozen or more to inform or entertain their readers with. Some were followed up in later editions, for example when a defendant was remanded for whatever reason, but others were not. Most cases at Thames concerned drunk and disorderly behaviour but, with notable exceptions in the coverage of media celebrities like Tottie Fay and Jane Cakebread, you would not know this from a reading of the newspapers alone.

There is a lesson here then for the student of history: sources may reveal as much by what they do not say as by what they do. Even the existence of a handful of years of court registers from Thames provokes as many questions as answers. The registers appear to cover two broad types of business. The first, used for this study, deals for the most part with crime and misdemeanours. Here are the drunk and disorderly, thieves, receivers, those charged with violence, with begging or vagrancy, and all manner of antisocial activity. The register I used is typical of others from the 1880s, so it is justified to rely on its veracity. But the other register is full of even more mundane business. Here are the parents prosecuted under the Education Act because their children are playing truant from school. Here too are prosecutions for bastardy, for keeping a dog without a licence, for obstructing the streets and polluting the environment.[4] Moreover, there are also prosecutions here for assault, including very many for assaults on police. This suggests the registers overlapped to some extent and that, given they each cover alternate months (when we know the courts sat six days a week, every month), there are missing registers. Studying the police courts is not easy but that should not mean we focus overmuch on the Old Bailey, which is so much better documented.

These courts were public spaces. This is important to stress because alongside the reportage that reached middle-class homes (and those of the more affluent and aspiring lower classes) we can be certain that ordinary people attended them. They would surely have recognized the coverage of the courts in the newspaper columns they read or had read to them. This helps to validate the newspapers as sources for this study. If what they described bore little relation to the way these courts functioned I expect this would be commented on, and so far I can see no evidence for this.

Thus, allowing for the bias of class and the demands of editors, it seems reasonable to accept the newspaper coverage of the Metropolitan Police courts as an accurate, if partial, description of life in this 'nether world'. As public spaces, widely reported by both London and regional newspapers, we should ask again what their purpose was.

The police courts were forums for regulating crime, morality and violence. Given the discretion allowed to police court magistrates it is hard to understand these as anything less than filters for the jury courts, with those filters being adjusted to take account of public opinion. That the definition of 'public opinion' was narrower than it might be today is indisputable given the restrictions on the franchise and the sharper divisions of class that existed in the 1800s. Davis described a magistracy that provided a service to the poor, with free legal advice and as a champion to help them stand up to over-officious overseers and beadles.[5] She argues that their role as a 'working-class resource' declined towards the end of the century as 'successive governments chose to divert non-criminal business away from the courts'.[6] This is a reasonable position to take but one that presumes much about working-class attitudes towards the law. As 'one-stop shops' for justice the police courts present as affordable arenas of negotiation for poor Londoners. The cost of a summons, at 2s, was a not inconsiderable outlay for a working-class family but it could be found, especially if it was believed that this might be recouped or even waived. Courts were local and easily accessible, much more so than the situation pertaining in many rural areas of the country. Until the later decades of the century the working class must have recognized that the magistrate was no obvious friend of the police either, which may have emboldened them. By the 1880s it seems this situation had changed, and the courts were more often reflecting the power dynamics of the streets, where the police had largely won their battle for control. Given this and the reality that the tentacles of the state were exacting an ever more widespread grip on working-class life, it is not unreasonable to agree that the image of the magistrate as the 'friend of the poor' began to evaporate as the twentieth century dawned.

Regardless, however, we should guard against seeing these as 'people's courts' even if they were venues in which the poor sought justice. It is entirely possible that working-class Londoners viewed the summary process as a useful tool on occasion without necessarily accepting its authority in others. Writing about the use of the law in an earlier period, John Brewer and John Styles noted: 'Even though the plebeian and the underdog were invariably disadvantaged when they clashed with those in authority or had recourse to the courts, they knew that they were never merely the passive victims of a process that they were powerless to effect.'[7] Their Victorian counterparts also enjoyed some agency in the courts, as we have seen, but overwhelmingly the occupants of a police court dock were working class, and while many of those bringing prosecutions were of a similar or equal social status, justice was still dispensed by men who were part of a broad social elite. When a working-class man or woman brought a complaint against an equal, be it for simple theft (where one-fifth to one-quarter of all prosecutors were working class)[8] or violence, the court quite often took their side. Similarly, we see plenty of examples in the press of the courts siding with the poor when they complained about treatment by parish officers. It is also apparent that in the first half of the century at least, itinerant traders found the summary process a possible bulwark against attempts by shopkeepers to undermine their traditional ways of working.

But in many other ways it is impossible not to view the police courts as an important part of the disciplinary armoury of the state. In tandem with the New Police, the magistracy enforced the rule of law as an intrinsic mechanism to preserve the inequalities of a society that was fundamentally unbalanced economically. Yes, magistrates may have frequently upbraided overseers for not assisting the poorest, or handed small doles to the needy, but they also upheld laws that punished begging, petty theft and pilfering, all of which were forms of survival for the poorest and for those existing on meagre wages. Magistrates handed down fines and prison sentences to those that did not or, in Tottie Fay's case, arguably could not abide by the social conventions of Victorian society. The prosecution of drunkenness, with all its subsidiary variations, is an example of class control of behaviour. The wealthy and powerful drank and got drunk, but they were rarely prosecuted, because their drinking took place behind closed doors and seldom brought them into conflict with the police. On the occasions it did and when arrests or summonses resulted in court appearances, they simply paid their fines and were discharged. Very often their names were concealed in press reports. This was also true for 'respectable' female shoplifters, or for rich men who used prostitutes; seldom did the papers print their names. By contrast working-class women who picked pockets, stole from shop counters or solicited for business were named and shamed for a largely middle-class readership. The image presented by the press was that the police and courts were engaged in a constant battle against a tide of working-class criminality and antisocial activity.

This undoubtedly played well to an audience that had been primed to believe that a 'criminal class' operated in Victorian London, an army of ne'er-do-wells and, in Mayhew's words, 'those who would not work'.[9] Historians of crime have rejected the idea that a criminal class existed but that does not undermine the contemporary belief in its existence. Dominique Kalifa has argued that the idea of an 'underworld' was fabricated in the nineteenth century (across Europe and America, as well as London), an underworld that included not just criminality but poverty, degradation and immorality.[10] This othering of aspects of working-class life allowed the rich and powerful, and the merely better off and comfortable, to conveniently offload their responsibility for the suffering of so many in the 1800s. Instead of seeing an unequal society they saw a society that was undermined at its roots by the inhabitants of the nether world who needed to be demonized, controlled and disciplined. Certainly there were members of the nether world who deserved support and rescue; ideas of the 'deserving' poor were as well established as the 'undeserving'. The Mendicity Society was happy to help those in genuine need, as they saw them, so long as they behaved in ways they decided were appropriate. The magistrates were also happy to help individuals who accepted their place in the social hierarchy and played by its rules. By contrast a 'Union man' like Charles Stephens represented a threat to the status quo and had to be brought down.

The newspapers were complicit in this. Then, as now, they overwhelmingly represented the opinions of a minority of Britons and attempted to shape the views of society to reflect their narrow perspective. The reporting of the police courts, while allowing for the occasional victory of the 'little man', validated the idea that respectability was a state into which the middle class and elite were born and to which the working class should aspire. The nether world this reportage exposed was a reminder to contemporaries of the dangers that their society faced. Crime and poverty were closely linked in the public consciousness and their inclusion side by side in the 'police intelligence' columns helped reinforce this. The prevailing belief was that individuals, and not society, were responsible for their own misery. Criminality and pauperism was a choice, not a consequence of environment or any inequality of life chances. We continue to view the poor as 'scroungers', 'lazy' and 'dependent'.[11] Our courts and prisons are full of poorly educated young men and women from communities that have been blighted by poverty and inequality for decades, if not longer. The nether world continues to exist today, and we ought to ask ourselves why. Finally, and more positively, the actions of many of the people we see coming into these courtrooms to be judged by, or to solicit help from, their social 'betters' is indicative as much of a determined resistance to the constraints that society placed upon working men and women as it is of any perceived acceptance of the authority of others to rule them.

REFERENCES

INTRODUCTION AND THEMES

1 Elizabeth McKellar, *Landscapes of London: The City, the Country and the Suburbs, 1660–1840* (New Haven, CT, and London, 2013), p. 3.
2 Ralph Hyde, *The A to Z of Georgian London* (London, 1982).
3 Ralph Hyde, *The A to Z of Victorian London* (London, 1987).
4 These were Cumberland, Durham, Northumberland and Westmorland.
5 Joseph Fletcher, 'Statistical Account of the Constitution and Operation of the Criminal Courts of the Metropolis', *Journal of the Statistical Society of London*, XI/4 (1846), p. 300. It should be noted that Middlesex's judicial area was considerable until boundary changes were made in 1889. This jurisdiction covered the capital north, east and west of the Thames, excluding the City of London, but including Westminster. Following the formation of the London County Council in 1889 the sessions were split into north and south under the umbrella of the London County Sessions.
6 Middlesex Justices Act (1792), 32 Geo III c 53.
7 See John Beattie, *The First English Detectives: The Bow Street Runners and the Policing of London, 1570–1840* (Oxford, 2021); David Cox, *A Certain Share of Low Cunning: A History of the Bow Street Runners, 1792–1839* (London, 2012).
8 Jennifer Davis, 'Law Breaking and Law Enforcement: The Creation of a Criminal Class in Mid-Victorian London', PhD thesis, Boston College, 1984, p. 316.
9 Ibid.
10 Charles Dickens [Jr], *Dickens's Dictionary of London* (London, 1879).
11 G. W. Bacon, *London Police Courts* map (London, 1913), LMA/SC/PM/TH/01/01/051.
12 Dudley Barker, *Laughter in Court* (London, 1935), p. 10.
13 Hugh R. P. Gamon, *The London Police Court To-day and To-morrow* (London, 1907), pp. 68–9.
14 James Greenwood, *The Prisoner in the Dock: My Four Years' Daily Experiences in the London Police Courts* (London, 1902), p. 218.

15 Sascha Auerbach, *Armed with Sword and Scales: Law, Culture and Local Courtrooms in London, 1860–1913* (Cambridge, 2021), p. 96.

16 Lucy Brown, *Victorian News and Newspapers* (Oxford, 1985), p. 96.

17 Robert B. Shoemaker, 'The Old Bailey Proceedings and the Representation of Crime and Criminal Justice in Eighteenth-Century London', *Journal of British Studies*, XLVII/3 (2008), pp. 559–80.

18 Fletcher, 'Statistical Account', pp. 294–5.

19 Auerbach, *Armed with Sword and Scales*, p. 98.

20 An Act for regulating the Police Courts in the Metropolis (1839), 2 and 3 Vict c 71; Henry Turner Waddy, *The Police Court and Its Work* (London, 1925), p. 48.

21 Auerbach, *Armed with Sword and Scales*, p. 80. A salary of £1,200 in 1839 might represent approximately £75,000 today, or the equivalent remuneration for a senior manager, MP or barrister.

22 Jennifer Davis, 'A Poor Man's System of Justice?: The London Police Courts in the Second Half of the Nineteenth Century', *Historical Journal*, XXVII/2 (1984) p. 309.

23 At each of the police courts there were two clerks, two ushers, a door and office keeper, and a gaoler. Fletcher, 'Statistical Account', p. 294.

24 Horace Cox, *Metropolitan Police Court Jottings: By a Magistrate* (London, 1882), p. 9.

25 Drew D. Gray, *Crime, Prosecution and Social Relations: The Summary Courts of the City of London in the Late Eighteenth Century* (Basingstoke, 2009); Greg T. Smith, ed., *Summary Justice in the City: A Selection of Cases Heard at the Guildhall Justice Room, 1752–1781* (Woodbridge, 2013).

26 Gamon, *The London Police Court*, p. 109.

27 Ibid., p. 67.

28 Sascha Auerbach, '"Beyond the Pale": Victorian Penal Culture, Police Court Missionaries, and the Origins of Probation in England', *Law and History Review*, XXXIII/3 (2015), p. 628.

29 Probation of First Offenders Act (1887), 50 and 51 Vict c 25; Dorothy Bochel, *Probation and Aftercare: Its Development in England and Wales* (Edinburgh, 1976), p. 15. See also Auerbach, '"Beyond the Pale"', for a full discussion of the role and development of police court missionaries and the move towards the creation of the Probation Service.

30 Thomas Holmes, *Pictures and Problems from the London Police Courts* (London, 1900).

31 Auerbach, '"Beyond the Pale"', p. 627.

32 Auerbach, *Armed with Sword and Scales*, p. 63.

33 J. M. Beattie, *The First English Detectives: The Bow Street Runners and the Policing of London, 1750–1840* (Oxford, 2012), p. 18.

34 Clive Emsley, *The English Police: A Political and Social History* (London, 1991), p. 24.

35 Leon Radzinowicz, *A History of the Criminal Law and Its Administration
    from 1750*, vol. II: *The Clash between Private Initiative and Public Interest in the
    Enforcement of the Law* (London, 1968), pp. 159–60.

36 G. A. Minto, *The Thin Blue Line* (London, 1965).

37 Stanley Palmer, *Police and Protest in England and Ireland, 1780–1850*
    (Cambridge, 1988), p. 292.

38 Beattie, *The First English Detectives*, p. 246.

39 Charles Reith, *A New Study of Police History* (London, 1956), pp. 135–6.

40 Robert D. Storch, 'The Plague of the Blue Locusts: Police Reform and Popular
    Resistance in Northern England, 1840–57', *International Review of Social History*,
    XX/1 (1975), pp. 61–90.

41 Quoted in Emsley, *The English Police*, p. 22.

42 Haia Shpayer-Makov, *The Making of a Policeman: A Social History of a Labour
    Force in Metropolitan London, 1829–1914* (Aldershot, 2002), p. 42.

43 David Churchill, *Crime Control and Everyday Life in the Victorian City: The
    Police and the Public* (Oxford, 2017), pp. 37–8.

44 Stephen Inwood, 'Policing London's Morals: The Metropolitan Police and
    Popular Culture, 1829–1850', *London Journal*, XV/2 (1990), pp. 129–46.

45 Cox, *Metropolitan Police Court Jottings*, p. 8.

46 Alfred Chichele Plowden, *Grain or Chaff? The Autobiography of a Police
    Magistrate* (London, 1903), p. 208.

47 Davis, 'Law Breaking and Law Enforcement', p. 292.

48 Auerbach, *Armed with Sword and Scales*, p. 64.

49 Gamon, *The London Police Court*, p. 92.

50 Gray, *Crime, Prosecution and Social Relations*.

51 Peter King, 'The Summary Courts and Social Relations in Eighteenth-Century
    England', *Past and Present*, 183 (May 2004), p. 162.

52 Ibid., pp. 168–9.

53 See, for example, Drew Gray, 'Making Law in Mid-Eighteenth-Century
    England: Legal Statutes and the Application in the Justicing Notebook of
    Phillip Ward of Stoke Doyle', *Journal of Legal History*, XXXIV/2 (2013), pp. 211–33;
    Gwenda Morgan and Peter Rushton, 'The Magistrate, the Community, and
    the Maintenance of an Orderly Society in Eighteenth-Century England',
    Historical Research, LXXVI/191 (2003), pp. 54–77.

54 Robert B. Shoemaker, *Prosecution and Punishment: Petty Crime and the Law in
    London and Rural Middlesex, c. 1660–1725* (Cambridge, 1991), pp. 318–19.

55 Gray, *Crime, Prosecution and Social Relations*, p. 174.

56 Davis, 'Law Breaking and Law Enforcement', p. 318.

57 From a letter from H. D'Eyncourt to 29/10/1880, HO45/9496/6739. Quoted in
    Davis, 'Law Breaking and Law Enforcement', p. 319.

58 Auerbach, *Armed with Sword and Scales*, p. 26.

59 Davis, 'A Poor Man's System of Justice', p. 335.

60 Churchill, *Crime Control*; Emsley, *The English Police*; Inwood, 'Policing
    London's Morals'; Robert D. Storch, 'The Policeman as Domestic Missionary:
    Urban Discipline and Popular Culture in Northern England, 1850–1880',
    Journal of Social History, IX/4 (1976), pp. 481–502; David Taylor, *The New Police in
    Nineteenth-Century England: Crime, Conflict, and Control* (Manchester, 1997).

61 The Old Bailey Proceedings online, www.oldbaileyonline.org, and The Digital
    Panopticon, www.digitalpanopticon.org, accessed 31 July 2023.

62 Rosalind Crone, *Violent Victorians: Popular Entertainment in Nineteenth-Century
    London* (Manchester, 2012); Judith Flanders, *The Invention of Murder: How the
    Victorians Revelled in Death and Detection and Created Modern Crime* (London,
    2011); Drew Gray, *Murder Maps: Crime Scenes Revisited* (London, 2021).

63 Heather Shore, *Artful Dodgers: Youth and Crime in Early 19th-Century London*
    (London, 1999).

64 William Stead, 'The Maiden Tribute of Modern Babylon', *Pall Mall Gazette*,
    4–10 July 1885.

1 THE POLICE, DRINK AND THE WORKING CLASSES

 1 The Metropolitan Police Act and Metropolitan Court Act, 2 and 3 Vict c 47
    and 2 and 3 Vict c 71.

 2 Thames Police court register, LMA/PS/TH/A1881.

 3 Neil R. A. Bell and Adam Wood, eds, *Sir Howard Vincent's Police Code 1889*
    (Coventry, 2015), pp. 70 and 128.

 4 An Act for Regulating the Sale of Intoxicating Liquors, 35 and 36 Vict c 94.

 5 *Morning Post*, 11 January 1850.

 6 *Lloyd's Illustrated Newspaper*, 30 May 1880.

 7 Charles Booth Police Notebooks Book 13.1 Police districts 2.3.4. (1898–9),
    pp. 102–3, available at www.booth.lse.ac.uk, accessed 8 July 2022.

 8 Anna Clark, *The Struggle for the Breeches: Gender and the Making of the British
    Working Class* (Berkeley, CA, 1997); Joanne Bailey [Begiato], *Unquiet Lives:
    Marriage and Marriage Breakdown in England, 1660–1800* (Cambridge, 2009).

 9 *Morning Chronicle*, 7 September 1850.

10 *Morning Chronicle*, 9 January 1861.

11 Henry Yeomans, 'What did the British Temperance Movement Accomplish?
    Attitudes to Alcohol, the Law and Moral Regulation', *Sociology*, XLV/1 (2011),
    p. 41.

12 Beerhouse Act (1830), 11 Geo IV and 1 Will IV c 64.

13 Yeomans, 'What did the British Temperance Movement Accomplish?', p. 43.

14 Erika Rappaport, 'Sacred and Useful Pleasures: The Temperance Tea Party and
    the Creation of a Sober Consumer Culture in Early Industrial Britain', *Journal
    of British Studies*, LII/4 (2013), pp. 990–1016.

15 Licensing Act (1872), 35 and 36 Vict c 94.

16 Lucia Zedner, *Women, Crime, and Custody in Victorian England* (Oxford, 1991), p. 222.

17 Roy McLeod, 'The Edge of Hope: Social Policy and Chronic Alcoholism, 1870–1900', *Journal of the History of Medicine and Allied Sciences*, XXII/3 (1967), p. 218.

18 Habitual Drunkards (Inebriates) Act (1879), 42 and 43 Vict c 19.

19 Martin J. Wiener, *Reconstructing the Criminal: Culture, Law, and Policy in England, 1830–1914* (Cambridge, 1990), p. 296.

20 *Morning Post*, 30 August 1880.

21 James Nicholls, *The Politics of Alcohol: A History of the Drink Question in England* (Manchester, 2009), p. 164.

22 Quoted ibid., p. 168.

23 Zedner, *Women, Crime, and Custody*, p. 222.

24 Ibid., p. 226.

25 Ibid., p. 230.

26 Inebriates Act (1898), 61 and 62 Vict c 60.

27 Zedner, *Women, Crime, and Custody*, p. 232; Claudia Soares, 'The Path to Reform? Problematic Treatments and Patient Experience in Nineteenth-Century Female Inebriate Institutions', *Cultural and Social History: The Journal of the Social History Society*, XII/3 (2015), p. 415; Wiener, *Reconstructing the Criminal*, pp. 299–300.

28 Zedner, *Women, Crime, and Custody*, p. 232.

29 Yeomans, 'What did the British Temperance Movement Accomplish?', p. 46.

30 Anon., '"Drink and Drunkenness in London", by a Police Court Magistrate', *North American Review* (March 1897), p. 325.

31 We do not know when Tottie was born, only when she died (1 February 1908).

32 Thomas Beames, *The Rookeries of London: Past, Present, and Prospective* (London, 1850); David R. Green, 'People of the Rookery: A Pauper Community in Victorian London', Occasional Paper no. 26, University of London, King's College (1986), pp. 36–7.

33 A list of these, probably far from exhaustive, was included in her record of previous convictions when she appeared before the Middlesex Sessions of the Peace in March 1886. *Calendar of Prisoners* (1 March 1886), LMA/MJ/SR/5718.

34 Judith R. Walkowitz, *Prostitution and Victorian Society: Women, Class, and the State* (Cambridge, 1980).

35 *Pall Mall Gazette*, 7 March, 1887; Fay may well have appeared in the reports of cases at the police courts, but 1887 appears to mark the first example of her 'story' being established.

36 *Dundee Courier*, Friday 27 July, 1888.

37 *Sheffield Evening Telegraph*, 19 February 1889.

38 *Birmingham Daily Post*, 2 January 1889.

39 A Bischoffsheim handcart and not a horse-drawn vehicle.

40 *Illustrated Police News*, 22 June 1889.

41 *Sheffield Evening Telegraph*, 9 August 1889; *Reynolds's Newspaper*, 25 August 1889.

42 *Illustrated Police News*, 31 August 1889.

43 *Portsmouth Evening News*, 26 April 1890.

44 On 25 August 1879 Fay was committed of stealing a sheet and a table cloth and given a four-month gaol sentence, LMA/MJ/SR/5718.

45 *Sheffield Evening Telegraph*, 19 May 1890.

46 *Daily News*, 28 May 1890; *London Adjourned General Sessions* (19 May 1890), LMA/LJ/SR/20.

47 *Sheffield Evening Telegraph*, 4 December 1890.

48 *Daily News*, 9 January 1891.

49 *Penny Illustrated Paper*, 25 April 1891.

50 *The Standard*, 11 April 1891.

51 *Sheffield Evening Telegraph*, 7 May 1891; *London General Sessions of the Peace* (4 May 1891), LMA/ LJ/SR/43.

52 *The Vaudeville*, 12 September 1891.

53 *Illustrated Police News*, 21 May 1892.

54 *Reynolds's Newspaper*, 15 May 1892.

55 *Leeds Times*, 1 August 1892.

56 *Yorkshire Evening Post*, 12 August 1892.

57 *Lloyd's Illustrated Paper*, 5 June 1892.

58 *Reynolds's Newspaper*, 12 June 1892.

59 *Reynolds's Newspaper*, 14 August 1892.

60 *Yorkshire Evening Post*, 15 August 1892.

61 *Manchester Courier and Lancashire General Advertiser*, 24 September 1892.

62 *Reynolds's Newspaper*, 25 September 1892.

63 *Daily Gazette for Middlesborough*, 7 October 1892.

64 *Daily News*, 27 October 1892; *London General Sessions of the Peace* (19 October 1892), LMA/LJ/SR/76.

65 *Sheffield Daily Telegraph*, 15 November 1892.

66 *York Herald*, 13 December 1892; *Portsmouth Evening News*, 14 December 1892.

67 *Yorkshire Evening Post*, 17 February 1894.

68 *Lloyd's Illustrated Newspaper*, 21 June 1896.

69 *Birmingham Daily Post*, 20 January 1893.

70 It seems Tottie Fay spent time in three asylums: Broadmoor, Fisherton (in Salisbury) and Colney Hatch. Isabel Knight, 'Fay, Tottie: The Worst and Wickedest Woman in London', The Friends of Horton Cemetery, 4 May 2021, www.hortoncemetery.org, accessed 23 September 2022.

71 McLeod, 'The Edge of Hope', p. 217.

72 *Evening Telegraph and Star*, 17 January 1896.

73 *Lloyd's Weekly Newspaper*, 22 August 1897.

74 E. P. Thompson, *The Making of the English Working Class* (London, 1963).

75 Anon., 'Drink and Drunkenness in London by a London Police Magistrate', *North American Review*, CLXIV/484 (1897), p. 318.

76 Anon., *The Life of Jane Johnson, the Champion Drunkard of the World (captured by the Salvation Army), as related by herself* (Leeds, 1883).

77 James Greenwood, *The Prisoner in the Dock: My Four Years' Daily Experiences in the London Police Courts* (London, 1902), pp. 184–5.

78 Gareth Stedman Jones, *Languages of Class: Studies in English Working Class History, 1832–1982* (Cambridge, 1983), p. 198.

2 REGULATING THE CAPITAL'S STREETS AND BUSINESSES

1 Neil A. Bell and Adam Wood, eds, *Sir Howard Vincent's Police Code 1889* (Coventry, 2015), p. 93.

2 Henry Mayhew, *London Labour and the London Poor: a cyclopædia of the condition and earnings of those that will work, those that cannot work, and those that will not work* (London, 1851).

3 David Churchill, *Crime Control and Everyday Life in the Victorian City: The Police and the Public* (Oxford, 2017), p. 100.

4 Ibid.

5 Clive Emsley, *The English Police: A Political and Social History* (London, 1991).

6 Stephen Inwood, 'Policing London's Morals: The Metropolitan Police and Popular Culture, 1829–1850', *London Journal*, XV/2 (1990), pp. 129–46.

7 Churchill, *Crime Control and Everyday Life*, p. 101.

8 Ibid., p. 58.

9 Marc Brodie, '"Jaunty Individualists" or Labour Activists? Costermongers, Trade Unions, and the Politics of the Poor', *Labour History Review*, LXVI/2 (2001), p. 147.

10 *The Sunday at Home: a family magazine for Sabbath reading*, 13 June 1868.

11 Gareth Stedman Jones, *Outcast London: A Study in the Relationship between Classes in Victorian Society* (New York, 1971), p. 62; Stephen Jankiewicz, 'A Dangerous Class: The Street Sellers of Nineteenth-Century London', *Journal of Social History*, XLII/2 (2012), p. 395.

12 Stedman Jones, *Outcast London*, p. 172.

13 Ibid., p. 185.

14 Artisans' and Labourers' Dwellings Improvement Act 1875, 38 and 39 Vict. c.36.

15 Stedman Jones, *Outcast London*, pp. 200–203.

16 David R. Green, 'People of the Rookery: A Pauper Community in Victorian London', Occasional Paper 26, University of London, King's College (1986), pp. 36–7.

17 Stedman Jones, *Outcast London*, p. 342.

18 Ole Münch, 'Henry Mayhew and the Street Traders of Victorian London: A Cultural Exchange with Material Consequences', *London Journal*, XLIII/1 (2018), p. 54.

19 Sections of his writings on *London Labour and the London Poor* were reproduced in the radical organ *Reynolds's Newspaper*. It was also serialized in weekly parts sold at a price casual labourers could afford. Münch, 'Henry Mayhew and the Street Traders of Victorian London', pp. 55 and 62.

20 Ibid., p. 57.

21 Ibid, p. 56.

22 *Punch, or the London Charivari*, 31 November 1863.

23 Stephen Inwood, *City of Cities: The Birth of Modern London* (Basingstoke, 2005); Jerry White, *London in the Nineteenth Century: 'A Human Awful Wonder of God'* (London, 2007).

24 *Morning Post*, 24 January 1870.

25 *Morning Post*, 22 October 1858.

26 *Morning Post*, 18 September 1860.

27 *Lloyd's Illustrated Newspaper*, 22 February 1874.

28 Inwood, 'Policing London's Morals'.

29 *Morning Chronicle*, 18 March 1856.

30 An Act for Regulating the Traffic in the Metropolis (1867), 30 and 31 Vict c 134.

31 *Morning Post*, 7 December 1870.

32 The act also carried penalties for those affixing advertisements to certain street furniture or carrying them about on horseback, in vehicles and on foot without permission. There were further regulations concerning the driving of cattle through the streets and some affecting hackney carriages.

33 *Morning Post*, 19 April 1872.

34 Ben Weinreb and Christopher Hibbert, eds, *The London Encyclopaedia* (Basingstoke, 1983), pp. 213–14.

35 *Morning Post*, 21 December 1853.

36 *Morning Post*, 1 August 1870.

37 Vagrant Act Amendment Act (1873), 36 and 37 Vict c 38.

38 *Morning Post*, 9 June 1870.

39 *Morning Post*, 6 April 1880.

40 *Lloyd's Weekly Newspaper*, 28 December 1873.

41 White, *London in the Nineteenth Century*, p. 130.

42 *Daily News*, 3 May 1890; *Illustrated Police News*, 10 May 1890.

43 *Reynolds's Newspaper*, 30 May 1869.

44 *The Standard*, 26 June 1889.

45 *The Standard*, 28 April 1896.

46 *Illustrated Police News*, 29 April 1882.

47 *Lloyd's Illustrated Newspaper*, 27 June 1880.

48 Metropolitan Street Act, 30 and 31 Vict c 5.

49 White, *London in the Nineteenth Century*, p. 189.

50 *Report of the Commissioners appointed to make inquiries relating to Smithfield Market and the markets in the City of London for the sale of meat* (London, 1850), CLA/016/AD/01/13.

51 Weinreb and Hibbert, eds, *London Encyclopaedia*, p. 790.

52 *The Standard*, 20 June 1889.

53 See Asa Briggs, *Victorian Cities* (London, 1963); Richard L. Schoenwald, 'Training Urban Man: A Hypothesis about the Sanitary Movement', in *The Victorian City: Images and Realities*, ed. H. J. Dyos and M. Wolff, 2 vols (London, 1999), vol. II, pp. 669–92; Tristram Hunt, *Building Jerusalem: The Rise and Fall of the Victorian City* (New York, 2005).

54 Adulteration of Food Act (1860), 23 and 24 Vict c 84 and the Sale of Food and Drugs Act (1875), 35 and 39 Vict c 63; P. J. Rowlinson, 'Food Adulteration: Its Control in 19th Century Britain', *Interdisciplinary Science Reviews*, VII/1 (1982), pp. 63–72.

55 *The Standard*, 30 July 1881.

56 *The Standard*, 7 April 1894.

57 *Reynolds's Newspaper*, 21 February 1869. In 1883 a butcher by the name of Charles Simmonds was sentenced to eight months imprisonment for stealing £3 worth of meat from his master. Simmonds was 38 in 1883 so it is just possible that this is the same Charles, or perhaps his son. See the Digital Panopticon, Charles Simmonds, Middlesex House of Detention Calendars, 1 January 1883, Record ID cpmMJ_CP_B_031_0009_0024, www.digitalpanopticon.org, accessed 14 July 2022.

58 *Daily News*, 6 February 1862.

59 *Morning Post*, 28 May 1875.

60 Lee Jackson, *Dirty Old London: The Victorian Fight against Filth* (New Haven, CT, and London, 2014), p. 62.

61 Edwin Chadwick, *An Inquiry into the Sanitary Condition of the Labouring Population of Great Britain* (London, 1842).

62 The first was preliminary, leading to *The Second Report of the Commissioners for Inquiring into the State of Large Towns and Populous Districts* (London, 1845).

63 11 and 12 Vict c 63 (August 1848).

64 Jackson, *Dirty Old London*, p. 93.

65 *Morning Post*, 28 September 1854.

66 Ibid.

67 Stedman Jones, *Outcast London*, pp. 19–21.

68 Norman McCord, *British History, 1815–1906* (Oxford, 1991), pp. 287–8.

69 Factories Act (1844), 7 and 8 Vict c 15 and Factories Act (1847), 10 and 11 Vict c 29.

70 Factories (Extension) Act (1867), 30 and 31 Vict c 103.

71 *The Era*, 3 January 1869.

72 *Reynolds's Newspaper*, 21 February 1869.

73 Sascha Auerbach, *Armed with Sword and Scales: Law, Culture and Local Courtrooms in London, 1860–1913* (Cambridge, 2021), p. 148.

74 *Morning Post*, 22 September 1870.

75 Auerbach, *Armed with Sword and Scales*, pp. 88–9.

76 *The Standard*, 8 August 1870.

77 *The Standard*, 11 March 1896.

78 Hugh R. P. Gamon, *The London Police Court To-day and To-morrow* (London, 1907), p. 100.

79 *Reynolds's Newspaper*, 24 August 1873; *Morning Post*, 4 October 1873.

80 *Morning Post*, 29 July 1868.

81 Offences Against the Person Act (1861), 24 and 25 Vict c 100 (section 35 covered furious driving).

82 Bell and Wood, eds, *Sir Howard Vincent's Police Code 1889*, pp. 88–9.

83 The offence of causing injury by 'wanton or furious driving' remains on the statute and is indictable (meaning it would only be heard before a Crown Court). It is rarely used because it only applies to 'non-mechanically propelled' vehicles, such as bicycles or horse-drawn carts. It does still carry the threat of imprisonment but a fine is more likely. The distinction between felony and misdemeanour was abolished in UK law under the Criminal Law Act 1967, c 58.

84 Thames Police court register, 1881.

85 *Morning Post*, 7 September 1870.

86 *Morning Post*, 29 August 1870.

3 THIEVES AND SWINDLERS

1 Juvenile Offenders Act (1847), 10 and 11 Vict c 82; the Summary Jurisdiction Act (1848), 10 and 11 Vict c 43; the Larceny Act (1850), 13 and 14 Vict c 37; and the Criminal Justice Act (1855), 18 and 19 Vict c 126.

2 V.A.C. Gatrell, 'The Decline of Theft and Violence in Victorian and Edwardian England', in *Crime and the Law: The Social History of Crime in Western Europe since 1500*, ed. V.A.C. Gatrell, Bruce Lenman and Geoffrey Parker (London, 1980), p. 274.

3 Shani D'Cruze and Louise A. Jackson, *Women, Crime and Justice in England since 1660* (Basingstoke, 2009), pp. 30–46; Lynn McKay, 'Why They Stole: Women in the Old Bailey, 1779–1789', *Journal of Social History*, XXXII/3 (1999), pp. 623–39; Deirdre Palk, *Gender, Crime and Judicial Discretion, 1780–1830* (Woodbridge, 2006); Tammy C. Whitlock, *Crime, Gender and Consumer Culture in Nineteenth-Century England* (Farnham, 2005); Lucia Zedner, *Women, Crime and Custody in Victorian England* (Oxford, 1991).

4 See Drew D. Gray, *Crime, Policing and Punishment in England, 1660–1914* (London, 2016), fig. 7.1, p. 160.

5 P. D'Sena, 'Perquisites and Casual Labour on the London Wharfside in the Eighteenth Century', *London Journal*, xiv/2 (1989), pp. 130–47.

6 Douglas Hay, ed., *Albion's Fatal Tree* (London, 1975); Eric Hobsbawm, 'Social Criminality: Distinctions between Socio-Political and other Forms of Crime', *Bulletin of the Society for the Study of Labour History*, xxv (1972), pp. 5–6; John Rule and Roger Wells, *Crime, Protest, and Popular Politics in Southern England, 1740–1850* (London, 1997).

7 So long as the defendant consented, all larcenies valued at under 5s could now be dealt with by a magistrate. Criminal Justice Act (1855), 18 and 19 Vict c 126.

8 Bruce P. Smith, 'The Presumption of Guilt and the English Law of Theft, 1750–1850', *Law and History Review*, xxiii/1 (2005), p. 154.

9 See J. M. Beattie, *Policing and Punishment in London, 1660-1750: Urban Crime and the Limits of Terror* (Oxford, 2001), and Drew D. Gray, *Crime, Prosecution and Social Relations: The Summary Courts and the City of London in the Late Eighteenth Century* (Basingstoke, 2009).

10 Tabulating decade against offence subcategory where offence category is theft, between January 1837 and December 1901. Counting by offence, www.oldbaileyonline.org, accessed 11 February 2022.

11 *The Standard*, 28 August 1848; Trial of Edward Shanox (t18480918-2200), www.oldbaileyonline.org, accessed 11 February 2022.

12 Eric Partridge, *A Dictionary of the Underworld* (London, 1949), p. 427, defines a 'magsman' as 'a fashionably dressed swindler' or, citing George W. Matsell's *Vocabulum; or, The Rogue's Lexicon* (New York, 1859), 'fellows who are too cowardly to steal, but prefer to cheat confiding persons by acting upon their cupidity'.

13 *Pall Mall Gazette*, 31 March 1870.

14 *Nottinghamshire Guardian*, 3 September 1880.

15 Trial of Henry Perry (t18800913-484), www.oldbaileyonline.org, accessed 25 February 2022.

16 Eloise Moss, *Night Raiders: Burglary and the Making of Modern Urban Life in London, 1860–1968* (Oxford, 2019).

17 Eloise Moss, 'Burglary Insurance and the Culture of Fear in Britain, 1899–1939', *Historical Journal*, liv/4 (2011), p. 1048.

18 *The Standard*, 16 November 1881.

19 Trial of Henry Watkins and Charles Edmonds (t18811212-123), www.oldbaileyonline.org, accessed 11 February 2022.

20 Trial of Charles Edmonds and Henry Watkins (t18811212-130), www.oldbaileyonline.org, accessed 11 February 2022.

21 Trial of Charles Edmonds and Henry Watkins (t18811212-131), www.oldbaileyonline.org, accessed 11 February 2022.

22 *Morning Chronicle*, 15 February 1861.

23 *Morning Post*, 5 April 1865.

24 Trial of John Campbell, James Roberts, Edmund Collins and Robert White (t18650410-381), www.oldbaileyonline.org, accessed 15 February 2022.

25 Moss, *Night Raiders*, p. 4.

26 *Morning Chronicle*, 12 August 1851.

27 Trial of George Andrews (t18510818-1664), www.oldbaileyonline.org, accessed 15 February 2022.

28 *Morning Post*, 18 November 1840.

29 *Morning Post*, 3 May 1841. Collins may have been self-medicating with mercury; it was used as disinfectant, diuretic and even as a laxative. At points in history mercury was also used to treat syphilis.

30 *Morning Post*, 9 April 1860.

31 Trial of Henry Mason and Margaret Sawyer (t18600507-413), www.oldbaileyonline.org, accessed 4 March 2022.

32 *The Standard*, 15 August 1864. A Charles Giles born in 1825 was convicted of an offence in 1846 (aged 21). He was accused of forgery and transported for seven years. He earned a ticket of leave in September 1851, but this was revoked just one year later. Could this be the same man? The gaoler had described him as 'a very old thief' but it might have meant he was an experienced offender not an aged one. See www.digitalpanopticon.org.

33 Matthew Bach has challenged the idea that the police could effectively track criminals using legislation passed in the 1860s and '70s. Matthew Bach, *Combating London's Criminal Class: A State Divided, 1869–95* (London, 2020).

34 *Morning Post*, 7 June 1883.

35 'Dip' or 'dipping' are both slang terms for the act of picking pockets in the nineteenth century. Partridge, *Dictionary of the Underworld*, pp. 189–90.

36 *Morning Post*, 23 March 1865.

37 *Morning Post*, 13 January 1864.

38 Tabulating decade where offence category is shoplifting, between January 1820 and December 1910. Counting by offence, www.oldbaileyonline.org, accessed 21 December 2021.

39 *Reynolds's Newspaper*, 16 April 1854.

40 William M. Meier, *Property Crime in London, 1850–Present* (Basingstoke, 2011), pp. 77–8.

41 *Morning Post*, 17 May 1832.

42 *Morning Chronicle*, 7 November 1860.

43 J.A.R. Cairns, *The Loom of the Law: The Experiences and Reflections of a Metropolitan Magistrate* (London, 1922), pp. 199–200.

44 D'Sena, 'Perquisites and Casual Labour'.

45 This practice, which persisted well into the twentieth century, was known as 'sucking the monkey'.

46 *Morning Post*, 29 August 1870.

47 Féidhlim McGowan, 'Brewing up a Storm: Investigating British Tea Prices from 1690–1914', *Student Economic Review*, 29 (2015), pp. 20–21.

48 *Morning Post*, 28 January 1871.

49 *Lloyd's Weekly London Newspaper*, 20 October 1872.

50 *Morning Post*, 16 August 1889.

51 *Morning Chronicle*, 20 May 1840.

52 *Morning Post*, 16 December 1852.

53 Thames Police court register, 1881.

54 *The Standard*, 27 September 1895.

55 *Lloyd's Illustrated Newspaper*, 4 April 1880; *Lloyd's Illustrated Newspaper*, 24 April 1880.

56 *Lloyd's Weekly Newspaper*, 9 July 1893.

57 Trial of George John Binet (t18930724-680), www.oldbaileyonline.org, accessed 28 January 2022.

58 Ibid.

59 Witchcraft Act (1735), 9 Geo II c 5.; Fraudulent Mediums Act (1951), 14 and 15 Geo VI c 33. The 1951 legislation was repealed in 2008 under legislation that brought Britain in line with EU regulations regarding 'unfair sales and marketing practices'.

60 Neil R. A. Bell and Adam Wood, eds, *Sir Howard Vincent's Police Code 1889* (Coventry, 2015), p. 88.

61 *The Standard*, 28 July 1883.

62 *The Standard*, 7 July 1882.

63 See Heather Shore, *London's Criminal Underworlds, c. 1720–c. 1930: A Social and Cultural History* (Basingstoke, 2015).

64 This reference is from the 1874 edition (p. 217), cited in Partridge, *Dictionary of the Underworld*, p. 415, which also cites an 1869 mention as 'the earliest record'.

65 *The Standard*, 19 May 1880.

66 Trial of Samuel John Holmes, Henry John Dover, Henry Lawrence, William Farrington, Frederick Hiscock, Alfred Vincent, Edward Simmonds and William Phillips (t18800803-449), www.oldbaileyonline.org, accessed 21 January 2022.

4 VIOLENCE AND HOMICIDE

1 Drew Gray, 'Settling their Differences: The Nature of Assault and Its Prosecution in the City of London in the Late Eighteenth and Early Nineteenth Centuries', in *Assaulting the Past: Violence and Civilization in Historical Context*, ed. Katherine D. Watson (Newcastle, 2007), pp. 141–59; Peter

King, 'Punishing Assault: The Transformation of Attitudes in the English Courts', *Journal of Interdisciplinary History*, XXVII/1 (1996), pp. 43–74.

2 V.A.C. Gatrell, 'The Decline of Theft and Violence in Victorian and Edwardian England', in *Crime and the Law: The Social History of Crime in Western Europe since 1500*, ed. V.A.C. Gatrell, Bruce Lenman and Geoffrey Parker (London, 1980), pp. 288–9.

3 Martin J. Wiener, *Men of Blood: Violence, Manliness, and Criminal Justice in Victorian England* (Cambridge, 2004).

4 Rosalind Crone, *Violent Victorians: Popular Entertainment in Nineteenth-Century London* (Manchester, 2012); Judith Flanders, *The Invention of Murder: How the Victorians Revelled in Death and Detection and Created Modern Crime* (London, 2011).

5 See Gatrell, 'The Decline of Theft and Violence', p. 287 (Table IV).

6 Lawrence Stone, 'Interpersonal Violence in English Society, 1300–1980', *Past and Present*, CI/1 (1983), pp. 22–33; John Carter Wood, *Violence and Crime in Nineteenth-Century England: The Shadow of Our Refinement* (London, 2004).

7 M. Beth Emmerichs, 'Getting Away with Murder? Homicide and the Coroners in Nineteenth-Century London', *Social Science History*, XXV/1 (2001), pp. 93–100; P. Fisher, 'Getting Away with Murder? The Suppression of Coroner's Inquests in Early Victorian England and Wales', *Local Population Studies*, 78 (2007), pp. 47–62.

8 Stone, 'Interpersonal Violence'.

9 Until 1996 murders were only prosecuted as such if the killing took place within a year and a day of the death of the victim. Moreover, under the 'felony murder rule' a criminal that killed another while committing a felony (a robbery for example) would be liable to a charge of murder. This was removed by the Homicide Act (1957).

10 Offences Against the Person Act (1861), 24 and 25 Vict c 100.

11 Neil R. A. Bell and Adam Wood, eds, *Sir Howard Vincent's Police Code 1889* (Coventry, 2015), p. 25

12 Gatrell, 'The Decline of Theft and Violence', p. 285.

13 Bell and Wood, eds, *Sir Howard Vincent's Police Code 1889*, p. 25.

14 Offences Against the Person Act (1828), 9 Geo IV c 31. This legislation (also known as Lord Lansdowne's Act) affected the law on sexual relationships with minors, specifically making it a felony to have sexual relations with a girl less than ten years of age, the penalty for which was death.

15 Barry Godfrey, 'Counting and Accounting for the Decline in Non-Lethal Violence in England, Australia and New Zealand, 1880–1920', *British Journal of Criminology*, XLIII/2 (2003), pp. 340–53.

16 Clive Emsley, *The English and Violence since 1750* (London, 2005), p. 40.

17 *Morning Post*, 8 March 1883.

18 Drew D. Gray, *Crime, Prosecution and Social Relations: The Summary Courts of the City of London in the Late Eighteenth Century* (Basingstoke, 2009), see p. 20 (Table 2.1), and see also pp. 93–4.

19 Thames Police court register, 23 March 1881 and 20 September 1881.

20 Thames Police court register, 18 July 1881 and 23 May 1881, respectively.

21 Wiener, *Men of Blood*.

22 *Morning Post*, 16 March 1867.

23 Tabulating decade against punishment subcategory where offence category is wounding and verdict category is guilty, between January 1862 and December 1900. Counting by offence, www.oldbaileyonline.org, accessed 22 July 2022.

24 *Middlesex General Sessions of the Peace* (19 November 1888), LMA/ MJ/5783.

25 *Morning Post*, 22 October 1888; *Reynolds's Newspaper*, 28 October 1888; *The Standard*, 23 November 1888.

26 *The Standard*, 10 November 1888.

27 Thames Police court register, 1 July 1881; *The Standard*, 2 July 1881.

28 Robinson was called to appear on 7 May, a Saturday, but was still too drunk. He was held over until Monday, when he paid his fines and was released. Thames Police court register, 9 May 1881.

29 Sascha Auerbach, *Armed with Sword and Scales: Law, Culture and Local Courtrooms in London, 1860–1913* (Cambridge, 2021), p. 62.

30 Thomas Holmes, *Pictures and Problems from the London Police Courts* (London, 1900), p. 62.

31 Thames Police court register, 18 March 1881.

32 Joanne Begiato, 'Beyond the Rule of Thumb: The Materiality of Marital Violence in England, *c.* 1700–1857', *Cultural and Social History*, XV/1 (2015), p. 10.

33 *The Standard*, 19 July 1875.

34 'The police should not interfere in domestic quarrels, unless there is ground to fear that actual violence is imminent'. Bell and Wood, eds, *Sir Howard Vincent's Police Code 1889*, p. 97.

35 *The Standard*, 19 July 1875.

36 Ibid.

37 *Morning Post*, 7 September 1869.

38 Thames Police court register, 9 July 1881; *Morning Post*, 11 July 1886.

39 Thames Police court register, 18 March 1881.

40 *Morning Post*, 3 August 1886.

41 *Lloyd's Illustrated Newspaper*, 10 October 1880.

42 See www.digitalpanopticon.org, accessed 22 April 2022.

43 Thames Police court register 1881.

44 *Morning Post*, 1 November 1865.

45 Thames Police court register, 3 November, 26 March and 20 September 1881, respectively.

46 *Morning Chronicle*, 20 October 1847.

47 Henry Mayhew, *London Labour and the London Poor: a cyclopædia of the condition and earnings of those that will work, those that cannot work, and those that will not work*, vol. 1 (London, 1851).

48 *Morning Post*, 15 October 1887.

49 *The Standard*, 13 June 1859

50 Trial of Jeremiah Coghlan (t18590613-633), www.oldbaileyonline.org, accessed 8 April 2022.

51 Jeremiah Coghlan (*b.* 1838), Life Archive ID obpdef1-633-18590613, www.digitalpanopticon.org, accessed 8 April 2022.

52 *Morning Post*, 24 May 1877.

53 Trial of John Wicks (t18770528-496), www.oldbaileyonline.org, accessed 29 April 2022.

54 *The Standard*, 1 January 1892.

55 Trial of James Muir (t18920208-270), www.oldbaileyonline.org, accessed 29 April 2022.

56 Auerbach, *Armed with Sword and Scales*, p. 61.

57 Matthew Sweet, *Inventing the Victorians: What We Think We Know about Them and Why We're Wrong* (New York, 2001), p. 217.

58 Flanders, *The Invention of Murder*. See also Drew Gray, *Murder Maps. Crime Scenes Revisited: Phrenology to Fingerprint, 1811–1911* (London, 2020).

5 JUVENILES IN THE POLICE COURTS

1 John Muncie, *Youth and Crime*, 3rd edn (London, 2009), p. 275.

2 Peter King, *Crime and Law in England, 1750–1840: Remaking Justice from the Margins* (Cambridge, 2006), p. 62.

3 *Report of the Committee for Investigating the Alarming Increase of Juvenile Delinquency in the Metropolis* (London, 1816).

4 Peter King and Joan Noel, 'The Origins of the "Problem of Juvenile Delinquency": The Growth of Juvenile Prosecutions in London in the Late Eighteenth and Early Nineteenth Centuries', *Criminal Justice History*, 14 (1993), pp. 17–41.

5 Heather Shore, *Artful Dodgers: Youth and Crime in Early 19th-Century London* (Woodbridge, 2002), p. 19.

6 Karl Ittmann, *Work, Gender and Family in Victorian England* (Basingstoke, 1995), p. 149.

7 John Springhall, *Youth, Popular Culture and Moral Panics: Penny Gaffs to Gangsta-Rap, 1830–1996* (Basingstoke, 1998), p. 74.

8 Ibid., p. 166.

9 Heather Shore, *London's Criminal Underworlds, c. 1720–c. 1930: A Social and Cultural History* (Basingstoke, 2015), p. 113.

10 J. J. Tobias, *Prince of Fences: The Life and Crimes of Ikey Solomons* (London, 1974).

11 Shore, *London's Criminal Underworlds*, pp. 114–15.

12 *Morning Chronicle*, 23 May 1823.

13 Henry Moir, Life Archive ID, www.digitalpanopticon.org, accessed 6 May 2022.

14 Ibid.

15 Trial of James Morgan and Edward Pettifer (t18230625-14), www.oldbaileyonline.org, accessed 6 May 2022.

16 National Archives, HO 73/16 William Augustus Miles, *Evidence of Thieves Collected by William Augustus Miles Esq.*

17 NA HO 73/16 Constabulary Force letters and papers.

18 Ibid.

19 *The Standard*, 8 August 1879.

20 Thames Police court register: 3, 10, 17 and 19 May.

21 Leon Radzinowicz and Roger Hood, *A History of the English Criminal Law and Its Administration from 1750*, vol. V: *The Emergence of Penal Policy* (London, 1986), pp. 717–19.

22 Thames court civil registers, PS/TH/A/02/008 and PS/TH/A/02/009.

23 Elementary Education Act 1876, 43 and 44 Vict. c. 23.

24 *Lloyd's Weekly Newspaper*, 12 June 1887.

25 Thames Police court register, 11 July 1881.

26 Thames Police court register, 23 May, 2 May and 16 May 1881, respectively.

27 *Daily News*, 24 July 1877.

28 *Lloyd's Illustrated Newspaper*, 3 October 1869.

29 David Churchill, *Crime Control and Everyday Life in the Victorian City: The Police and the Public* (Oxford, 2017), pp. 116–17.

30 Robert D. Storch, 'The Plague of the Blue Locusts: Police Reform and Popular Resistance in Northern England, 1840–57', *International Review of Social History*, XX/1 (1975), pp. 61–90.

31 Churchill, *Crime Control and Everyday Life*, pp. 120–21.

32 'Street arab' was a prejorative term used by contemporaries to refer to homeless children who roamed the streets begging or committing acts of petty crime. While the term may have longer origins it became more commonly used from the mid-1860s.

33 Clarence Rook, *The Hooligan Nights: Being the Life and Opinions of a Young and Impertinent Criminal Recounted by Himself and Set Forth by Clarence Rook* (London, 1899).

34 *Morning Post*, 3 January 1877.

35 Thomas Robson, Middlesex House of Detention Calendars, 8 January 1877, www.digitalpanopticon.org, accessed 6 May 2022.

36 Stanley Cohen, *Folk Devils and Moral Panics* (London, 1972); Geoffrey Pearson, *Hooligan: A History of Respectable Fears* (Basingstoke, 1983).

37 John E. Archer, *The Monster Evil: Policing and Violence in Victorian Liverpool* (Liverpool, 2011); Andrew Davies, 'Youth Gangs, Masculinity and Violence in Late Victorian Manchester and Salford', *Journal of Social History*, XXXII/2 (Winter 1998), pp. 349–69; Stephen Humphries, *Hooligans or Rebels? An Oral History of Working-Class Childhood and Youth, 1889–1939* (Oxford, 1981): Michael Macilwee, *Gangs of Liverpool: From the Cornermen to the High Rip* (Wrea Green, 2006). See also Drew D. Gray, 'Gang Crime and the Media in Late Nineteenth-Century London: The Regent's Park Murder of 1888', *Cultural and Social History*, X/4 (2015), pp. 559–75.

38 Pearson, *Hooligan*, p. 112; Humphries, *Hooligans or Rebels?*, p. 190.

39 *Paddington Times*, 2 June 1888.

40 *Pall Mall Gazette*, 13 October 1888.

41 Mr St John Wontner, *Daily News*, 2 February 1862, quoted in Shore, *London's Criminal Underworlds*, p. 153.

42 *Pall Mall Gazette*, 26 May 1888.

43 Trial of George Galletly, Peter Lee, William Joseph Graefe, William Henshaw, (Charles Henry Govier, Francis Cole, William Elvis, Michael Doolan), (t18880730-759), www.oldbaileyonline.org, accessed 6 May 2022.

44 Gray, 'Gang Crime', p. 564.

45 *Borough of Marylebone Mercury*, 7 July 1888; *Pall Mall Gazette*, 15 August 1888; he is listed as either seventeen or eighteen in August 1888.

46 George Galletly (b. 1871), Life Archive ID, www.digitalpanopticon.org, accessed 6 May 2022.

47 Youthful Offenders Act (Reformatory Schools Act) (1854), 17 and 18 Vict c 86.

48 Jeannie Duckworth, *Fagin's Children: Criminal Children in Victorian London* (London, 2002), p. 43.

49 Mary Carpenter, *Reformatory Schools for the Children of the Perishing and Dangerous Classes and for Juvenile Offenders* (London, 1851), pp. 38–9.

50 Radzinowicz and Hood, *A History of the English Criminal Law*, p. 177.

51 Gillian Carol Gear, 'Industrial Schools in England, 1857–1933: "Moral Hospitals" or "Oppressive Institutions"?', PhD thesis, University of London Institute of Education, 1999, p. 10.

52 J.A.R. Cairns, *The Loom of the Law* (London, 1922), p. 123.

53 Thomas Holmes, *Pictures and Problems from the London Police Courts* (London, 1900), pp. 101 and 118.

54 *Morning Chronicle*, 2 May 1860.

55 Lucy Williams, "At Large": Women's Lives and Offending in Victorian Liverpool and London', PhD thesis, University of Liverpool, 2014, p. 96.

56 Barry S. Godfrey, David. J. Cox and Stephen Farrell, *Criminal Lives: Family Life, Employment, and Offending* (Oxford, 2012), p. 39.

57 *The Standard*, 24 January 1878.

58 *Morning Post*, 21 October 1876.

59 Gear, 'Industrial Schools in England', p. 52.

60 The Probation of First Offenders Act (1887), 50 and 51 Vict c 25.

61 Dorothy Bochel, *Probation and Aftercare: Its Development in England and Wales* (Edinburgh, 1976), p. 15.

62 John E. Zucchi, *Little Slaves of the Harp: Italian Child Street Musicians in Nineteenth-Century Paris, London, and New York* (Liverpool, 1999), p. 77.

63 Michael Thomas Bass, *Street Music in the Metropolis: Correspondence of the Existing Law, and Proposed Amendments* (London, 1864).

64 Ibid., p. 51.

65 *An Act for the Better Regulation of Street Music within the Metropolitan Police District* (1864), 27 and 28 Vict c 55.

66 Julia Quilter and Luke McNamara, '"Long May the Buskers Carry on Busking": Street Music and the Law in Melbourne and Sydney', *Melbourne University Law Review*, XXXIX/2 (2015), pp. 539–91.

67 Infant Life Protection Act (1872), 35 and 36 Vict c 38.

68 *Morning Post*, 3 August 1872.

69 *The Standard*, 27 May 1889; *Lloyd's Weekly Newspaper*, 9 June 1889.

70 Prevention of Cruelty to Children Act (1889), 52 and 53 Vict c 44.

6 PROSTITUTION AND THE POLICE COURTS

1 Thames Police court register 1881: 18 March, 21 and 28 May.

2 William Acton, *Prostitution, Considered in Its Moral, Social and Sanitary Aspects* (1857) (London, rev. 1869), pp. 33–5.

3 Henry Mayhew, *London Labour and the London Poor*, vol. IV: *Those that Will not Work* (London, 1861).

4 Hallie Rubenhold, *The Five: The Untold Lives of the Women Killed by Jack the Ripper* (London, 2019).

5 Nina Attwood, *The Prostitute's Body: Rewriting Prostitution in Victorian Britain* (London, 2015), p. 3.

6 Mayhew, *London Labour and the London Poor*, vol. IV, p. 264.

7 Judith R. Walkowitz, *City of Dreadful Delight: Narratives of Sexual Danger in Late-Victorian London* (London, 1992), p. 21.

8 Acton, *Prostitution*.

9 Jeffrey Weeks, *Sex, Politics and Society: The Regulation of Sexuality since 1800* (London, 1981), p. 86.

10 Vagrancy Act (1824), 5 Geo IV c 83.

11 Metropolitan Police Act (1839), 2 and 3 Vict c 47.

12 Julia Laite, *Common Prostitutes and Ordinary Citizens: Commercial Sex in London, 1885–1960* (Basingstoke, 2011), p. 6.

13 Hugh R. P. Gamon, *The London Police Court To-day and To-morrow* (London, 1907), p. 30.

14 Horace Cox, *Metropolitan Police Court Jottings: By a Magistrate* (London, 1882), p. 47.

15 *Morning Chronicle*, 16 November 1858.

16 Anon., *The Practice of the Mendicity Society by 'One who knows it'* (London, 1847), p. 7.

17 Judith Walkowitz, *Prostitution and Victorian Society: Women, Class, and the State* (Cambridge, 1980), pp. 19–21.

18 Lucy Williams, '"At Large": Women's Lives and Offending in Victorian Liverpool and London', PhD thesis, University of Liverpool, 2014, pp. 216–17.

19 Neil A. Bell and Adam Wood, eds, *Sir Howard Vincent's Police Code 1889* (Coventry, 2015), p. 143.

20 *Morning Post*, 5 January 1865.

21 *Morning Post*, 16 October 1870.

22 *Portsmouth Evening News*, 8 February 1886.

23 *The Standard*, 9 February 1886.

24 *Daily News*, 9 February 1886.

25 Criminal Law Amendment Act (1885), 48 and 49 Vict c 69.

26 Antony E. Simpson, ed., *The Maiden Tribute of Modern Babylon: The Report of the Secret Commission by W. T. Stead* (Lambertville, NJ, 2007).

27 Walkowitz, *City of Dreadful Delight*, p. 82.

28 *Daily News*, 17 February 1886.

29 *The Standard*, 24 February 1886.

30 *Reynolds's Newspaper*, 11 April 1886.

31 *The Standard*, 24 February 1886.

32 *Pall Mall Gazette*, 24 February 1886.

33 *Pall Mall Gazette*, 3 March 1886.

34 *Reynolds's Newspaper*, 14 March 1886.

35 *Pall Mall Gazette*, 9 March 1886.

36 *Daily News*, 10 March 1886.

37 Trial of Louisa Hart (t18860503-597), www.oldbaileyonline.org, accessed 13 May 2022.

38 *Pall Mall Gazette*, 9 April 1886.

39 *Reynolds's Newspaper*, 11 April 1886.

40 Ibid.

41 *Pall Mall Gazette*, 10 April 1886

42 Judith Rowbotham, Kim Stevenson and Samantha Pegg, eds, *Crime News in Modern Britain: Press Reporting and Responsibility, 1820–2020* (Basingstoke, 2013), p. 80.

43 Louisa Hart (b. 1865), Life Archive ID, www.digitalpanopticon.org, accessed 13 May 2022.

7 POVERTY AND HOMELESSNESS

1 Andrew Mearns, *The Bitter Cry of Outcast London: An Inquiry into the Condition of the Abject Poor* (London, 1883).

2 George Sims, *How the Poor Live: and, Horrible London* (London, 1889), p. 42.

3 *The Standard*, 28 February 1888.

4 Gareth Stedman Jones, *Outcast London: A Study in the Relationship between Classes in Victorian Society* (Oxford, 1971), pp. 200–202.

5 *The Standard*, 28 February 1888.

6 *Morning Post*, 24 November 1865.

7 Mary S. Morgan, 'Introduction', in *Charles Booth's Poverty Maps* (London, 2019), pp. 40–41.

8 Mary K. Matossian, 'Death in London, 1750–1909', *Journal of Interdisciplinary History*, XVI/2 (1985), p. 186.

9 Metropolitan Poor Act (1867), 30 Vict c 6.

10 David R. Green, *Pauper Capital: London and the Poor Law, 1790–1870* (Farnham, 2010), pp. 165–6.

11 The West Street workhouse was situated between Sharp's Alley and Dunsham Yard. Until 1840 female paupers were admitted to the union's workhouse on Shoe Lane. When the male house at West Street was enlarged female paupers were sent there.

12 *Morning Post*, 10 August 1849.

13 Green, *Pauper Capital*, pp. 173–4.

14 Charles B. P. Bosanquet, *A Handy Book for Visitors of the Poor in London* (London, 1874), p. 35.

15 James Greenwood, 'A Night in a Workhouse' (1866), in *Into Unknown England, 1866–1913: Selections from the Social Explorers*, ed. Peter Keating (Glasgow, 1978), pp. 31–54.

16 James Greenwood, *The Prisoner in the Dock: My Four Years' Daily Experiences in the London Police Courts* (London, 1902), p. 117.

17 *Morning Chronicle*, 8 March 1841.

18 Green, *Pauper Capital*, pp. 169–70.

19 *Morning Post*, 10 December 1864.

20 Vagrancy Act (1824), 5 Geo IV c 83.

21 Neil A. Bell and Adam Wood, eds, *Sir Howard Vincent's Police Code 1889* (Coventry, 2015), p. 185.

22 Peter Cunningham, *Hand-Book of London* (London, 1850).

23 *Morning Post*, 6 December 1839.

24 *The Standard*, 30 June 1886.

25 *Reynolds's Newspaper*, 11 July 1886.

26 See Stephen King, *Fraudulent Lives: Benefit Cheats in the Popular and Policy Imagination, c. 1601–2023* [forthcoming].

27 *Morning Post*, 26 May 1868.

28 The 1961 act decriminalized the act of suicide. Suicide Act (1961), 9 and 10 Eliz II c 60.

29 P. D. James and T. A. Critchley, *The Maul and the Pear Tree: The Ratcliffe Highway Murders, 1811* (London, 1971).

30 An Act to Alter and Amend the Law Relating to the Internment of the remains of any person found *felo de se* (1823), 4 Geo IV c 2.

31 Burial Laws Amendment Act (1880), 43 and 44 Vict c 41; The Interments (*felo de se*) Act (1882), 45 and 46 Vict c 19.

32 Attempted suicide was formally recognized as an offence in law in 1850, 'if not before'. Michael MacDonald and Terence R. Murphy, *Sleepless Souls: Suicide in Early Modern England* (Oxford, 1990), p. 350.

33 Olive Anderson, *Suicide in Victorian and Edwardian England* (Oxford, 1987), p. 423.

34 Ibid., pp. 282–3.

35 Ibid., p. 284.

36 Ibid., p. 423.

37 Victor Bailey, *'This Rash Act': Suicide Across the Life Cycle in the Victorian City* (Stanford, CA, 1998), p. 130.

38 Thames Police court register, 24 March 1881.

39 *Morning Post*, 16 July 1849.

40 Thames Police court register, 8 September 1881.

41 *Daily News*, 29 March 1881.

42 All Thames register 1881: 20 July, 30 September, 27 September.

43 *Illustrated Police News*, 5 March 1881.

44 *Daily News*, 13 May 1881.

45 Anderson, *Suicide in Victorian and Edwardian England*, p. 423.

46 Elaine Showalter, *The Female Malady: Women, Madness and English Culture, 1830–1980* (London, 1987).

47 Anderson, *Suicide in Victorian and Edwardian England*, p. 115.

48 *Morning Post*, 11 March 1865.

49 *Morning Chronicle*, 1 May 1860.

50 Anderson, *Suicide in Victorian and Edwardian England*, p. 122.

51 Coroner's Records, LMA/ COR/MW/1890/01/01/66.

52 I. O'Donnell and R.D.T. Farmer, 'The Epidemiology of Suicide on the London Underground', *Social Science and Medicine*, XXXVIII/3 (1994), pp. 409–18.

53 *The Standard*, 29 June 1893.
54 Today it is estimated that a dose of 15–30 grams could be lethal if ingested orally.
55 *Morning Post*, 24 March 1866.
56 Anderson, *Suicide in Victorian and Edwardian England*, p. 284.
57 Ibid., p. 115.
58 *The Standard*, 10 May 1847.
59 *Morning Post*, 24 May 1893.
60 *Birmingham Daily Post*, 25 May 1893.
61 *Morning Post*, 25 May 1893.
62 Anderson, *Suicide in Victorian and Edwardian England*, p. 335.

8 POLITICS, RIOT AND TRADE UNIONISM

1 Gareth Stedman Jones, 'Rethinking Chartism', in *Languages of Class: Studies in English Working Class History, 1832–1982* (Cambridge, 1983), p. 191.
2 Philip Priestley, *Victorian Prison Lives: English Prison Biography, 1830–1914* (London, 1985).
3 Henry Mayhew, *London Labour and the London Poor*, vol. IV (London, 1861–2).
4 K.R.M. Short, *The Dynamite War: Irish-American Bombers in Victorian Britain* (Dublin, 1979), p. 8.
5 *Morning Post*, 11 December 1867.
6 Short, *The Dynamite War*, p. 11.
7 Karl Marx and Frederick Engels, *Ireland and the Irish Question* (London, 1978), p. 159, quoted in Michael O'Riordan, 'Marx: The Irish Connection', *The Crane Bag*, VII/1 (1983), pp. 163–6.
8 Short, *The Dynamite War*, p. 184.
9 *Pall Mall Gazette*, 31 May 1884.
10 Short, *The Dynamite War*, pp. 200–201.
11 Trial of James George Gilbert, alias James Gilbert Cunningham, and Harry Burton (t18850420-532), www.oldbaileyonline.org, accessed 17 June 2022.
12 *Morning Post*, 10 February 1886.
13 Trial of Frederick Barton and Thomas Barton (t18860531-606), www.oldbaileyonline.org, accessed 17 June 2022.
14 Jerry White, *London in the Nineteenth Century* (London, 2007), p. 369.
15 Riot was a felony under the 1714 Riot Act and had carried the death penalty until 1837 when it was reduced to transportation. The Act itself was repealed in 1973.
16 *Reynolds's Newspaper*, 15 July 1855.
17 *Morning Chronicle*, 23 July 1852.
18 Louise Raw, *Striking a Light: The Bryant and May Matchwomen and Their Place in History* (London, 2009).
19 *The Standard*, 21 August 1889.
20 *The Standard*, 21 December 1889.

CONCLUSION: THE PEOPLE'S COURTS?

1 Jennifer Davis, 'Law Breaking and Law Enforcement: The Creation of a Criminal Class in Mid-Victorian London', PhD thesis, Boston College, 1984; Jennifer Davis, 'A Poor Man's System of Justice?: The London Police Courts in the Second Half of the Nineteenth Century', *Historical Journal*, XXVII/2 (1984), pp. 309–35.

2 Sascha Auerbach, *Armed with Sword and Scales: Law, Culture and Local Courtrooms in London, 1860–1913* (Cambridge, 2021).

3 For exceptions see Norma Landau, *The Justices of the Peace, 1679–1760* (Berkeley, CA, 1984); Drew D. Gray, *Crime, Prosecution and Social Relations: The Summary Courts of the City of London in the Late Eighteenth Century* (Basingstoke, 2009); Robert B. Shoemaker, *Prosecution and Punishment: Petty Crime and the Law in London and Rural Middlesex, c. 1660–1725* (Cambridge, 1991).

4 Thames Police court register, court 1, part 11, 1887, LMA/PS/TH/A/02/008.

5 Davis, 'Law Breaking and Law Enforcement', pp. 267–8.

6 Ibid., pp. 328–9.

7 John Brewer and John Styles, *An Ungovernable People: The English and Their Law in the Seventeenth and Eighteenth Centuries* (London, 1980), pp. 19–20.

8 Davis, 'Law Breaking and Law Enforcement', p. 292.

9 Henry Mayhew, *London Labour and the London Poor: a cyclopædia of the condition and earnings of those that will work, those that cannot work, and those that will not work* (London, 1851).

10 Dominique Kalifa, *Vice, Crime, and Poverty: How the Western Imagination Invented the Underworld* (New York, 2013).

11 Stephen King, *Fraudulent Lives: Benefit Cheats in the Popular and Policy Imagination, c. 1601–2023* [forthcoming].

SUGGESTED READING

The Victorian period is well served by books and articles but, while crime and punishment feature prominently, the history of the non-jury courts is much less well covered. Alongside the work of Jennifer Davis, who broke new ground in the 1980s with her article 'A Poor Man's System of Justice?: The London Police Courts in the Second Half of the Nineteenth Century', *Historical Journal*, XXVII/2 (1984), pp. 309–35, readers are directed to Sascha Auerbach, *Armed with Sword and Scales: Law, Culture and Local Courtrooms in London, 1860–1913* (Cambridge, 2021) as one of the handful of authors working on the late Victorian and Edwardian periods. For studies of the summary process in the capital in earlier periods, see my own work – Drew D. Gray, *Crime, Prosecution and Social Relations: The Summary Courts of the City of London in the Late Eighteenth Century* (Basingstoke, 2009) – and Robert Shoemaker's *Prosecution and Punishment: Petty Crime and the Law in London and Rural Middlesex, c. 1660–1725* (Cambridge, 1991).

There are numerous histories of London, but readers might enjoy Jerry White's *London in the Nineteenth Century: 'A Human Awful Wonder of God'* (London, 2007), and Stephen Inwood's *City of Cities: The Birth of Modern London* (Basingstoke, 2005), both of which provide modern and well-researched introductions to London in the 1900s.

Readers interested in finding out more about the Victorian criminal justice system will find the work of the late Clive Emsley invaluable. His work on police is essential reading but also his study of violence – Clive Emsley, *The English and Violence since 1750* (London, 2005) – provides an accessible introduction to the topic. For other work on violent crime and murder, see Rosalind Crone, *Violent Victorians: Popular Entertainment in Nineteenth-Century London* (Manchester, 2012); Martin J. Wiener, *Men of Blood: Violence, Manliness, and Criminal Justice in Victorian England* (Cambridge, 2004); Judith Flanders, *The Invention of Murder: How the Victorians Revelled in Death and Detection and Created Modern Crime* (London, 2011); and my own *Murder Maps. Crime Scenes Revisited: Phrenology to Fingerprint, 1811–1911* (London, 2020).

Those interested in juvenile crime should look at Jeannie Duckworth's *Fagin's Children: Criminal Children in Victorian London* (London, 2002) and Heather Shore's seminal study *Artful Dodgers: Youth and Crime in Early 19th-Century London* (Woodbridge, 2002). Shore's second book – Heather Shore, *London's Criminal Underworlds, c. 1720–c. 1930: A Social and Cultural History* (Basingstoke, 2015) – is a fascinating study of underground criminality and well worth your time. In the same vein, an academic study by David Churchill – *Crime Control and Everyday Life in the Victorian City: The Police and the Public* (Oxford, 2017) – offers important analysis of the role of the police and courts in urban Britain.

For a clear overview that covers two centuries, my textbook – Drew D. Gray, *Crime, Policing and Punishment in England, 1660–1914* (London, 2016) – should provide a solid basis for students and general readers alike. I have always turned to Philip Priestley's *Victorian Prison Lives: English Prison Biography, 1830–1914* (London, 1985) as one of the few studies we have that brings us the voices of those incarcerated by the Victorian state. For work on property crime in the 1800s, I found William M. Meier's *Property Crime in London, 1850–Present* (Basingstoke, 2011) to be extremely useful.

Likewise, Julia Laite's *Common Prostitutes and Ordinary Citizens: Commercial Sex in London, 1885–1960* (Basingstoke, 2011) and Judith R. Walkowitz's *Prostitution and Victorian Society: Women, Class, and the State* (Cambridge, 1980) are essential reading for anyone interested in the reality of the sex trade in Victorian London. Those interested in women's experiences of the justice system are recommended to read Lucia Zedner's *Women, Crime, and Custody in Victorian England* (Oxford, 1991), while Olive Anderson's *Suicide in Victorian and Edwardian England* (Oxford, 1987) is an important starting point for research into this disturbing topic.

ACKNOWLEDGEMENTS

Creating a book is collaborative and I must thank my publishers at Reaktion Books. First, for giving me the chance to tell the stories of the many 'ordinary' people whose lives briefly made the pages of the nineteenth-century newspapers. And second, for all their help in selecting images, correcting my mistakes and translating my ideas into print. To Alan Clarke for being a critical friend; all remaining mistakes are my own. My thanks again to my wife who has had to put up with me as I tried to research and write a book during a global pandemic and struggled with my frustrations of being confined to my home office for such long periods.

I would also like to thank my colleagues at the University of Northampton whose support has enabled me to research, write and complete this study while juggling a growing variety of other tasks. In particular I am grateful to Anthony Stepniak, Lisa Lapidge and Sarah Mullan, who have made my life so much easier the last couple of years. Thanks to the Centre for Historical Research for helping fund some of the images, and a mention too to Kate Williams, who I hope will enjoy reading this; and to Sarah Field and Jessica Lynch, who quietly make sure life runs smoothly in our faculty. More broadly I want to thank the university, which has supported me and given me a space to write about the things that matter to me. Universities are the centre of the culture wars at the moment, with accusations of 'wokeness' and suggestions that they do not offer students 'value for money'. As someone who left school in 1981 with one A level and few academic prospects, I'd like to thank Northampton for giving me the chance to fulfil my potential. I hope society recognizes that everyone should be given that chance, not just those who were born with a proverbial silver spoon in their mouths. For me history is about more than 'chaps and maps', it is about real people and their lives. So *Nether World* is respectfully dedicated to all those, past and present, that society neglects and forgets.

PHOTO ACKNOWLEDGEMENTS

The author and publishers wish to express their thanks to the sources listed below for illustrative material and/or permission to reproduce it:

The Getty Research Institute, Los Angeles: pp. 10, 23, 71, 73, 77, 80, 89, 90, 132, 183, 203, 214, 216, 246; The J. Paul Getty Museum, Los Angeles: pp. 11, 126, 127, 145, 224, 260, 268; Lewis Walpole Library, Yale University, Farmington, CT: p. 43; Look and Learn/ Illustrated Papers Collection/Bridgeman Images: pp. 14, 26, 169, 230; Philadelphia Museum of Art, PA: pp. 114–15; Rijksmuseum, Amsterdam: p. 8; Royal Holloway, University of London, photo Wellcome Collection, London: p. 233.

INDEX

Page numbers in *italics* refer to illustrations